Fodor's

CHICAGO

T0049571

Welcome to Chicago

Chicago is a city with an appetite: for food, of course, but also for design, history, and culture. Come here to marvel at the architecture or take in the gorgeous views of Lake Michigan; to spend a day cheering with baseball fans and a night laughing at a comedy show; and to visit renowned institutions like the Field Museum and the Adler Planetarium. This book was produced during the COVID-19 pandemic. As you plan your upcoming travels to Chicago, please confirm that places are still open and let us know when we need to make updates by writing to us at: editors@fodors.com.

TOP REASONS TO GO

★ **Architecture:** The skyline dazzles with some of the country's most iconic buildings.

★ **Local Eats:** Cheap ethnic bites and gourmet chefs make Chicago a great food town.

★ **Art:** See everything from Old Masters at the Art Institute to outdoor sculptures in Millennium Park.

★ **Jazz and Blues:** Music venues are filled with both big-name legends and up-and-comers.

★ **Shopping:** Shop on the Magnificent Mile or in funky Wicker Park boutiques.

★ **Comedy:** Chicago improv venues are training grounds for comedy superstars.

Contents

Fodor's Features

A Guide to the Art Institute........... 74
The Sky's the Limit.................. 116
Chicago Sings the Blues............ 175
Frank Lloyd Wright 240

MAPS

Chapter 1

EXPERIENCE CHICAGO

18 ULTIMATE EXPERIENCES

Chicago offers terrific experiences that should be on every traveler's list. Here are Fodor's top picks for a memorable trip.

1 Explore the Park

Millennium Park is a 25-acre public green space filled with art and right on North Michigan Avenue in the Loop. See the stainless-steel mirrored *Cloud Gate*, the Frank Gehry-designed band shell, and the Crown Fountain. (Ch. 3)

2 Learn About Architecture

For an immersive look at Chicago's architectural history, book a walking tour with the Chicago Architecture Center. (Ch. 2)

3 See Beautiful Art

From one of the world's largest collection of French Impressionist paintings to blockbuster exhibitions, the Art Institute is a must-not-miss for art lovers. (Ch. 3)

4 Roar at the Zoo

Brookfield Zoo often gets all the glory but Lincoln Park Zoo is free, centrally located, and hugs the city's scenic lakefront. (Ch. 6)

5 Shop the Mag Mile

Michigan Avenue's famous Magnificent Mile draws avid shoppers its upscale shops, luxury malls, and top-notch restaurants. The architecture here is stunning as well. (Ch. 4)

6 Bike the Lakefront

See some of the biggest attractions in the city by riding down Chicago's glorious 18-mile long Lakefront Trail. (Ch. 3)

7 Laugh It Up

If you adore Saturday Night Live, then you must catch a Second City comedy show. Joan Rivers, Tina Fey, Bill Murray, and Mike Myers are all Second City alums. (Ch. 6)

8 Explore History

The Field Museum of Natural History has amazing exhibits, like Sue the *T. rex*, a 67-million-year-old complete fossil found in South Dakota. (Ch. 3)

9 Discover Pilsen

Celebrate the city's Hispanic heritage in the Pilsen neighborhood. Visit the National Museum of Mexican Art, eat great Mexican food, and admire outdoor murals. (Ch. 5)

10 Get Your Science On

The Museum of Science & Industry has stellar permanent collections as well as rotating exhibits. Must-sees include Apollo 8's command module. (Ch. 8)

11 Eat Deep-Dish Pizza

Chi-town's signature pizza style is super-thick, composed of layers of sauce and cheese. And if that's not indulgent enough for you, opt for a stuffed version.

12 Tour Historic Houses

Illinois' most famous architect—Frank Lloyd Wright—is widely known for his Prairie style of architecture. Visit his birthplace in Oak Park and tour his most notable houses. (Ch. 9)

13 Cheer the Cubs

The Cubbies have always been a draw but even more so now after their historic World Series win in 2016. Wrigley Field—built in 1914—is a local legend. (Ch. 6)

14 Drink with a View

Grab a drink and admire the views at the 96th floor Signature Lounge in the former John Hancock Center (now called 360 Chicago). (Ch. 4)

15 Explore the Oceans

Shedd Aquarium is for anyone who is curious about the mammals and fish who occupy oceans and freshwater lakes. (Ch. 3)

16 Willis Skydeck

Take the ear-popping ride to the 103rd floor of the Willis Tower, where on a clear day you can see as far as Michigan, Wisconsin, and Indiana. (Ch. 3)

17 Hear Live Music

Chicago's rep as a jazz and blues destination hasn't hit a bad note—ever. In addition to summer music festivals, the city is littered with live music venues.

18 Sail the Chicago River

There are many ways to get out on the water in downtown Chicago. Take one of the many fascinating boat cruises, or rent a kayak or canoe. (Ch. 1)

WHAT'S WHERE

1 **The Loop, West Loop, and South Loop.** Bounded by El tracks, the city's business center is full of architectural landmarks. Restaurants and galleries dominate the West Loop; the South Loop now teems with college students and condo dwellers.

2 **Near North and River North.** Shoppers stroll the Magnificent Mile between the stately tower at 875 N. Michigan Ave. (formerly the John Hancock Center, the name most locals still use) and the Chicago River, passing landmarks such as the Water Tower and Tribune Tower. Just north, stately mansions dominate the Gold Coast, while River North has a thriving gallery scene.

3 **Lincoln Park and Wicker Park.** Beyond its huge park, Lincoln Park boasts cafés and high-end boutiques, while Wicker Park, Bucktown, and Logan Square have become increasingly trendy, with cafés, cocktail bars, and cool shops.

4 **Lakeview and Far North Side.** Baseball fans pilgrimage to Wrigley Field: just south of the ballpark, on Clark Street, are memorabilia shops and sports bars; two blocks east is Halsted Street, epicenter of gay enclave Boystown, now called Northalsted. Farther north is Swedish-settled Andersonville, which has a quiet, residential feel.

5 **Pilsen, Little Italy, and Chinatown.** Mexican restaurants, mom-and-pop shops, and Spanish signage line 18th Street, the heart of Pilsen. Gone are many of the Near West Side's Italian groceries and shops, but you can still get a mean veal marsala on Taylor Street. In Chinatown, check out the restaurants, teahouses, and bakeries.

6 **Hyde Park.** The big draw of this South Side neighborhood is the University of Chicago, while Promontory Point has breathtaking lake and skyline views.

7 **Day Trips From Chicago.** Just outside the city, Evanston is the site of Northwestern University and its leafy campus. Suburban Oak Park is known for native sons Frank Lloyd Wright and Ernest Hemingway; Wright's home and studio are here, along with notable examples of his architecture.

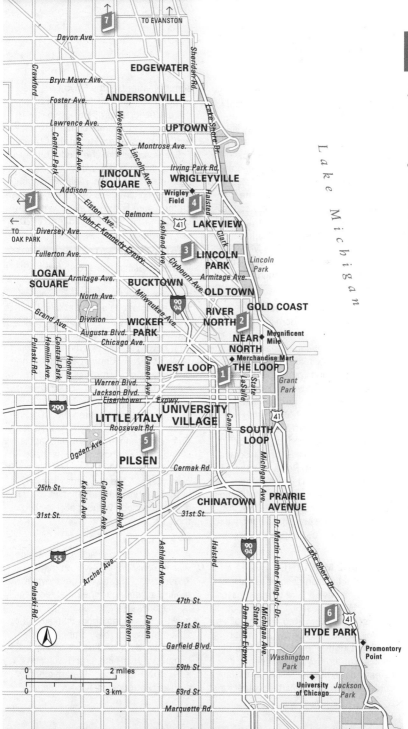

TO EVANSTON

Devon Ave.

EDGEWATER

Bryn Mawr Ave.

ANDERSONVILLE

Foster Ave.

Lawrence Ave.

UPTOWN

Montrose Ave.

LINCOLN SQUARE

Irving Park Rd.

WRIGLEYVILLE

Wrigley Field

Addison

Belmont

LAKEVIEW

TO OAK PARK

Diversey Ave.

Fullerton Ave.

LINCOLN PARK

Lincoln Park

LOGAN SQUARE

Armitage Ave.

BUCKTOWN

Armitage Ave.

OLD TOWN

North Ave.

Division

WICKER PARK

Augusta Blvd.

Chicago Ave.

RIVER NORTH

GOLD COAST

NEAR NORTH

Magnificent Mile

Merchandise Mart

WEST LOOP

THE LOOP

Grant Park

Warren Blvd.

Jackson Blvd.

Eisenhower Expwy.

UNIVERSITY VILLAGE

SOUTH LOOP

LITTLE ITALY

Roosevelt Rd.

PILSEN

Ogden Ave.

Cermak Rd.

25th St.

31st St.

CHINATOWN

PRAIRIE AVENUE

31st St.

47th St.

51st St.

Garfield Blvd.

59th St.

63rd St

Marquette Rd.

HYDE PARK

Promontory Point

Washington Park

University of Chicago

Jackson Park

Lake Michigan

0   2 miles

0   3 km

Chicago Today

A century ago, poet Carl Sandburg called Chicago the "stormy, husky, brawling / city of the Big Shoulders" in an eponymous poem that still echoes city life today. Indeed, Chicago is stormier and huskier than ever, with political scandals breaking more frequently than the El train circles the Loop. But it's also cleaner, greener, and more urbane than expected—with bold new architecture, abundant green spaces, and a vibrant dining scene. So what will you find when you visit: a rough-and-tumble Midwestern town or a sophisticated metropolis? The answer is both, and much, much more.

BUILDING AND REBUILDING

The imposing skyline dominates postcards and tourist snapshots—and for good reason. Architecture fans are excited to see the city that Daniel Burnham, Louis Sullivan, and Frank Lloyd Wright built, but modern development has also brought new energy. Recent years have seen the birth of the Millennium Park lakefront, an overhaul of the Riverwalk, and major new additions to the skyline such as the Aqua residential skyscraper and the 101-story St. Regis Chicago. Development doesn't come without controversy, however. Some older buildings have been torn down to make way for the new, and preservationists decry each loss of a historic building to the wrecking ball.

POLITICAL MACHINE

Rahm Emanuel surprised observers by declining to seek a third term as mayor in 2019. His successor, Lori Lightfoot, is the first Black woman to hold the office, as well as the first openly gay mayor. In 2020, Lightfoot earned praise for her handling of the Covid-19 pandemic in its early days, but her response to the surge of Black Lives Matter protests that summer, after George Floyd was killed by police in Minneapolis—prioritizing the protection of property in wealthy neighborhoods—angered many. Lightfoot, who was president of the Chicago Police Board before she ran for office, is frequently at odds with the city's powerful police union; meanwhile, gun violence continues to be a major concern on the South and West sides. Whether Lightfoot runs for a second term in 2023 is a matter of much speculation.

FOODIE'S PARADISE

Visitors expecting deep-dish pizza and Italian beef sandwiches won't be disappointed, but they will have to elevate their expectations a hundredfold. Chicago is—dare we say it?—one of the most exciting cities in the country for dining right now. It seems like there's a *Food & Wine* Best New Chef or Top Chef winner on every block. Sample cutting-edge cuisine from chef Grant Achatz at Next and Alinea and Noah Sandoval at Oriole. Or just spend your entire visit in Logan Square, where such stalwarts as Lula Café and Longman & Eagle are regularly joined by newer go-tos like Giant and Mi Tocaya Antojería. Satisfied yet? We didn't even mention the hundreds of neighborhood ethnic eateries that let you dine across the globe without ever leaving the city.

BREW CREW

A couple of decades ago, Goose Island was the only craft brewer on the scene. These days, Chicago is a beer lover's dream: according to the most recent tally by the Brewers Association, Chicago has 167 breweries, more than any other U.S. metro area. That number includes national and regional heavy hitters like Lagunitas, Half Acre, and Revolution, as well as more specialized microbrewers like Metropolitan, Moody Tongue, and Marz. Many operate their own taprooms, where you can sip flagship flavors and limited edition batches. Craft beer megastores like the Beer Temple in Avondale and Bitter Pops in Lakeview have their own tasting rooms so you can sample the goods before taking a six-pack or growler to go.

IMPACT OF COVID-19

Like much of the world, Chicago saw grievous effects from the pandemic—the lives lost, of course (more than 25,000 in Illinois), as well as the horrible stresses on the health-care system and schools and scores of lost jobs. The hospitality industry's landscape was changed by Covid, as well. One report showed that 19% of the city's restaurants closed permanently between March 2020 and August 2021, including newer favorites as well as institutions like Spiaggia and Blackbird. Not all the news was bad: lawmakers cleared the way for restaurants and bars to continue selling to-go cocktails, initially an emergency measure, until at least 2024.

ROOMS TO GROW

The travel slowdown didn't impede the continuing expansion of hotels in the city. New and impending openings in the Loop and River North include the Pendry Chicago, the towering St. Regis (opening in 2022), and the Sable—the first hotel on Navy Pier. They join a growing number of options in neighborhoods away from downtown, like the Robey in Wicker Park. You'll have your pick of places to lay your head.

SPORTING GOODS (AND BADS)

Chicagoans love their sports teams. Even if most of their pro franchises have struggled since the Cubs finally broke their World Series curse in 2016, you can still find the bars packed on game days,

cheering on the Bears, Cubs, White Sox, Blackhawks, and Bulls. There are some changes to the sporting landscape: The Chicago Fire FC hope their move from the suburbs to Soldier Field will win over new soccer fans, even as the Bears are contemplating a move out of Soldier Field to suburban Arlington Heights. And with their first WNBA championship in 2021, the Chicago Sky showed everyone how to make their city proud.

FULL OF PRIDE

Sure, Chicagoans like to complain—about the weather, about the sports teams, and especially about our politicians. But if an out-of-towner dares to diss our beloved city, you can bet there will be fireworks bigger than the ones over Navy Pier in summer. Sandburg was right again about Chicago when he wrote, "come and show me another city with lifted head singing / so proud to be alive and coarse and strong and cunning."

What to Eat and Drink in Chicago

MEXICAN FOOD

Chicago may not be your first thought as a haven for Mexican food, but the city has long been a draw for Mexican immigrants. You'll find many restaurants owned and staffed by first- and second-generation Mexican-Americans, ranging from corner taquerias to high-end sit-down spots.

PIZZA

Chicago deep-dish pizza is unique, and worth seeking out at least once, but the typical pie, known as "tavern style," has a thin-but-sturdy cracker crust. In Chicago, the round pizza is typically cut into squares, leaving you to decide between crispy edge pieces or center slices.

HOT DOGS

Many believe the assembly of a classic Chicago dog is sacrosanct: a charred frank on a poppy seed bun is piled with sliced tomatoes, chopped onions, whole sport peppers, sweet relish and a pickle spear, plus mustard and celery salt—and absolutely no ketchup.

THE STEAK HOUSE

Grass-fed beef is to the Midwest, what fresh-caught seafood is to coastal cities, and Chicago's reputation as a meat-and-potatoes town has a basis in truth. Old-school steak houses, settings for a dinner of filet mignon or New York strip, still thrive downtown, and on a Monday or Tuesday night, when many restaurants are closed, a steak house can be your best bet.

ITALIAN BEEF

Thin-sliced, seasoned roast beef, topped with sweet peppers (usually roasted green bells) or hot peppers (pickled, oil-packed *giardiniera*), and piled into an Italian roll is a local delicacy. Order it "dipped," and it'll be submerged, bread and all, in warm au jus before serving.

MALÖRT

This bitter wormwood liqueur can only be found for sale in the Chicago area. Once confined to working-class Polish and Swedish bars, Malört has become a point of civic pride alongside the craft cocktail surge of recent decades. Many finer bars have incorporated it into cocktail recipes, but shooting it straight—tasting its jolt of grapefruit, heavy on the pith, followed by a lingering deep-bitter finish—has become a rite of Chicago passage.

Craft beer in Chicago

HAROLD'S CHICKEN SHACK

Black-owned at its founding in 1950, this South Side and West Side chain is so beloved for its fried-to-order chicken and signature "mild sauce" (a proprietary blend generally believed to be made from barbecue sauce, ketchup, and hot sauce) that it's been namechecked in lyrics by musicians including Common, Kanye, and others.

JIBARITO

This creation is a product of the city's thriving Puerto Rican community, and the *jibarito's* genius move is replacing bread with smashed and fried slices of crispy plantain (aka tostones). These are the vessel for seared steak or another protein, and toppings like lettuce, tomato, and cheese. Most agree it first appeared in the mid-1990s.

CRAFT BEER

Local microbreweries have proliferated across the U.S. but Chicago was at the forefront of the trend. Two decades ago, Goose Island was the city's only local brew but these days, you can barely swing an empty growler without hitting a new taproom or two. Expect to find everything from IPAs to lagers, to sours and stouts.

FLAMING SAGANAKI

The theatrical presentation of a pan of fried cheese, flambéed tableside to cries of *Opa!* is said to have started at Chicago's Parthenon restaurant in Greektown in the 1950s. The dish was adopted by Greek restaurants across the U.S. and beyond, and you can still find it at some Chicago spots.

An Architecture Lover's Guide to Chicago

WILLIS TOWER

Most locals still call it the Sears Tower, and likely will continue to do so. The sleek, black bundle of component towers—an innovation in wind resistance at great heights—was the world's tallest building for nearly 25 years and it's still the king of Chicago's skyline.

BAHÁ'Í HOUSE OF WORSHIP

One of just nine Bahá'í temples in the world, it's worth the trip to see the intricate tracery in French-Canadian architect Louis Bourgeois's concrete dome surrounded by nine towers. Crushed quartz mixed into the concrete makes the structure sparkle in the sun.

MARINA CITY

Architect Bertrand Goldberg's aversion to right angles gets one of its purest expressions in these twin residential towers, which are sometimes compared to corncobs but which Goldberg likened to the shape of sunflowers—each wedge-shape apartment's curved balcony is a petal.

CHICAGO ARCHITECTURE CENTER

Any architecture buff's first stop, the CAC features scale models of many of the city's best-known skyscrapers, including the Chicago City Model Experience, which gives you a bird's-eye view of more than 4,000 buildings in and around the Loop. This is also the place to buy tickets for the center's excellent walking tours and river cruises.

CHICAGO CULTURAL CENTER

Originally the city's first public library, this Beaux Arts beauty is now a hub for art exhibitions, music, and theater performances, and more—all free to attend. The building's lavish interior, awash in marble and brass, has been lovingly restored; head upstairs to Preston Bradley Hall to ogle the world's largest Tiffany dome, 38 feet in diameter.

ROBIE HOUSE

Completed in 1909, this Prairie-style layer cake is peak Frank Lloyd Wright, all horizontal lines and cantilevered eaves. The Hyde Park residence, now a National Historic Landmark and a UNESCO World Heritage Site, underwent a $2.9 million restoration in 2019; tours are available Thursday through Monday.

Tribune Tower

TRIBUNE TOWER

The *Chicago Tribune* newspaper moved out of its namesake building on Michigan Avenue in 2018 and the neo-Gothic skyscraper has been converted into condominiums, but the tower's signature flying buttresses and stately crown are still a striking part of the skyline.

THE CHICAGO BUNGALOW

The Chicago bungalow was an evolution of the California cottage, adapted by early-20th-century architects to fit Chicago's narrow standard lot size. Instantly identifiable by their 1½-story build, with a single dormer window protruding from the center of a low-pitched roof, the bungalow proliferated in the city's outer neighborhoods from north to south, in what became known as "the bungalow belt"; large clusters still survive.

AQUA TOWER

With its undulating concrete balconies suggesting rippling liquid, Aqua's addition to the skyline in 2009 made Jeanne Gang a household name in architectural circles; the building was not just a critical hit, it was also the world's tallest building designed by a woman. Aqua recently lost that designation to another Gang design, the nearby St. Regis Chicago, which is also currently the third-tallest building in the city.

THE ROOKERY

This 1888 office building was designed by Chicago master planners Burnham and Root—reason enough to add it to your list—but a 1907 interior redesign was completed by Frank Lloyd Wright, and it's the only surviving example of Wright's work you can find downtown.

Chicago's Best Outdoor Adventures

PADDLEBOARD ON LAKE MICHIGAN

Vendors at several beaches and harbors on the lakefront have stand-up paddleboards for rent so you can test your balance on the water. Some, including Chicago SUP at North Avenue Beach, also offer lessons, but check ahead of time.

LAKEFRONT BEACHES

One of the bonuses of summer in Chicago is that there are more than two dozen public beaches along the lakefront. Different beaches have different draws—beach volleyball, Jet Ski rentals, waterfront dining. Beach access is free of charge, so go ahead and dig your toes into the sand.

GRANT PARK SKATE PARK

Near the southern end of Grant Park, at 9th Street and Columbus Drive, this skate park opened in 2014 with three acres of ramps, curbs, rails, and half-pipes for skaters, rollerbladers, and BMX riders looking to master their moves.

KAYAK THE CHICAGO RIVER

For a truly unique view of the city, rent a kayak and paddle down Chicago's main waterway. Start on the North Side and circumnavigate Goose Island, or head all the way downtown and wend your way through the skyscraper canyon of the Main Branch. Rental outfits are located at various spots along the river.

BIKE OR RUN THE LAKEFRONT TRAIL

The paved trail running alongside the Lake Michigan shore doesn't quite span the entire length of the city—but it comes close, stretching 18.5 miles from Edgewater at the north trailhead down to South Shore. Recent upgrades created separate paths for cyclists and runners.

THE 606

A decommissioned elevated rail line running east-west from Bucktown to Humboldt Park was transformed into a 2.7-mile recreational trail, with lush greenery and public art. Named for the first three digits of Chicago's ZIP Codes, the 606 is so popular there's talk of extending it.

MAGGIE DALEY PARK

Nestled between Millennium Park to the west and DuSable Lake Shore Drive to the east, this newer park is rife with outdoor activities for families, from rock-climbing walls to miniature golf to the irresistible skating ribbon (ice skates in the winter, roller skates and scooters in warmer months).

Nature walk in LaBagh Woods

312 RIVERRUN

Completed in 2021, this pedestrian and cycling path connects three previously existing parks along the North Branch of the Chicago River via a new bridge that crosses 18 feet above the water while weaving underneath vehicular bridges, allowing nearly 2 miles of continuous, car-free travel.

NATURE WALK IN LABAGH WOODS

LaBagh Woods, on the city's Far Northwest Side and managed by the Cook County Forest Preserve, offers roughly 5 miles of unpaved trails, in an area that's great for bird-watching and wildlife spotting; you'll forget you're still in the city.

SNOWTREKKING AT NORTHERLY ISLAND

Adjacent to the Museum Campus, much of this man-made peninsula is kept "natural," with a walking path that lets you stroll through prairie grasses and wildflowers but it also has a killer view of the skyline. When winter weather cooperates, you can rent snowshoes or cross-country skis from the park's fieldhouse.

Under the Radar Chicago

MUSEUM OF CONTEMPORARY PHOTOGRAPHY
The MoCP holds works by more than 1,500 photographers. Special exhibits often highlight rising stars.

RICHARD H. DRIEHAUS MUSEUM
Reflecting the interests of its namesake and founder, a philanthropist, the Driehaus is devoted to art and architecture of the Gilded Age. The building, a lovingly restored 1883 mansion, is part of the collection.

PULLMAN NATIONAL MONUMENT
America's first planned industrial community (aka a company town) this former home of the workers employed by a railcar manufacturer is notable for its architecture as well as its role in the civil rights and labor movements.

GARDEN OF THE PHOENIX
A serene retreat on an island at the center of Jackson Park's lagoon, this Japanese ornamental garden (also known as Osaka Garden, for Chicago's sister city) was originally established as Japan's pavilion for the World's Columbian Exhibition of 1893. Visit in the spring to see the cherry blossoms.

THE LINCOLN LODGE
This comedy showcase started in the back room of a Lincoln Square diner, where young comics like Hannibal Buress, Cameron Esposito, and Kumail Nanjiani honed their stand-up. It now has its own venue in Bucktown, where you can find the next generation of comedians working the room.

NATIONAL MUSEUM OF MEXICAN ART
In Pilsen, the neighborhood that's long been the hub of Chicago's Mexican-American community, you can browse a collection of 18,000 works ranging from ancient sculptural figures to contemporary paintings, or catch a theater or dance performance by a local Latinx troupe.

THE LIGHT OF TRUTH
Completed in 2021, this sculpture in Bronzeville is a monument to the Black journalist and activist Ida B. Wells. Designed by sculptor and Chicago native Richard Hunt, it features three bronze pillars supporting a metal swirl that suggests a torch. It's a new beacon for the historically Black neighborhood.

Wabash Arts Corridor

WABASH ARTS CORRIDOR

Running along both sides of Wabash Avenue from Ida B. Wells Drive south to 16th Street, this mile-long stretch is a curated gallery for muralists and street artists. The district contains nearly 40 permanent installations and an ever-evolving set of temporary exhibitions, and has included work by prominent Chicago illustrators like Shepard Fairey, Hebru Brantley, and Sam Kirk.

MIRÓ'S *CHICAGO*

It might be overshadowed by the iconic, untitled Picasso across the street in Daley Plaza, but Spanish surrealist Joan Miró's 39-foot-tall abstract sculpture, which sits next to the Chicago Temple building, deserves just as much attention. With a curvy concrete base inset with ceramics and a bronze upper body, the work suggests a celestial goddess presiding over Loop passersby.

BRIDGEPORT ART CENTER

Originally a Spiegel Catalog warehouse, this massive facility (500,000 square feet across six stories) is home to artists' studios, galleries, shops, and event spaces. It's not convenient to public transit, but take a cab on the third Friday of the month for Open Studios night to see resident artists' work. The small Chicago Maritime Museum on the bottom floor explains the importance of water to the city's history.

Chicago Then and Now

THE EARLY DAYS

Before Chicago was officially "discovered" by the team of Father Jacques Marquette, a French missionary, and Louis Jolliet, a French-Canadian mapmaker and trader, in 1673, the area served as a center of trade and seasonal hunting grounds for several Native American tribes, including the Miami, Illinois, and Potawatomi. Villages kept close trading ties with the French, though scuffles with the Fox tribe kept the French influence at bay until 1779. That year, Black French trader Jean Baptiste Point du Sable built a five-room "mansion" by the mouth of the Chicago River on the shore of Lake Michigan.

THE GREAT FIRE

The city grew until 1871, when a fire in the barn of Catherine and Patrick O'Leary spread across the city, killing hundreds. (Contrary to the legend, it was probably not started by a cow kicking over a lantern.) A recent drought coupled with crowded wooden buildings and wood-brick streets allowed the blaze to take hold quickly, destroying 18,000 structures within 36 hours.

GANGSTERS TO THE GREAT MIGRATION

World War I (aka the Great War) changed the face of Chicago. Postwar—and especially during Prohibition (1920–33)—the Torrio–Capone organization expanded its gambling and liquor distribution operations, consolidating its power during the violent "beer wars" from 1924 to 1930. Hundreds of casualties include the seven victims of the infamous 1929 St. Valentine's Day Massacre. In 1934 the FBI gunned down bank robber and "Public Enemy No. 1" John Dillinger outside the

Important Dates in Chicago History

1673: Chicago discovered by Marquette and Jolliet

1837: Chicago incorporated as a city

1860: First national political convention. Abraham Lincoln nominated as the Republican candidate for president

1871: Great Chicago Fire

1886: Haymarket Riot

1893: World's Columbian Exposition

1968: Democratic National Convention

1973: Sears (now Willis) Tower, tallest building in North America, completed

2008: Then Illinois senator Barack Obama elected 44th president of the United States

Biograph Theater on the North Side, now a theater venue and a Chicago landmark.

The Great War also led to the Great Migration, when African Americans from the South moved to the northern cities between 1916 and 1970. World War I slowed immigration from Europe but increased jobs in Chicago's manufacturing industry. More than 500,000 African Americans came to the city to find work, and by the mid-20th century African Americans were a strong force in Chicago's political, economic, and cultural life.

THE DALEY DYNASTY

The Daley family's unmatched influence began when Richard J. Daley became mayor in 1955. He was reelected five times, and his son Richard M. Daley later served six terms himself until opting out in 2011, when President Barack Obama's former chief of staff, Rahm Emanuel, won.

The first Mayor Daley redrew Chicago's landscape, overseeing the construction of O'Hare International Airport, the expressway system, the University of Illinois at Chicago, and a towering skyline. He also helped John F. Kennedy get elected.

Despite these advances, Mayor Richard J. Daley is perhaps best known for his crackdown on student protesters during the 1968 Democratic National Convention. Americans watched on their televisions as the Chicago police beat the city's youth with sticks and blinded them with tear gas. That incident, plus his "shoot-to-kill" order during the riots that followed the assassination of Dr. Martin Luther King Jr., and his use of public funds to build giant, disastrous public housing projects like Cabrini–Green, eventually led to the temporary dissolution of the Democratic machine in Chicago. After Daley's death, Chicago's first Black—and beloved—mayor, Harold Washington, took office in 1983.

CHICAGO TODAY

The thriving commercial and financial "City of Broad Shoulders" is spiked with gorgeous architecture and set with cultural and recreational gems, including the Art Institute, Millennium Park, 250 theater companies, and 30 miles of shoreline. Approximately 2.7 million residents live within the city limits, and tens of thousands commute from the ever-sprawling suburbs to work downtown.

Mayor Daley (who served 6 terms, from 1989 to 2011) gave downtown a makeover, with his focus on eco-friendly building initiatives that led to a green roof on City Hall and new bike paths throughout town. But parts of the South and West sides remain mired in poverty and suffer the brunt of the gun violence that has made international headlines.

There are always controversies (former governor Rod Blagojevich was convicted of federal corruption charges in 2011 and current Mayor Lightfoot is no stranger to contention), but most Chicagoans are fiercely proud to call the city home.

Chicago Sports Teams

You can't talk about Chicago for long without hearing the name of at least one of its storied sports legends: Michael Jordan, Scottie Pippen, Walter "Sweetness" Payton, William "The Refrigerator" Perry, Ernie Banks, "Slammin'" Sammy Sosa, and "Shoeless" Joe Jackson. One of the best ways to experience the spirit of Chicago is to join its fiercely loyal fans at a game.

CHICAGO BEARS

Chicago's hard-fought brand of football has made the Monsters of the Midway the winningest franchise in NFL history; they've won more than 750 games. The team last made it to the Super Bowl in 2006, but has not fared particularly well in the years since. The organization announced in 2021 that it would purchase the 326-acre Arlington Park property in suburban Arlington Heights, which could become the site of a new stadium, though Mayor Lightfoot said she wants the team to remain at Soldier Field.

Where They Play: Soldier Field

Season: August–December

How to Buy Tickets: Ticketmaster ☎312/559–1212.

Most Notable Players: Dick Butkus, Mike Ditka, Sid Luckman, Bronko Nagurski, Walter Payton, Gale Sayers

CHICAGO BULLS

Although the days of Air Jordan, three-peats, and Dennis Rodman in wedding dresses are long gone, the legacy established by winning six championships in eight years has sustained the Bulls's popularity, even through the leaner years that followed. Hope is everlasting, though, as the team rebuilds around a new roster of young stars.

Where They Play: United Center

Season: October–April

How to Buy Tickets: Ticket office ☎312/455–4000.

Most Notable Players: Michael Jordan, Dennis Rodman, Scottie Pippen, Luol Deng, Joakim Noah

Past Highlights: The Bulls owned the 1990s, becoming the only team in NBA history to win more than 70 games in a season in 1995–96 with an incredible 72–10 record.

CHICAGO CUBS

The Cubbies certainly earned their reputation as "Lovable Losers," leading on generations of ever-hopeful fans for more than 100 championship-free years. The streak was broken with a World Series win in 2016—only 108 years after the Cubs' last championship. Some fans complain that the Cubs' current owners are investing more in upgrades to both Wrigley Field and the surrounding real estate than in winning, but there's still always next year.

Where They Play: Wrigley Field

Season: April–September

How to Buy Tickets: Ticket office ☎773/404–2827 ⊕ chicago.cubs.mlb.com

Most Notable Players: Ernie Banks, Ron Santo, Ryne Sandberg, Sammy Sosa

Past Highlights: "Slammin'" Sammy Sosa played a major role in reawakening Americans' interest in baseball in 1998 as he battled Mark McGwire in a historic chase for the home-run record, finishing with 66 home runs during the height of the steroid era.

CHICAGO WHITE SOX

The South Side favorites won the World Series in 2005 and then made the playoffs only once in the next 14 seasons but they've seen postseason play in both 2020 and 2021. The Sox's win against the Yankees in the nationally televised "Field of Dreams" game in August 2021 marked them as a team to watch, with more promise in coming seasons than their North Side rivals.

Where They Play: Guaranteed Rate Field

Season: April–September

How to Buy Tickets: Ticket office ☎ 312/674–1000.

Most Notable Players: "Shoeless" Joe Jackson, Nellie Fox, Luis Aparicio, Harold Baines, Frank Thomas

Past Highlights: In July 2009 Mark Buehrle, a veteran pitcher who had spent his entire career with the White Sox, notched the second perfect game in the team's history, earning him a congratulatory phone call from President Obama (an avowed Sox fan).

CHICAGO BLACKHAWKS

Though the Hawks have led the NHL in attendance for the last three seasons, they too were hit by the seemingly city-wide championship drought, having failed to win a Stanley Cup since 1961. That's changed in recent years, with three championships in the span of six seasons (2010, 2013, and 2015). But fans who got used to the hockey season extending into late spring had a rude awakening in 2018, when the Blackhawks missed the playoffs for the first time in 10 years. The team made it back in 2020 but were knocked out in the first round; the Hawks missed the playoffs again in 2021.

Where They Play: United Center

Season: October–April

How to Buy Tickets: Ticket office ☎ 800/745–3000 ⊕ blackhawks.nhl.com

Most Notable Players: Stan Mikita, Pierre Pilote, Bobby Hull, Denis Savard, Tony Esposito

Past Highlights: The Hawks brought the Cup home to Chicago in 2010 on a thrilling sudden-death overtime goal by Patrick Kane to beat the Flyers in Game 6. Even the Chicago Picasso donned a hockey mask in celebration.

CHICAGO SKY

The WNBA team's 2006 debut ended in last place in the Eastern Conference, but they improved steadily, making it to the WNBA Finals in 2014. In 2021, under head coach James Wade and with the addition of Candace Parker, a two-time league MVP who grew up in suburban Naperville, Illinois, the Sky clinched their first WNBA championship in front of a sold-out home court crowd.

Where They Play: Wintrust Arena

Season: May–September

How to Buy Tickets: Ticket office ☎ 866/759–9622 ⊕ sky.wnba.com.

Most Notable Players: Sylvia Fowles, Elena Delle Donne, Courtney Vandersloot, Candace Parker

CHICAGO FIRE FC

The Chicago Fire Football Club ended its first season in 1998 by taking home the MLS Cup and the U.S. Open Cup. They've had their ups and downs since, with a fallow stretch coinciding with their 14-season residency at SeatGeek Stadium in suburban Bridgeview. In 2020, new owner and chairman Joe Mansueto brought the team back to Soldier Field, where the Fire had played prior to the stadium's renovation in 2002.

Where They Play: Soldier Field

Season: April–November

How to Buy Tickets: Ticket office ☎ 872/710–0800

Most Notable Players: Zach Thornton, Chris Armas, Peter Nowak

Best Tours

Whether you're interested in architecture, food, history, or something else, there's a tour for you in Chicago.

ARCHITECTURE TOURS

Great cities might have great buildings, but few compare to Chicago. At trip to Chicago is not complete with an architectural tour. There are many throughout the city from which to choose. Take one to discover the skyscraping Loop or one of the Prairie School buildings created by Frank Lloyd Wright.

Chicago Architecture Center. The Chicago Architecture Center conducts excellent docent-led boat, walking, and bus tours of the Loop and beyond. To get a panoramic view of Chicago's magnificent skyline, try the boat tours. ⊠ *111 E. Wacker Dr., Chicago Loop* ☎ *312/922–3432* ⊕ *www.architecture.org* ⊠ *From $15 walking tours.*

Chicago Greeter. At Greeter, savvy local volunteers run free two- to four-hour walking tours of the city's neighborhoods and areas of interest, such as fashion, film, and public art. Tours run Friday and weekends at 11:30 am and 1:30 pm and should be booked well in advance. Those who don't sign up in advance for a Chicago Greeter tour can show up for an on-the-spot InstaGreeter tour, offered Friday through Sunday at 11:30 am and 1:30 pm. Tours depart from the visitor information center at Chicago Cultural Center. ⊠ *77 E. Randolph St.* ☎ *312/744–8000* ⊕ *www.chicagogreeter.com* ⊠ *Free.*

BEHIND THE SCENES

For a look at what (or who) makes the city tick, check out the following tours.

BUS TOURS

Big Bus Tours. Big Bus Tours does hop-on, hop-off rides that take visitors to many downtown and Loop highlights and allow the flexibility to stop at attractions that catch your fancy. ⊠ *Chicago* ⊕ *www.bigbustours.com/en/chicago/chicago-bus-tours/* ⊠ *starting at $49.*

KAYAKING AND CANOEING TOURS

For a more adventurous spin down the river, rent a canoe or a kayak. Just beware of large boats and crew shells.

Chicago River Canoe and Kayak. This company offers seasonal boat rentals from its launch on the North Branch of the river, in the North Center neighborhood. You can paddle out on your own, or arrange a guided trip. ⊠ *3400 N. Rockwell St.* ☎ *773/704–2663* ⊕ *www.chicagoriverpaddle.com* ⊠ *from $20.*

Kayak Chicago. Tours focusing on everything from the city's varied architecture to the nighttime skyline are available at this well-regarded outfit. ⊠ *1220 W. Le Moyne St.* ☎ *312/852–9258* ⊕ *www.kayakchicago.com* ⊠ *rentals start at $30/hr.*

Urban Kayaks. At this popular outfitter you can join 90-minute tours of the main branch of the Chicago River. ⊠ *435 E. Chicago Riverwalk* ☎ *312/965–0035* ⊕ *www.urbankayaks.com* ⊠ *rentals start at $35/hr.*

Wateriders. Architectural tours and themed tours like "Ghosts and Gangsters Tour" are some of the offerings at Wateriders. ⊠ *East Bank Club, 500 N. Kingsbury St.* ☎ *312/953–9287* ⊕ *www.wateriders.com* ⊠ *starts at $65.*

RIVER AND LAKEFRONT TOURS

Hop into a boat and sail down the Chicago River for some of the prettiest views of the city. Some tours even head out to the lake for a skyscraper-studded panorama.

Shoreline Sightseeing. Shoreline's been plying these waters since 1939, and has tours of both the river and Lake Michigan. They also have seasonal water taxis; you won't get running narration, but it's not crowded and it's affordable—single rides range from $6 to $10 with stops at the Michigan Avenue Bridge, Polk Bros Park, Navy Pier, Union Station/Willis Tower, and Museum Campus. ⊠ *Chicago* ☏ *312/222–9328* ⊕ *www.shorelinesightseeing.com* ⊠ *starting at $27; water taxi starts at $6.*

Tall Ship *Windy*. Adventure and education meet on lake tours that illuminate Chicago's maritime history, the life of lake sailors, and environmentalism. Former Mayor Richard M. Daley declared the tall ship *Windy* the flagship of Chicago. ⊠ *Navy Pier – Tall Ship Windy, 600 E Gand Ave* ☏ *312/451–2700* ⊕ *tallshipwindy.com* ⊠ *starting at $39.*

Wendella. See the city at dusk on the Chicago at Sunset tour. There's also a river architecture tour and a combined river and lake tour. ⊠ *400 N. Michigan Ave., at the Wrigley Bldg.* ☏ *312/337–1446* ⊕ *www.wendellaboats.com* ⊠ *starting at $29.*

SPECIAL-INTEREST TOURS

Whether you're a foodie or a history buff, there's a tour for you.

Chicago Food Planet Food Tours. Sample local delicacies like deep-dish pizza, Polish pastries, Chicago-style hot dogs, and Szechuan cuisine on a Near North, Bucktown–Wicker Park, or Chinatown food-and-cultural tour. ⊠ *Chicago* ☏ *312/932–0800* ⊕ *www.chicagofoodplanet.com/#tour_section* ⊠ *starting at $65.*

Untouchable Tours: Chicago's Original Gangster Tour. Your guides, in character as Prohibition era goons, take you on a bus tour through Chicago's checkered mafia past. Though the kitsch factor is high, the tours are stuffed with history and will take you to neighborhoods you might otherwise miss. ⊠ *Chicago* ☏ *773/881–1195* ⊕ *www.gangstertour.com* ⊠ *$35.*

CHICAGO TOURISM

Choose Chicago. A comprehensive collection of sightseeing excursions by air, water, and land can be found through the city's tourism bureau, Choose Chicago. ⊠ *Chicago* ☏ *312/567–8500* ⊕ *www.choosechicago.com/things-to-do/tours-attractions/.*

Free and Almost Free

It's easy to spend money in Chicago, what with shopping, museum-entrance fees, restaurants, and theater, but if you'd like to put your wallet away for a while, here are some options. The Lincoln Park Zoo is also free.

FREE MUSEUMS AND GALLERIES

■ Block Museum of Art

■ DePaul Art Museum

■ Design Museum of Chicago

■ DuSable Museum of African-American History: free Wed.

■ Museum of Contemporary Photography

■ National Museum of Mexican Art

■ National Museum of Puerto Rican Arts and Culture

■ National Veterans Art Museum

■ Smart Museum of Art

■ Swedish American Museum: free 2nd Tues. of month

NOTABLE PUBLIC ART

■ Chicago has some of the most famous public art in the country, including a Picasso in Daley Plaza, Alexander Calder's *Flamingo* in Federal Plaza, and Anish Kapoor's *Cloud Gate* sculpture in Millennium Park. For a fairly comprehensive list, see www.cityofchicago.org/publicart or pick up a Chicago Public Art guide at a visitor center.

■ The City Gallery (806 N. Michigan Ave.) in the Historic Water Tower has rotatingexhibits of Chicago-themed photography.

■ Five different galleries showcase contemporary visual art by local artists at the Chicago Cultural Center (*www.chicagoculturalcenter.org*).

FREE CONCERTS

■ Free concerts—from classic and jazz to electronica and world beat—are performed Wednesdays and some Mondays in season at 12:15 in the Chicago Cultural Center (*www.chicagoculturalcenter.org*).

■ Grant Park and Millennium Park host regular classical and pop concerts in summer. For a schedule, pick up the Chicago Reader or visit the Time Out Chicago website at www.timeout.chicago.

MORE GREAT EXPERIENCES FOR $7 OR LESS

■ Take a free guided tour of selected River North art galleries on the second Saturday of every month in season. To RSVP, see www.chicagogallerynews.com/organizations/free-cgn-saturday-gallery-tours.

■ Spend an afternoon in the gardens at the Garfield Park Conservatory, with 12 acres of indoor and outdoor botanical habitats. Admission is free but timed reservations may be required; see www.garfieldconservatory.org.

■ Book a neighborhood walking tour with the Chicago Greeters. Led by knowledgeable local residents, Greeter tours can be tailored to your interests. They're free but you'll need to book at www.chicagogreeter.com at least 10 business days in advance.

■ Listen to some Statue Stories. This public art program recruited 28 celebrities with Chicago connections to lend their voices to monologues written for some of the city's most familiar sculptures—enter a unique URL on your smartphone and hear John C. Reilly voice Abraham Lincoln, or Shonda Rhimes speak as Miró's *Chicago*. Go to www.statuestorieschicago.com to set your itinerary.

Chicago with Kids

Chicago sometimes seems to have been designed with kids in mind. There are many places to play and things to do, from building sand castles at one of the lakefront's many beaches to playing 18-hole minigolf at Maggie Daley Park in summer. Here are some suggestions for ways to show kids the sights.

MUSEUMS

Several area museums are specifically designed for kids. At the **Chicago Children's Museum**, three floors of exhibits cast off with a play structure in the shape of a schooner, where kids can walk the gangplank and slide down to the lower level, and make a splash with a water playground, featuring a scaled-down river and a waterwheel.

Also at **Navy Pier** you'll find a Ferris wheel and Viennese swings (the kind that go around in a circle like a merry-go-round). In summer, crowds of kids make the most of Pier Park's light tower ride, musical carousel, and funhouse maze.

Many other Chicago museums are also kid-friendly, especially the butterfly haven and the animal habitat exhibit with its climbable tree house at the **Peggy Notebaert Nature Museum,** the replica coal mine and hands-on Idea Factory at the **Museum of Science and Industry,** the dinosaur exhibits at the **Field Museum,** and the sharks and dolphins at the **John G. Shedd Aquarium.**

PARKS, ZOOS, AND OUTSIDE ACTIVITIES

Chicago's neighborhoods are dotted with area play lots that have playground equipment as well as several ice-skating rinks for winter months. On scorching days, visit the **63rd Street Beach House,** at 63rd Street and Lake Shore Drive in Woodlawn. The interactive spiral fountain in the courtyard jumps and splashes, leaving kids giggling and jumping. The **North Park Village Nature Center** on the Far Northwest Side (on Pulaski Road north of Bryn Mawr Avenue) is a wilderness oasis, serving up 46 acres of trails and a kid-oriented Nature Center with hands-on activities and fun educational programs. Deer sightings are common here.

Millennium Park has a 16,000-square-foot ice-skating rink. Skaters have an unparalleled view of downtown as they whiz around the ice. Nearby **Maggie Daley Park** offers a looping skating ribbon, in addition to climbing walls and other rugged equipment for summer play.

For more structured fun, there are two zoos: the free **Lincoln Park Zoo** and the large, suburban **Brookfield Zoo,** which has surprising exhibits such as a wall of pulsing jellyfish.

What to Watch and Read

A RAISIN IN THE SUN

Lorraine Hansberry's 1959 play (and its 1961 movie adaptation), center on a Black family on Chicago's South Side contemplating using an insurance windfall to buy a house in a white neighborhood. The resistance faced by the Younger family was inspired by similar housing discrimination Hansberry's own family faced when she was a child in Chicago, when restrictive housing covenants helped ingrain the city's enduring segregation.

THE BLUES BROTHERS

When John Belushi and Dan Aykroyd took a couple of their *Saturday Night Live* characters to the big screen, they set Jake and Elwood Blues loose across a dementedly wacky, fantasyland version of Chicago. The location shots, though, were for the most part quite real, including the epic car chase through Lower Wacker Drive and the climactic crash into the Richard J. Daley Center.

THE GREAT BELIEVERS

A finalist for the National Book Award, Rebecca Makkai's 2018 novel is set largely in Chicago's Boystown neighborhood (now commonly called Northalsted) across the 1980s, as the city's gay community is coalescing only to be faced with the AIDS crisis. Makkai's attention to geographic detail fixes the plot firmly in the real neighborhood, underscoring the all-too-recent reality of the epidemic.

HIGH FIDELITY

John Cusack moved Nick Hornby's novel about a mopey pop-music obsessive from London to Chicago for this 2000 film adaptation. Building out a real Wicker Park storefront into the record shop owned by Cusack's character and filming scenes on CTA trains, the movie feels like an affectionate wrap party for the city's alternative music scene of the 1990s.

THE JUNGLE

Upton Sinclair's muckraking novel of 1906 exposed the widespread corruption and dangerous working conditions that surrounded Chicago's stockyards and meatpacking industry. Sinclair intended it as a socialist rallying cry against capitalism, but its real-world impact was instead a push for better sanitation in slaughterhouses and the establishment of the agency that became the Food and Drug Administration.

HOOP DREAMS

This low-budget 1994 documentary follows Arthur Agee and William Gates, talented high-school basketball players who aspire to get college scholarships and make it to the NBA. Both come from impoverished backgrounds in disadvantaged Chicago neighborhoods; both are recruited by a well-off suburban private school. The filmmakers initially intended to make a 30-minute short but ended up following Gates and Agee for six years.

DIVISION STREET

The late Studs Terkel pivoted from top-tier radio interviewer to oral historian with this 1967 book, his first in a format he would come to define. Terkel interviewed 70 Chicago residents across a spectrum of backgrounds, eliciting their unguarded opinions about the state of the world. Then, rather than editorializing about their responses, he simply arranged them: each subject, in their own words, put into conversation with each other by a worthy chronicler.

NEVER A CITY SO REAL:
A WALK IN CHICAGO

Journalist and author Alex Kotlowitz's 2004 book is a biography of his adopted city by way of its residents. Each chapter is a portrait of a Chicagoan whose unique story Kotlowitz connects back to Chicago's larger contradictions, both frustrating and beautiful.

Chapter 2

TRAVEL SMART CHICAGO

Updated by
Jessica Mlinaric

👤 POPULATION:
8,877,000

💬 LANGUAGE:
English

$ CURRENCY:
U.S. Dollar

☎ AREA CODE:
312, 773, 708

⚠ EMERGENCIES:
911

🚗 DRIVING:
On the right side of the road

⚡ ELECTRICITY:
120-240 v/60 cycles;
plugs have two or three
rectangular prongs

� TIME:
One hour behind New York

🌐 WEB RESOURCES:
www.choosechicago.com
www.gochicago.com
www.enjoyillinois.com

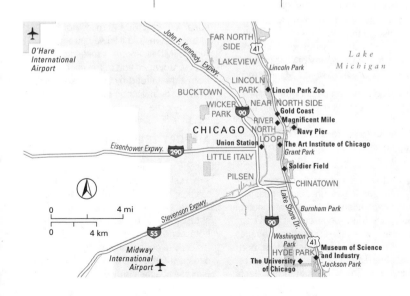

Getting Here and Around

Chicago is famously known as a city of neighborhoods. The Loop is Chicago's epicenter of business, finance, and government. Neighborhoods surrounding the Loop are River North (an area populated by art galleries and high-end boutiques), Near North (bordered by Lake Michigan and Navy Pier), and the West Loop and South Loop, both areas with trendy residential areas plus hip dining and shopping options.

Moving north, you'll encounter the Magnificent Mile (North Michigan Avenue), which gives way to the Gold Coast, so named for its luxurious mansions, stately museums, and deluxe entertainment venues. Lincoln Park, Lakeview, Wrigleyville, Lincoln Square, and Andersonville all lie north of these areas, and each has considerable charm.

Neighborhoods west of the Loop are River West, Wicker Park, Bucktown, and Logan Square, the latest place for of-the-moment art, shopping, dining, and nightlife.

Beyond the South Loop lie Chinatown; Pilsen, where long-standing Mexican murals and taquerias intermingle with a burgeoning arts scene; and Hyde Park, home to the University of Chicago and the Museum of Science and Industry.

Traveling between neighborhoods is a relatively sane experience, thanks to the matrix of bus and train routes managed by the Chicago Transit Authority. Driving can be harried, but taxis are normally plentiful in most parts of town.

Chicago streets generally follow a grid pattern, running north–south or east–west and radiating from a center point at State and Madison streets in the Loop. East and west street numbers go up as you move away from State Street; north and south street numbers rise as you move away from Madison Street. Each block is represented by a hundred number (so the 12th block north of Madison will be the 1200 block).

■ TIP→ **The Chicago tourism bureau, known as Choose Chicago (choosechicago.com) often has hotel and local transportation packages that include tickets to major museum exhibits, theater productions, or other special events.**

Air

There are national and international direct flights to Chicago. From New York, travel time by air to Chicago is 2 hours; from Dallas, 2½ hours; from San Francisco, 4¾ hours; from Los Angeles, 4½ hours; from London, 9 hours. There are no direct flights from Sydney, but travel time is about 19 hours (not including layovers). In Chicago the general rule is to arrive at the airport two hours before an international flight; for a domestic flight, plan to arrive 90 minutes early if you're checking luggage and 60 minutes if you're not.

Chicago has two airports: O'Hare International Airport (ORD; 19 miles northwest of downtown) and Midway International Airport (MDW; about 11 miles southwest of downtown). If you're traveling to or from either airport by bus or car during morning or afternoon rush hours, factor in some extra time—ground transport can be slow.

AIRPORT TRANSFERS

There are shuttles from each airport to various points in the city. When taking an airport shuttle bus to O'Hare or Midway to catch a departing flight, be sure to allow at least 1½ hours. Though some shuttles make regular stops at the major hotels and don't require reservations, it's best to check. Reservations are not necessary from the airports. GO Airport Express coaches provide service from both airports to major downtown and Near North locations as well as to most suburbs.

To and from O'Hare: It can take anywhere from 30 to 90 minutes to travel between downtown and O'Hare by car, based on time of day, weather conditions, and construction on the Kennedy Expressway (Interstate 90).

Chicago Transit Authority (CTA) trains, called elevated or El trains, are the cheapest way to and from the airports; they can also be the most convenient transfer: The Blue Line El train offers a reliable 45-minute trip between the Loop and O'Hare. Shared ride services like Uber and Lyft to downtown from O'Hare take at least 45 minutes and one-way fares start at $25. Metered cab service is available at O'Hare. Expect to pay about $40 to $50 plus tip from O'Hare to Near North and downtown locations.

To and from Midway: Driving between Midway and downtown can take 30 to 60 minutes, depending on traffic conditions on the Stevenson Expressway (Interstate 55).

Chicago Transit Authority (CTA) trains, called elevated or El trains, are the cheapest way to and from the airports; they can also be the most convenient transfer: The Orange Line El train runs from the Loop to Midway in about 30 minutes. From Midway to downtown, a shared ride service like Uber or Lyft takes at least a half hour and a one-way fare starts at $15. Metered cab service is available at both O'Hare and Midway airports. Expect to pay about $25 to $35 plus tip from Midway.

Transfers between airports: O'Hare and Midway airports are on opposite ends of the city, so moving between them can be an arduous, time-consuming task. Your best and cheapest move is hopping on the El. You will travel the Blue Line to the Orange Line, transferring at the Clark/Lake stop to get from O'Hare to Midway, reversing the trip to go from Midway to O'Hare. The entire journey should take you less than two hours.

Bicycle

Mayor Richard Daley (served 1989 to 2011) worked to establish Chicago as one of the most bike-friendly cities in the United States, and it remains that way today. There are more than 300 miles of designated bike routes in the city, running through historic areas, beautiful parks, and along city streets (look for the words "bike lane"). Bicycling on busy city streets can be a challenge and is not for the faint of heart—cars come within inches of riders, and the doors of parked cars can swing open at any time. The best bet for a scenic ride is the lakefront, which has a traffic-free 18-mile asphalt trail with scenic views of the skyline. When your bike is unattended, always lock it; there are bike racks throughout the city.

In 2013, the Divvy Bikes bike share program launched in Chicago. The network now boasts 6,000 bikes at more than 600 stations throughout the city (though there are far fewer, and in some cases none, on large swaths of the South and West sides). You can purchase a 24-hour pass at any of the Divvy stations for $15, which allows riders to take unlimited 3-hour rides during that period. A single ride costs $3.30 for 30 minutes. Ride for more than 30 minutes at a time, and you'll incur extra charges.

In Millennium Park at Michigan Avenue and Randolph Street, Hub312 offers 244 indoor bike-parking spaces plus showers and lockers for $15 a day. Bike rentals include adult and kids bikes and child

Getting Here and Around

bike trailers and start at $20 per hour. Bike rentals are also readily available at Bike and Roll Chicago, which has three locations, one at Millennium Park, one at Navy Pier, and one at Lakeshore Sports & Fitness in the Loop. Bike and Roll Chicago carries a good selection of mountain and cross bikes. Rates start at $29 per hour. The Chicago Department of Transportation publishes free route maps. The Active Transportation Alliance provides information on bike safety and local updates. Bobby's Bike Hike takes guests on year-round cycling tours of Chicago. The three-hour tours begin at 540 N. Lake Shore Drive and cycle through historic neighborhoods, shopping areas, and the lakefront. A $40 to $80 fee includes bikes, helmets, and guides.

 Boat

Water taxis are an economical, in-the-know way to cruise parts of the Chicago River and Lake Michigan. A combination of working stiffs and tourists boards these boats daily. You won't get the in-depth narrative of an architecture tour, but the views of Chicago's waterways are just as good—and you can't beat the price: $6 per one-way ticket and $10 for a day pass.

Wendella Boats operates Chicago Water Taxis, which use six docks along the Chicago River (Michigan Avenue, West Loop, Riverwalk, Chicago Avenue, Goose Island, and Chinatown). The entire ride takes about a half hour, and you'll get to see a good portion of the downtown part of the river. The boats operate seven days a week, April through October. You can purchase tickets at any dock or on the company's website.

Shoreline Sightseeing's water taxis run two routes: the River Taxi cruises between the Willis (formerly Sears) Tower and Navy Pier, while the Lake Taxi navigates Lake Michigan between Navy Pier and the Museum Campus. Late May to early September, water taxis run from 10 am to 6 pm. You can purchase tickets at any dock or in advance on the company's website.

 Car

Chicago traffic is often heavy, on-street parking is nearly impossible to find, parking lots are expensive, congestion creates frustrating delays (especially during rush-hour snarls), and other drivers may be impatient with those who are unfamiliar with the city and its roads. On the other hand, Chicago's network of buses and rapid-transit rail is extensive, and taxis and limousines are readily available (the latter often priced competitively with metered cabs), so rent a car *only* if you plan to visit outlying suburbs that are not accessible by public transportation.

If you do need to rent one, you'll have plenty of options, from the big chains to luxury options. If you rent from the airport, expect to pay slightly more because of airport taxes.

The Illinois tollways snake around the outskirts of the city. Interstate 294 runs north and south between Wisconsin and Indiana. Interstate 90 runs northwest to western Wisconsin, including Madison and Wisconsin Dells. Interstate 88 runs east–west and goes from Eisenhower to Interstate 55. Traffic on all is sometimes just as congested as on the regular expressways. Most tollgates are unmanned, so bring lots of change if you don't have an I-Pass, which is sometimes included with rental cars. Even though tolls are double without the I-Pass, it's not cost-effective to purchase one for a couple of days.

The Illinois Department of Transportation gives information on expressway congestion, travel times, and lane closures and directions on state roadways.

GASOLINE
Gas stations are less numerous in downtown Chicago than in the outlying neighborhoods and suburbs. Filling up is about 50¢ higher per gallon downtown, when you can find a station. Major credit cards are accepted at all gas stations, and the majority of stations are completely self-serve.

PARKING
Most of Chicago's streets have metered parking, but during peak hours it's hard to find a spot. Most parking pay boxes accept quarters and credit cards in increments as small as five minutes in high-traffic areas, up to an hour in less crowded neighborhoods. Prices average $2–$6.50 an hour. Parking lots and garages are plentiful downtown, but they're expensive. You could pay anywhere from $15 for three hours prepaid with the SpotHero app to more than double for three hours in a private lot. Some neighborhoods, such as the area of Lakeview known as Wrigleyville, enforce restricted parking (especially strict on Cubs' game nights) and will tow cars without permits. You won't find many public parking lots in the neighborhoods. Many major thoroughfares restrict parking during peak travel hours, generally from 7 to 9 am heading toward downtown and from 4 to 6 pm heading away. Read street signs carefully to determine whether a parking spot is legal. On snow days in winter cars parked in designated "snow route areas" will be towed. There's a $150 plus

$30 per day fine plus the cost of towing the car. In sum, Chicago isn't the most car-friendly place for visitors. Unless it's a necessity, it's best to forget renting a car and use public transportation.

ROAD CONDITIONS
The Loop and some residential neighborhoods such as Lincoln Park, Lakeview, and Bucktown are made up of mostly one-way streets, so be sure to read signs carefully.

Rush hours are 6:30 to 9:30 am and 4 to 7 pm, but don't be surprised if the rush starts earlier or ends later, depending on weather conditions, big events, and holiday weekends. There are always bottlenecks on the expressways, particularly where the Edens and Kennedy merge, and downtown on the Dan Ryan from 22nd Street into the Loop. Sometimes anything around the airport is rough. There are electronic signs on the expressways that post updates on the congestion. Additionally, summertime is high time for construction on highways and inner-city roads. Drive with patience.

ROADSIDE EMERGENCIES
Dial 911 in an emergency to reach police, fire, or ambulance services. AAA Chicago provides roadside assistance to members. Mr. Locks Security Systems will unlock your vehicle 24 hours a day.

RULES OF THE ROAD
Speed limits in Chicago vary, but on most city roads it's 30 mph. Most interstate highways, except in congested areas, have a speed limit of 55 to 70 mph. In Chicago you may turn right at a red light after stopping if there's no oncoming traffic and no restrictions are posted. When in doubt, wait for the green. Cameras have been installed at many major intersections in the city to catch drivers who run red lights and commit other infractions. There are many one-way

Getting Here and Around

streets in Chicago, particularly in and around the Loop, so be alert to signs and other cars. Illinois drunk-driving laws are quite strict. Anyone caught driving with a blood-alcohol content of .08 or more will automatically have his or her license seized and be issued a ticket; authorities in home states will also be notified. Those with Illinois driver's licenses can have their licenses suspended for three months on the first offense.

Passengers are required to wear seat belts. Always strap children under age eight into approved child-safety seats.

It's illegal to use handheld cellular phones while driving in the city; restrictions vary in the suburbs. Headlights are compulsory if you're using windshield wipers. Radar detectors are legal in Illinois.

Ⓜ Public Transportation

Chicago's extensive public transportation network includes rapid-transit trains, buses, and a commuter-rail network. The Chicago Transit Authority, or CTA, operates the city buses, rapid-transit trains (the El), and suburban buses (Pace). Metra runs the commuter rail.

The Regional Transportation Authority (RTA) for northeastern Illinois oversees and coordinates the activities of the CTA and Metra. The RTA's website can be a useful first stop if you are planning to combine suburban and city public transit while in Chicago.

CTA: THE EL AND BUSES

The Chicago Transit Authority (CTA) operates rapid-transit trains and buses. Chicago's rapid-transit train system is known as the El. Each of the eight lines has a color name as well as a route name: Blue (O'Hare–Congress–Douglas),

Brown (Ravenswood), Green (Lake–Englewood–Jackson Park), Orange (Midway), Purple (Evanston), Red (Howard–Dan Ryan), Yellow (Skokie Swift), and Pink (Cermak). In general, the route names indicate the first and last stop on the train. Chicagoans refer to trains both by the color and the route name. Most, but not all, rapid-transit lines operate 24 hours; some stations are closed at night. The El, though very crowded during rush hours, is the fastest way to get around (unless you're coming from the suburbs, in which case the Metra is quicker but doesn't run as often). Trains run about every 10 minutes during rush hours, every 30 minutes on weekends, and every 15 minutes at other times. Pick up the brochure "Downtown Transit Sightseeing Guide" for hours, fares, and other pertinent information. (You can also download it at ⊕ www.transitchicago. com/assets/1/6/ctamap_downtown-transitsightseeingguide.pdf). In general, late-night CTA travel is not recommended. Note that many of the Red and Blue line stations are subways; the rest are elevated. This means if you're heading to O'Hare and looking for the Blue Line, you may have to look for a stairway down, not up.

The basic fee for rapid-transit trains is $2.50, which must be paid using a Ventra transit card. The basic fare for buses is $2.25 using a Ventra card and an addtional 25¢ for a transfer. Rechargable Ventra cards can be purchased at CTA station vending machines as well as at Jewel and CVS stores; they can be topped up with any amount or loaded with a pass valid for 1, 3, 7, or 30 days of unlimited travel (costing $10, $20, $28, and $105 respectively). You can also purchase single-ride Ventra cards at any CTA stop.

These easy-to-use cards (which can be shared) are inserted into the turnstiles at CTA train stations and into machines as you board CTA buses; directions are clearly posted. To transfer between the Loop's elevated lines and the subway or between trains and buses, you must either use a Ventra card with at least 25¢ stored on it or, if you're not using a transit card, buy a transfer when you first board. If two CTA train lines meet, you can transfer for free. You can also obtain free train-to-train transfers from specially marked turnstiles at the Washington/State subway station or the State/Lake El station, or ask for a transfer card, good on downtown trains, at the ticket booth. Transfers can be used twice within a two-hour time period.

Buses generally stop on every other corner northbound and southbound (on State Street they stop at every corner). Eastbound and westbound buses generally stop on every corner. Buses from the Loop generally run north–south. Principal transfer points are on Michigan Avenue at the north side of Randolph Street for northbound buses, Adams Street and Wabash Avenue for westbound buses and the El, and State and Lake streets for southbound buses.

Bus schedules vary depending on the time of day and route; they typically run every 8 to 15 minutes, though service is less frequent on weekends, very early in the morning, and late at night. Schedules are available online at ⊕ www.transitchicago.com.

METRA: COMMUTER TRAINS

Metra serves the city and suburbs. The Metra Electric railroad has a line close to Lake Michigan; its trains stop in Hyde Park. The Metra commuter rail system has 11 lines to suburbs and surrounding

cities, including Aurora, Elgin, Joliet, and Waukegan; one line serves the North Shore suburbs, and another has a stop at McCormick Place. Trains leave from several downtown terminals.

Metra trains use a fare structure based on distance. A Metra weekend pass costs $10 and is valid for all-day use on any line except for the South Shore line.

🚕 Taxi

You can hail a cab on just about any busy street in Chicago. Hotel doormen will hail one for you as well. Cabs aren't all yellow anymore; look for standard-size sedans or, in some cases, minivans. Available taxis are sometimes indicated by an illuminated rooftop light. Chicago taxis are metered, with fares beginning at $3.25 (including a $1 fuel surcharge) upon entering the cab and 20¢ for each additional 1/9 mile or 36 seconds of wait time. A charge of $1 is made for the first additional passenger and 50¢ for each passenger after that. There's no extra baggage or credit-card charge. Taxi drivers expect at least a 15% tip.

🚆 Train

Amtrak offers nationwide service to Chicago's Union Station, at 225 South Canal Street.

Essentials

🍴 Dining

Sure, this city has great architecture, museums, and sports venues. But at its heart, Chicago is really a food town. This is evident in the priority that good eating takes, no matter the occasion. Rain or shine, locals will wait in a line that snakes around the corner for dolled-up dough-nuts at Doughnut Vault. They'll reserve part of their paychecks to dine at inventive Alinea. And they love to talk about their most recent meal—just ask.

It's no wonder that outdoor festivals are often centered on food, from Taste of Chicago in summer, which packs the grounds at Grant Park, to smaller celebrations, like the German-American fest in Lincoln Square, a mini-Oktoberfest in fall.

Although the city has always had options on the extreme ends of the spectrum—from the hole-in-the wall Italian beef sandwich shops to the special-occasion spots—it's now easier to find eateries in the middle that serve seasonal menus with a farm-to-table mantra. For the budget conscious, it's also a great time to dine: some talented chefs aren't bothering to wait for a liquor license, opening BYOB spots turning out polished fare (just try Han 202 in Chinatown).

EATING OUT STRATEGY

Where should we eat? With thousands of Chicago eateries competing for your attention, it may seem like a daunting question. But fret not—our expert writers and editors have done most of the legwork. The selections here represent the best this city has to offer—from hot dogs to haute cuisine. Find a review quickly in the listings, organized alphabetically within each neighborhood. Dig in, and enjoy!

WITH KIDS

Though it's unusual to see children in the dining rooms of Chicago's elite restaurants, dining with youngsters in the city does not have to mean culinary exile. Many of the restaurants in Chicago are excellent choices for families, and we've noted these in our reviews.

RESERVATIONS

Plan ahead if you're determined to snag a sought-after reservation. Some renowned restaurants are booked weeks or months in advance. If you're a large group, always call ahead, as even restaurants that don't take reservations often will make exceptions for groups of six or larger.

But you can get lucky at the last minute if you're flexible—and friendly. Most restaurants keep a few tables open for walk-ins and VIPs. Show up for dinner early (5:30 pm) or late (after 9 pm) and politely inquire about any last-minute vacancies or cancellations.

If you're calling a few days ahead of time, ask whether you can be put on a waiting list. Occasionally, an eatery may ask you to call the day before your scheduled meal to reconfirm: don't forget, or you could lose out.

WHAT TO WEAR

In general, Chicagoans are neat but casual dressers; only at the top-notch dining rooms do you see a more formal style. But the way you look can influence how you're treated—and where you're seated. Generally speaking, jeans will suffice at casual restaurants, although shorts, sweatpants, and sports jerseys are rarely appropriate. Moving up from there, a few pricier restaurants require jackets.

TIPPING AND TAXES

In most restaurants, tip the waiter 18% to 20%. (To figure the amount quickly, just take 10% of the bill and double it.) Bills for parties of six or more sometimes include the tip already. The city's tax on restaurant food is 10.75%.

SMOKING

Smoking is prohibited in all enclosed public spaces in Chicago, including restaurants and bars.

WINE

Although some of the city's top restaurants still include historic French vintages, most sommeliers are now focusing on small-production, lesser-known new-world wineries. Some are even keeping their wine lists purposefully small, so that they can change them frequently to match the season and the menu. Half bottles are becoming more prevalent, and good wines by the glass are everywhere. Don't hesitate to ask for recommendations. Even restaurants without a sommelier on staff will appoint knowledgeable servers to lend a hand with wine selections.

PRICES

If you're watching your budget, be sure to ask the price of daily specials recited by the waiter or captain. The charge for specials at some restaurants is noticeably out of line with the other prices on the menu. Beware of the $10 bottle of water; ask for tap water instead. And always review your bill.

If you eat early or late, you may be able to take advantage of a prix-fixe deal not offered at peak hours. Most upscale restaurants offer great lunch deals, with special menus at cut-rate prices designed to give customers a true taste of the place.

Many restaurants (particularly smaller ones downtown) accept only cash. If you plan to use a credit card, it's a good idea to double-check its acceptability when making reservations or before sitting down to eat.

Restaurant reviews have been shortened. For full information, visit Fodors.com.

What It Costs			
$	$$	$$$	$$$$
RESTAURANTS			
under $18	$18–$27	$28–$36	over $36

⊙ Discounts and Deals

Buying a Chicago CityPASS ($109, good for nine days from the date of first use) includes admission to the Shedd Aquarium, the Field Museum, and the Willis Tower Skydeck, plus the Museum of Science and Industry or 360 Chicago, and the Adler Planetarium or Art Institute of Chicago. Using it saves around 50%.

With the All-Inclusive Go Chicago Card you have options for one, two, three, or five consecutive days, which gets you admission to more than two-dozen local attractions, plus assorted discounts. There is also an Explorer Pass, which lets you choose the number of sights that you can see in a 60-day period. Prices start at $95.

Essentials

Health

COVID-19

Although COVID-19 brought travel to a virtual standstill for most of 2020 and into 2021, vaccinations have made travel possible again. Remaining requirements and restrictions—including those for non-vaccinated travelers—can, however, vary from one place (or even business) to the next. Check out the websites of the CDC and the U.S. Department of State, both of which have destination-specific, COVID-19 guidance. Also, in case travel is curtailed abruptly again, consider buying trip insurance. Just be sure to read the fine print: not all travel-insurance policies cover pandemic-related cancellations.

As of this writing, most places in Chicago require proof of vaccination or a negative COVID test in order to enter.

🛏 Lodging

Chicago hotels are as charming and individual as the city itself. Chalk it up in part to the city's magnificent architecture—and the fact that developers have morphed many historic buildings into boutique hotels. It's true that the places to stay come in all shapes and sizes, the majority being downtown high-rises ideally located to the action. Still, hotels are trickling into more remote neighborhoods, providing a different experience for the do-like-the-locals-do traveler.

Fair warning: room rates can be as temperamental as the city's climate. And just as snow in April and balmy weather in November are not uncommon, it's widely accepted that a hotel's room rates may drop $50 to $100 overnight—and rise again the next day. It all depends on the season and what festivals, conferences, and other events are happening around town.

Even so, it's wise to shop around. Focus on a neighborhood of interest, like the Near North Side, and you'll find budget chains such as Embassy Suites and luxury properties such as the Four Seasons Hotel Chicago within a few blocks of each other.

Ask yourself what kind of vibe you're up for. Luxe and sophisticated? Lounge under the handblown glass art installation at The Langham Chicago. Fun-loving and scene-y? Mingle with the culturati at Ace Hotel Chicago. Romantic and oh-so quiet? Take in the neighborhood scene by the lake at The Willows. There truly is something for every mood, every whim.

In many cases, a hotel's lively bar scene and artful design are what seals the deal, as is the case at The Godfrey Hotel, Chicago Athletic Association, and theWit. Rooms at these hot spots usually don't go for less than $250, but you'll walk away with bragging rights—and some pretty amazing Instagram pics.

LODGING STRATEGY

There are hundreds of hotels in Chicago to choose from. But don't worry—our expert writers and editors have researched them for you, and whittled the list down to the best. Here you'll find a wide variety, from friendly budget motels to sleek designer hot spots.

FACILITIES

Unless otherwise noted in the individual descriptions, all the hotels listed have private baths, central heating, and private phones. Almost all have Internet capability and Wi-Fi access as well as valet service.

RESERVATIONS

Reservations are an absolute necessity when planning your trip to Chicago—hotels often fill up with convention traffic, so book your room in advance.

WITH KIDS

In the listings, look for the word "Family," which indicates the property is particularly good for kids.

PRICES

Prices in the reviews are the lowest cost of a standard double room in high season; they do not take into account discounts or package deals you may find on consolidator websites.

Hotel reviews have been shortened. For full information, visit Fodors.com.

What It Costs			
$	**$$**	**$$$**	**$$$$**
UNDER $220			
under $220	$220–$319	$320–$420	over $420

🄨 Nightlife

Chicago's entertainment varies from loud and loose to sophisticated and sedate. You'll find classic Chicago corner bars in most neighborhoods, along with trendier alternatives like wine bars and lounges. The strains of blues and jazz provide much of the backbeat to the city's groove, and an alternative country scene is flourishing. As far as dancing is concerned, take your pick from cavernous clubs to smaller spots with DJs spinning dance tunes; there's everything from hip-hop to swing. Wicker Park/Bucktown and River North have the hottest nightlife, but prime spots are spread throughout the city.

Shows usually begin at 9 pm; cover charges generally range from $3 to $20, depending on the day of the week (Friday and Saturday nights are the most expensive). The list of blues and jazz clubs includes several South Side locations: be cautious about transportation here late at night, because some of these neighborhoods can be unsafe. Use a ride-share app or ask the bartender to call you a cab.

RESOURCES

To find out what's happening in the Windy City, head to *www.timeout.com/chicago* or *do312.com* for club listings, rotating parties, and DJ appearances. Time Out Chicago and the *Chicago Reader* also dish on the hottest bars and clubs. (You'll find theater and music listings in these publications as well.)

TIMING

Live music begins around 9 pm at bars around town. If you want to guarantee a seat, arrive well before the band's scheduled start and stake out a spot. Most bars close at 2 am Sunday through Friday and 3 am Saturday. A few dance clubs and late-night bars remain open until 4 am or 5 am (Berlin and the Mine Music Hall are very popular). Outdoor beer gardens such as Sheffield's are the exception; these close at 11 pm on weeknights and midnight on weekends. Some bars are not open seven days a week, so call before you go. Curtain times for performances are usually at 7:30 or 8 pm.

🄨 Performing Arts

If you're even mildly interested in the performing arts, Chicago has the means to put you in your seat—be it floor, mezzanine, or balcony. Just pick your preference (theater, dance, or symphony orchestra), and let an impressive body of artists do the rest. From critically

Where Should I Stay?

Neighborhood	Vibe	Pros	Cons
The Loop	Many historic hotels of architectural interest in an area filled with businesspeople on weekdays, and shoppers and theatergoers on weekends.	Accessible public transportation and abundant cabs and Ubers; great proximity to lakeside parks and museums, too.	El train noise; construction common; streets can sometimes be bare in late evening. It draws an older, more established crowd.
West Loop and South Loop	Mixed residential and business neighborhoods that are gentrifying quickly.	Trendy hotels; the restaurant and bar scene is booming.	Sometimes long walks to public transportation; minimal shopping. If you're looking for entertainment beyond the food and drink scene, it might require a quick drive or a long walk.
Near North	The pulse of the city, on and around North Michigan Avenue, has ritzy high-rise hotels and plenty of shopping and restaurants.	Many lodging options, including some of the city's most luxurious hotels. Lively streets abuzz until late night; safe.	Some hotels on the pricey side; crowded sidewalks; lots of tourists. And don't expect to find many bargains here.
River North	Lots of chains, from hotels to restaurants to shops, with a solid sprinkling of galleries, too.	Affordable lodging; easy access to public transportation; attractions nearby are family-friendly, especially during the day; high concentration of nightclubs.	Area might be too touristy for some. This is Chicago's home for chain restaurants; parking is a drag.
Lincoln Park and Wicker Park	Small, boutique hotels tucked on quiet, tree-lined streets with many independent shops and restaurants. Pedestrian-friendly area; you don't need a car to find a restaurant, bar, or bank.	Low crime; great paths for walks; lots of parkland. Eclectic collection of shops and restaurants, ranging from superaffordable to ultrapricey; from hot dogs to sushi, this place has it all.	Limited hotel selection; long walks to El train. Parking is almost impossible in some spots, and garages don't come cheap.
Lakeview and Far North Side	Busy around Wrigley Field, where both Chicagoans and travelers congregate in summertime; the area's lodging is midsize boutique hotels and B&Bs.	Low crime; moderately priced hotels; dining and shopping options (include some cool vintage-clothing boutiques) for all budgets; a slew of sports bars.	Congested traffic; panhandlers common, especially around El stations and Wrigley Field. Parking is a nightmare when the Cubs are playing in town.

acclaimed big names to fringe groups that specialize in experimental work, there truly is a performance art for everyone.

Ticket prices vary wildly, depending on whether you're seeing a high-profile group or venturing into more obscure territory. Chicago Symphony tickets range from $15 to $200, the Lyric Opera from $30 to $180 (if you can get them). Smaller choruses and orchestras charge from $10 to $30; watch the listings for free performances. Commercial theater tickets cost between $15 and $90; smaller experimental ensembles might charge $5, $10, or pay-what-you-can. Movie prices range from $14 for first-run houses to as low as $5 for some weekday matinees or second-run houses.

TICKETS

You can save money on seats for theater, dance, and comedy shows at **Hot Tix** (*www.hottix.org*), where unsold tickets are available, usually at half price (plus a service charge) on the day of the performance or up to several weeks in advance, depending on the show. Hot Tix booths are located across from the Chicago Cultural Center at 72 East Randolph Street and in the Block 37 shopping complex at 108 North State Street. Only the latter is open on Sunday and Monday. Full-price tickets for many performances can be purchased by phone or online through **Ticketmaster** (*800/653-8000, www.ticketmaster.com*).

For a cheaper, more intimate, and—arguably—equally rewarding theater experience, Chicago has a lively fringe theater scene. You'll find smaller storefront theater spaces scattered across the city (but concentrated on the North Side), where you can catch everything from dramatic classics mounted on tiny stages to edgy works by emerging writers. Best

of all, tickets often go for $20 or less and are usually available at the box office on the day of performance.

For hot, sold-out shows, such as performances by the Chicago Symphony Orchestra or the Lyric Opera of Chicago, call a day or two before the performance to see if there are any subscriber returns. Another option is to show up at the box office on concert day—a surprising number of people strike it lucky with on-the-spot tickets because of cancellations.

Small fees can have big payoffs! Many of the smaller neighborhood street festivals (there are hundreds in summer) request $5 to $10 donations upon entry, but it's often worth the expense: big-name bands are known to take the stage of even the most under-publicized festivals. For moment-to-moment festival coverage, check out *do312.com* or *www. timeout.com/chicago*.

 Safety

As in most large cities, the most common crimes in public places are pickpocketing, purse snatching, jewelry theft, and gambling scams. Keep your wallet in a front coat or pants pocket. Close your bag or purse securely and keep it close to you. Also beware of someone jostling you and of loud arguments; these could be ploys to distract your attention while another person grabs your wallet. Leave unnecessary credit cards at home, and hide valuables and jewelry from view.

Although crime on CTA buses and trains in general has declined, recently robbers have been targeting travelers with smartphones; keep your phone and other portable electronic devices out of sight on train platforms. Several additional precautions can reduce the chance of your

Essentials

becoming a victim: look alert and purposeful; know your route ahead of time; have your fare ready before boarding; and keep an eye on your purse or packages during the ride. Avoid taking public transit late at night.

The city has gained a reputation in recent years for being somewhat dangerous. While certain parts of Chicago are plagued by gun violence, they are largely segregated on the West and South Sides in areas that have long struggled with deep, intergenerational poverty. The city's tourist areas remain generally quite safe.

■TIP→ **Distribute your cash, credit cards, IDs, and other valuables between a deep front pocket, an inside jacket or vest pocket, and a hidden money pouch. Don't reach for the money pouch once you're in public.**

🛍 Shopping

If you haven't ventured into Chicago's vibrant neighborhoods, then you haven't shopped. So flex those biceps (you're going to have bags to carry), open your mind, and go beyond downtown. Indie boutiques you can't find anywhere else thrive in Wicker Park/Bucktown, Logan Square, Lincoln Park, and beyond.

Be aware: Chicago is as intellectual as it is fashionable. That means that in addition to on-trend clothing and accessories shops you're sure to lose yourself in bookstores, antiques shops, and gift boutiques, all with a quirk factor you can only find here. Of course, downtown's Magnificent Mile continues to attract the masses, and justifiably so, thanks to its block-after-block of luxury shops and department stores. And, just over the river, popular State Street refuses to be overshadowed; it's regained its former glory and now not only has big-box shops and department stores, but some only-in-Chicago gems like the Block 37 retail development.

Word of caution: a rather steep 10.25% sales tax is added to all purchases in the city, except groceries and prescription drugs. Neighborhood shops on the North Side, especially those in Wicker Park/Bucktown and Logan Square, tend to open late—around 11 or noon. The good news is that most stores, particularly those on Michigan Avenue and State Street, are open on Sunday, although this varies by type of business (galleries, for example, are often closed on Monday); where applicable, more information is provided at the beginning of each category.

💲 Taxes

At restaurants you'll pay approximately 10.75% for meal tax (thanks to special taxing initiatives, some parts of town are lower than others).

The hotel tax is 17.4% in the city, and slightly less in suburban areas.

In Chicago a steep 10.25% state and county sales tax is added to all purchases except groceries, which have a 2.25% tax. Sales tax is already added into the initial price of prescription drugs.

💲 Tipping

You should tip 15% for adequate service in restaurants and up to 20% if you feel you've been treated well. At higher-end restaurants, where more service personnel per table must divide the tip, increase these measures by a few percentage points. An especially helpful wine steward should be acknowledged with $2 or $3. It's not necessary to tip the maître d' unless you've been done a very special favor and you intend to visit again. Tip $1 per checked coat.

Taxi drivers, bartenders, and hairdressers expect about 15%. Bellhops and porters should get about $1 per bag; hotel maids about $2 to $5 per day of your stay; and valet-parking attendants $1 or $2 (but only after they bring your car to you, not when they park it). On package tours, conductors and drivers usually get about $2 to $3 per day from each group member. Concierges should get tips of $5 to $10 for special service.

📍 Visitor Information

Choose Chicago, the Chicago Convention and Tourism Bureau is a great place to start planning your visit to the Windy City. The organization's website is a veritable gold mine of information, from hotel packages to sample itineraries, event calendars, and maps. Start with their visitor guide at *www.choosechicago.com/plan-your-trip/visitor-resources.* You can also call the toll-free number to speak with a travel consultant. The Illinois Bureau of Tourism offers detailed information about what to do and see in Chicago and is especially helpful if your travel plans will take you outside the downtown area.

ONLINE TRAVEL TOOLS
ART
For a preview of the Art Institute of Chicago, check out *www.artic.edu.*

 When to Go

The best time to visit the Windy City is in June, September, and October. Those are the mild and sunny times. November through March the temperature ranges from cold, snowy, and colder. April and May are the rainy seasons but can fluctuate between cold/soggy and bright/warm. Another good time to visit. Deadly heat and humidity can make visitors uncomfortable in July and August but then it can be sunny and balmy. Locals will tell you that if you don't like the weather, stick around, it can change in a heartbeat. That said, in the warmer months suffer the heat and enjoy some fabulous outdoor festivals. Also, the city decks itself out in lights, especially Michigan Avenue, during the holiday season.

2

Travel Smart Chicago ESSENTIALS

Contacts

Air

Chicago Midway Airport. ✉ *Chicago* ☎ *773/838–0600* ⊕ *https://www.flychicago.com/midway/home/pages/default.aspx.* **O'Hare International Airport.** ☎ *773/686–2200, 800/832–6352* ⊕ *https://www.flychicago.com/ohare/home/pages/default.aspx.* **GO Airport Express.** ☎ *773/247–1200* ⊕ *www.airportexpress.com.*

🚲 Bicycle

Active Transportation Alliance. ☎ *312/427–3325* ⊕ *www.activetrans.org.* **Bike and Roll Chicago.** ☎ *312/729–1000* ⊕ *www.bikechicago.com.* **Bobby's Bike Hike.** ☎ *312/245–9300* ⊕ *www.bobbysbikehike.com.* **City of Chicago.** ☎ *312/744–5000.* **Divvy Bikes.** ☎ *855/553–4889* ⊕ *www.divvybikes.com.*

🚤 Boat

Shoreline Sightseeing. ☎ *312/222–9328* ⊕ *www.shorelinesightseeing.com.* **Wendella Boats.** ☎ *312/337–1446* ⊕ *www.wendellaboats.com.*

Car

AAA Chicago. ☎ *800/222–4357 AAA–HELP* ⊕ *www.aaa.com.* **Mr. Locks Security Systems.** ☎ *866/675–6257* ⊕ *www.mr-locks.com.*

Discounts and Deals

Chicago CityPASS. ✉ *Chicago* ☎ *888/330–5008* ⊕ *www.citypass.com/chicago.* **Go Chicago Card.** ✉ *Chicago* ☎ *800/887–9103* ⊕ *gocity.com/chicago.*

ublic Transportation

Regional Transportation Authority. ✉ *Chicago* ☎ *312/913–3110* ⊕ *www.rtachicago.com.* **CTA.** ✉ *Chicago* ☎ *888/968–7282* ⊕ *www.transitchicago.com.* **Metra information line.** ☎ *312/322–6777* ⊕ *www.metra.com.*

🚆 Train

Amtrak. ☎ *800/872–7245* ⊕ *www.amtrak.com.*

Visitor Information

Chicago Reader. ⊕ *www.chicagoreader.com.* **Chicago Sun-Times.** ⊕ *www.suntimes.com.* **Chicago Tribune.** ⊕ *www.chicagotribune.com.* **Choose Chicago.** ✉ *Chicago* ☎ *312/567–8500* ⊕ *www.choosechicago.com/things-to-do/tours-attractions/.* **Do312.** ✉ *Chicago* ⊕ *do312.com.* **Illinois Bureau of Tourism.** ☎ *800/226–6632* ⊕ *www.enjoyillinois.com.* **Time Out Chicago.** ⊕ *www.timeoutchicago.com.*

On the Calendar

March

St. Patrick's Day Parade. The St. Patrick's Day Parade turns the city on its head: the Chicago River is dyed green, shamrocks decorate the street, and the center stripe of Dearborn Street is painted the color of the Irish from Wacker Drive to Van Buren Street. This is your chance to get your fill of bagpipes and green beer. It's more than four hours long, so you probably won't see the whole thing. ⊠ *Chicago* ☎ *312/942–9188* ⊕ *www.cityofchicago. org/city/en/depts/dca/supp_info/parade7. html.*

June

Chicago Blues Festival. One of Chicago's most popular festivals, The Chicago Blues Festival in Millennium Park, is a very popular three-day, four-stage event in June. It attracts blues greats not only from from Chicago but from around the country. It should not be missed. ⊠ *Chicago* ☎ *312/744-5000* ⊕ *www.cityofchicago. org/city/en/depts/dca/supp_info/chica-go_blues_festival.html.*

July

Taste of Chicago. Taste of Chicago dishes out pizza, cheesecake, and other Chicago specialties to 3.5 million people after the Fourth of July holiday. ⊠ *Grant Park, Columbus Dr. between Jackson and Randolph Sts.* ☎ *312/744–3315* ⊕ *www. cityofchicago.org/city/en/depts/dca/ supp_info/taste_of_chicago.html.*

August

Chicago Air & Water Show. Thrill-seekers and families flock to the Chicago Air & Water Show, a lakefront spectacle featuring aerial acrobatics and daredevil water acts. See the U.S. Navy Blue Angels perform precision flying maneuvers at the two-day event in mid-August. ⊠ *Lakeshore, Fullerton Ave. to Oak St.; focal point at North Ave. Beach* ☎ *312/744–3315* ⊕ *www.cityofchicago. org/city/en/depts/dca/supp_info/chica-go_air_and_watershow.html.*

Northalsted Market Days. Street fairs are held every week in summer. Northalsted Market Days, in August, is the city's largest street festival. It's held in the heart of the gay community of Lakeview and has blocks and blocks of vendors as well as some wild entertainment such as zany drag queens and radical cheerleaders. ⊠ *Chicago* ⊕ *www.northalsted.com/ marketdays.*

September

Chicago Jazz Festival. The Chicago Jazz Festival holds sway for four days during Labor Day weekend in Millenium and Grant Parks. ⊠ *Chicago* ☎ *312/744–3315* ⊕ *www.cityofchicago.org/city/en/depts/ dca/supp_info/chicago_jazz_festival.html.*

World Music Festival. Over three weekends in September, international artists play traditional and contemporary music at venues across the city. ⊠ *Chicago* ⊕ *www.worldmusicfestivalchicago.org.*

November

Magnificent Mile Lights Festival. The holiday season officially starts with the Magnificent Mile Lights Festival, a weekend-long event in mid-November with tons of family-friendly activities including musical performances and ice-carving contests. The fanfare culminates in a parade and the illumination of more than 1 million lights along Michigan Avenue. ✉ *Chicago* ⊕ *www.themagnificentmile. com/events/lights-festival.*

Chapter 3

THE LOOP

Updated by
Kris Vire

◉ Sights	🍴 Restaurants	🛏 Hotels	🛍 Shopping	🍸 Nightlife
★★★★☆	★★★☆☆	★★★☆☆	★★☆☆☆	★★★★☆

NEIGHBORHOOD SPOTLIGHT

MAKING THE MOST OF YOUR TIME

The Loop has many "must-sees," including the Art Institute and the architectural boat tour (see Experience Chicago chapter), so prepare for a long day. Browse the shops on State Street, then take a trip out on the Ledge at Willis Tower and snap a selfie at Millennium Park's "Bean." Later, catch a play or a Chicago Symphony concert. Set aside another full day to explore the South Loop's Museum Campus: the Field Museum, Shedd Aquarium, and Adler Planetarium are all top-notch choices.

TOP REASONS TO GO

Get cultured: Spend an afternoon at the Art Institute perusing everything from ancient mosaics and old master paintings to contemporary photographs.

See fabulous fountains: Watch the faces screened onto Millennium Park's Crown Fountain spit at delighted onlookers, then admire the rococo splendor of Grant Park's Buckingham Fountain.

Appreciate architecture: From late 19th-century beauties, like the Rookery, to late 20th-century marvels, such as the Willis Tower, the Loop contains some of the country's architectural gems.

Get a taste of Chicago: Make a reservation for a trendy new spot in the West Loop's restaurant row, or opt for authentic Mediterranean food in the Greektown district a few blocks south.

Explore the world and beyond: Spot stars at the Adler Planetarium, spy your favorite fish at the John G. Shedd Aquarium, and see Sue the *T. rex* at the Field Museum.

PUBLIC ART

One of downtown Chicago's many attractive features is the abundance of public art. Look for sculptures by Chagall, Miró, and Picasso; street art murals along the Wabash Arts Corridor; and, of course, British artist Anish Kapoor's *Cloud Gate*, aka "the Bean," in Millennium Park, among other things.

GETTING HERE

■ If you're driving, you'll probably be taking the expressways—Kennedy from the northwest, Edens/Kennedy from the north, Dan Ryan from the south, and Congress from the west. Lake Shore Drive runs north and south along Lake Michigan.

■ If you're relying on public transportation, you can come by CTA bus, by El, or by rail. In the suburbs, hop on the Metra or South Shore Line and arrive at Union Station (Canal and Jackson streets). CTA's Red, Green, Blue, Yellow, Purple, Brown, and Pink lines link the city with the Loop.

Defined by the El (the elevated train that makes a circuit around the area), the Loop is Chicago at its big-city best. Noisy and mesmerizing, it's a living architectural museum alongside shimmering Lake Michigan. Gleaming modern towers vie for space with late 19th- and early 20th-century buildings, and striking sculptures by Picasso, Miró, and Chagall watch over plazas that come alive with music and farmers' markets in summer.

The Loop

The Loop oozes with charm and culture—it has a world-class symphony, top-rate theaters, fine restaurants, tempting shops, and swinging nightlife. There's no shortage of sights to see either. A slew of impressive buildings representing different styles and eras makes it feel like a theme park for architecture enthusiasts. (*You won't be able to go inside every architecturally notable building, but where you can, we explain what to look for in the interiors as well.*) Internationally known landmarks, including Millennium Park's *Cloud Gate* sculpture, blanket the Loop landscape, and visitors and locals alike gush over the masterpieces displayed inside the renowned Art Institute, this country's second-largest art museum.

 Sights

Aon Center

NOTABLE BUILDING | With the open space of Millennium Park at its doorstep, the Aon Center really stands out. Originally built as the Standard Oil Building, the 83-story skyscraper (first referred to as Big Stan) has changed names and appearances twice. Not long after the building went up in 1972, its marble cladding came crashing down, and the whole thing was resheathed in granite. Plans to add an observation deck on the 82nd and 83rd floors have met with delays, and likely won't be completed until 2024. ⊠ *200 E. Randolph Dr., Chicago Loop* ☎ *312/381–1000.*

Aqua

NOTABLE BUILDING | With its undulating concrete balconies suggesting rippling liquid, Aqua's addition to the skyline in 2009 made Jeanne Gang a household name in architectural circles; the building

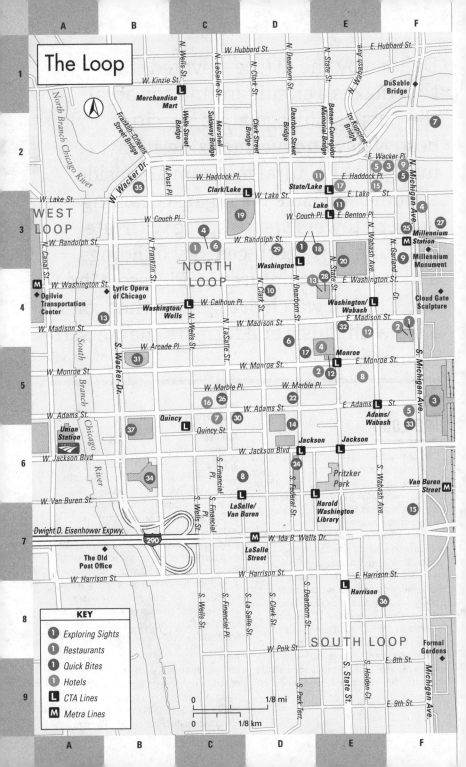

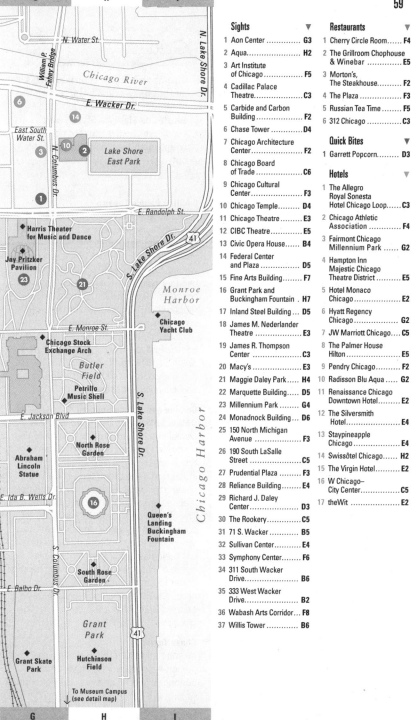

Sights ▼

1 Aon Center **G3**
2 Aqua...................... **H2**
3 Art Institute
 of Chicago **F5**
4 Cadillac Palace
 Theatre.................... **C3**
5 Carbide and Carbon
 Building **F2**
6 Chase Tower **D4**
7 Chicago Architecture
 Center.................... **F2**
8 Chicago Board
 of Trade **C6**
9 Chicago Cultural
 Center.................... **F3**
10 Chicago Temple........ **D4**
11 Chicago Theatre **E3**
12 CIBC Theatre.......... **E5**
13 Civic Opera House...... **B4**
14 Federal Center
 and Plaza **D5**
15 Fine Arts Building........ **F7**
16 Grant Park and
 Buckingham Fountain . **H7**
17 Inland Steel Building ... **D5**
18 James M. Nederlander
 Theatre **E3**
19 James R. Thompson
 Center **C3**
20 Macy's **E3**
21 Maggie Daley Park..... **H4**
22 Marquette Building..... **D5**
23 Millennium Park **G4**
24 Monadnock Building... **D6**
25 150 North Michigan
 Avenue **F3**
26 190 South LaSalle
 Street **C5**
27 Prudential Plaza **F3**
28 Reliance Building........ **E4**
29 Richard J. Daley
 Center.................... **D3**
30 The Rookery.............. **C5**
31 71 S. Wacker **B5**
32 Sullivan Center........... **E4**
33 Symphony Center........ **F6**
34 311 South Wacker
 Drive...................... **B6**
35 333 West Wacker
 Drive...................... **B2**
36 Wabash Arts Corridor... **F8**
37 Willis Tower **B6**

Restaurants ▼

1 Cherry Circle Room...... **F4**
2 The Grillroom Chophouse
 & Winebar **E5**
3 Morton's,
 The Steakhouse.......... **F2**
4 The Plaza **F3**
5 Russian Tea Time **F5**
6 312 Chicago **C3**

Quick Bites ▼

1 Garrett Popcorn.......... **D3**

Hotels ▼

1 The Allegro
 Royal Sonesta
 Hotel Chicago Loop...... **C3**
2 Chicago Athletic
 Association **F4**
3 Fairmont Chicago
 Millennium Park **G2**
4 Hampton Inn
 Majestic Chicago
 Theatre District **E5**
5 Hotel Monaco
 Chicago **E2**
6 Hyatt Regency
 Chicago **G2**
7 JW Marriott Chicago.... **C5**
8 The Palmer House
 Hilton **E5**
9 Pendry Chicago.......... **F2**
10 Radisson Blu Aqua **G2**
11 Renaissance Chicago
 Downtown Hotel.......... **E2**
12 The Silversmith
 Hotel...................... **E4**
13 Staypineapple
 Chicago **E4**
14 Swissôtel Chicago....... **H2**
15 The Virgin Hotel.......... **E2**
16 W Chicago–
 City Center................ **C5**
17 theWit **E2**

was not just a critical hit, it was also the world's tallest building designed by a woman. Aqua recently lost that designation to another Gang design, the nearby St. Regis Chicago, which is currently the third-tallest building in the city. It's a residential tower, so it's not open to the public. ⊠ *225 N. Columbus Dr., Chicago Loop.*

★ Art Institute of Chicago

ART MUSEUM | FAMILY | Come for the sterling collection of old masters and impressionists (an entire room is dedicated to Monet); linger over the extraordinary and comprehensive photography collection; take in a number of fine American works; and discover paintings, drawings, sculpture, and design spanning the ancient to the contemporary world.

With its flanking lions and marble lobby, the Michigan Avenue main building was once part of the World's Columbian Exposition. It opened as the Art Institute on December 8, 1893. While the collection is best known for its impressionist and postimpressionist pieces, visitors will find works from a vast range of periods and places, including Greek, Roman, Byzantine, European, Asian, African, and Native American art. Such iconic works as Grant Wood's *American Gothic* and Edward Hopper's *Nighthawks* can be found in the American galleries. Chicago favorites like the Thorne Miniature Room and Chagall's stained-glass *American Windows* are must-sees as well.

After the Renzo Piano–designed Modern Wing opened in 2009, the Art Institute became one of the largest art museums in the country. The 264,000-square-foot building contains the finest 20th- and 21st-century art in many mediums. ⊠ *111 S. Michigan Ave., Chicago Loop* ☎ *312/443–3600* ⊕ *www.artic.edu/ aic* 🎟 *$25 advance purchase online* ⊙ *Closed Tues.-Wed.* ⚠ *Advance reservations required for non-members.*

Grid City

Getting around the Loop is easy. It's laid out like a grid. The intersection of State Street, which runs north–south, and Madison Street, which runs east–west, is the zero point from which the rest of the city fans out.

Cadillac Palace Theatre

PERFORMANCE VENUE | Opened in 1926 as a vaudeville venue, the theater was designed to evoke the Palace of Versailles. As time went on, its popularity waned. During the 1970s, it became a banquet hall; in the '80s, it hosted rock concerts. Renovated in the '90s and reopened in 1999 as a performing arts space for long-run Broadway shows, the Cadillac Palace Theatre has recaptured some of its former glory. ⊠ *151 W. Randolph St., Chicago Loop* ☎ *312/977–1702* ⊕ *broadwayinchicago.com/theatre/ cadillac-palace-theatre.*

Carbide and Carbon Building

NOTABLE BUILDING | Designed in 1929 by Daniel and Hubert Burnham, sons of the renowned architect Daniel Burnham, this is arguably the jazziest skyscraper in town. A deep-green terra-cotta tower rising from a black-granite base, its upper reaches are embellished with gold leaf. The original public spaces are a luxurious composition in marble and bronze. The story goes that the brothers Burnham got their inspiration from a gold-foiled bottle of champagne. The building is now home to the swanky Pendry Chicago hotel. ⊠ *230 N. Michigan Ave., Chicago Loop* ☎ *312/777–9000* ⊕ *pendry.com/ chicago.*

Chase Tower

NOTABLE BUILDING | This building's graceful swoop—a novelty when it went up—continues to offer an eye-pleasing respite

from all the surrounding right angles; and its spacious, sunken bi-level plaza, with Marc Chagall's mosaic *The Four Seasons,* is one of the most enjoyable public spaces in the neighborhood. Designed by Perkins & Will and C.F. Murphy Associates in 1969, Chase Tower has been home to a succession of financial institutions. Name changes aside, it remains one of the more distinctive buildings around, not to mention one of the highest in the heart of the Loop. ⊠ *10 S. Dearborn St., Chicago Loop.*

★ Chicago Architecture Center

OTHER MUSEUM | After more than 25 years flying under the radar inside the Railway Exchange Building a few blocks south, the Chicago Architecture Foundation opened this sparkling new home in 2018. The 20,000-square-foot facility features interactive exhibits about the city's built environment, and it sits right above the dock where the center's indispensable river cruise tours board. Tours by bus and on foot also depart from the facility, which houses a terrific gift shop as well. ⊠ *111 E. Wacker Dr., Chicago Loop* ☎ *312/922–3432* ⊕ *architecture.org* ⌨ *$14.*

Chicago Board of Trade

NOTABLE BUILDING | Home of the thriving financial district, relatively narrow LaSalle Street earned the moniker "The Canyon" (and it feels like one) because of the large buildings that flank either end. This one was designed by Holabird & Root and completed in 1930. The streamlined, 45-story giant recalls the days when art deco was all the rage. The artfully lighted marble lobby soars three stories, and Ceres (the Roman goddess of agriculture) stands atop its roof. Trading is no longer done here, but it's worth a look at what was the city's tallest skyscraper until 1955, when the Prudential Center topped it. ⊠ *141 W. Jackson Blvd., Chicago Loop* ☎ *312/435–7180* ⊕ *www.cbotbuilding.com.*

Did You Know?

Terracotta, a baked clay that can be produced as tiles or shaped ornamentally, was commonly used by Chicago architects after the Great Fire of 1871.

Heat resistant and malleable, the material proved an effective and attractive fireproofing agent for the metal-frame buildings that otherwise would melt and collapse. The facade of the Marquette Building at 140 South Dearborn Street is a particularly fine example.

★ Chicago Cultural Center

NOTABLE BUILDING | Built in 1897 as the city's original public library, this huge building houses the Chicago Office of Tourism Visitor Information Center, as well as a gift shop, galleries, and a concert hall. Designed by the Boston firm Shepley, Rutan & Coolidge—the team behind the Art Institute of Chicago—it's a palatial affair notable for its Carrara marble, mosaics, gold leaf, and the world's largest Tiffany glass dome. ⊠ *78 E. Washington St., Chicago Loop* ☎ *312/744–3316* ⊕ *www.chicagoculturalcenter.org.*

Chicago Temple

NOTABLE BUILDING | The Gothic-inspired headquarters of the First United Methodist Church of Chicago, built in 1923 by Holabird & Roche, comes complete with a first-floor sanctuary, 21 floors of office space, a sky-high chapel (free tours are available), and an eight-story spire, which is best viewed from the bridge across the Chicago River at Dearborn Street. Outside, along the building's east wall at ground level, stained-glass windows relate the history of Methodism in Chicago. Joan Miró's sculpture *Chicago* (1981) is in the small plaza just east of the church. ⊠ *77 W. Washington*

Make sure to look up at the stunning Tiffany stained-glass dome at the Chicago Cultural Center.

St., Chicago Loop ☎ *312/236–4548* ⊕ *www.chicagotemple.org.*

Chicago Theatre

PERFORMANCE VENUE | When it opened in 1921, the grand and glitzy Chicago Theatre was tagged "the Wonder Theatre of the World." Its exterior features a shrunken version of the Arc de Triomphe, and its lobby is patterned after the Royal Chapel at Versailles with a staircase copied from the Paris Opera House. Murals decorate the auditorium walls and ceiling. The seven-story, 3,600-seat space has served as a venue for films and famed entertainers ranging from John Philip Sousa and Duke Ellington to Ellen DeGeneres and Beyoncé. Tours let you stand on the stage where they performed, go backstage, and peruse its autographed walls. ✉ *175 N. State St., Chicago Loop* ☎ *312/462–6318* ⊕ *www.thechicagotheatre.com* 🎫 *Tours $18.*

CIBC Theatre

PERFORMANCE VENUE | On Monroe, near State Street, the ornate CIBC Theatre (formerly the Bank of America Theatre and before that the LaSalle Bank Theatre and the Shubert Theatre) stages major Broadway plays and musicals. It was the tallest building in Chicago when it opened in 1906. ✉ *18 W. Monroe St., Chicago Loop* ☎ *800/775–2000* ⊕ *www.broadwayinchicago.com/theatre/cibc-theatre/.*

Civic Opera House

PERFORMANCE VENUE | The handsome home of the Lyric Opera of Chicago and the Joffrey Ballet is grand indeed, with pink-and-gray Tennessee-marble floors, pillars with carved capitals, crystal chandeliers, and a sweeping staircase to the second floor. Designed by Graham, Anderson, Probst & White, the second-largest opera house in North America combines lavish art deco details with art nouveau touches. Tours are given a few times a year. ✉ *20 N. Wacker Dr., Chicago Loop* ☎ *312/827–5600 Lyric Opera, 312/386–8905 Joffrey Ballet* ⊕ *www.civicoperahouse.com.*

Federal Center and Plaza

GOVERNMENT BUILDING | This center is spread over three separate buildings: the Everett McKinley Dirksen Building; the John C. Kluczynski Building (*230 S. Dearborn*), which includes the Loop's post office; and the Metcalfe Building (*77 W. Jackson*). Designed in 1959, but not completed until 1974, the severe constellation of buildings around a sweeping plaza was Mies van der Rohe's first mixed-use urban project. Fans of the International Style will groove on this pocket of pure modernism, while others can take comfort in the presence of the Marquette Building, which marks the north side of the site. In contrast to this dark ensemble are the great red arches of Alexander Calder's *Flamingo*. The area is bounded by Dearborn, Clark, and Adams streets and Jackson Boulevard. ✉ *Dirksen Bldg., 219 S. Dearborn St., Chicago Loop* ☎ *312/353–6996* ⊕ *www. gsa.gov/portal/content/101841.*

Fine Arts Building

NOTABLE BUILDING | This creaky building was constructed in 1895 to house the showrooms of the Studebaker Company, then makers of carriages. Once counting architect Frank Lloyd Wright among its tenants, the building today provides space for more than 200 musicians, visual artists, and designers. Take a look at the handsome exterior; then step inside the marble-and-woodwork lobby, noting the motto engraved in marble as you enter: "All passes—art alone endures." The building has an interior courtyard, across which strains of piano music and sopranos' voices compete with tenors' as they run through exercises. Visitors can get a peek at the studios and hear live music during "Open Studios" events, held on the second Friday of each month between 5 and 9 pm. ✉ *410 S. Michigan Ave., Chicago Loop* ☎ *312/566–9800* ⊕ *fineartsbuilding-studios.com.*

Finding Facts

For information about the city's architectural treasures, contact the **Chicago Architecture Center** (312/922–3432) or the Chicago Convention and Tourism Bureau (312/567–8500).

Grant Park and Buckingham Fountain

CITY PARK | **FAMILY** | Bordered by Lake Michigan to the east, a spectacular skyline to the west, and the Museum Campus to the south, Grant Park serves as the city's front yard and unofficial gathering place. This pristine open space has walking paths, a stand of stately elm trees, and formal rose gardens, where Loop dwellers and 9-to-5ers take refuge from the concrete and steel. It also hosts many of the city's largest outdoor events, including the annual Taste of Chicago, a vast picnic featuring foods from more than 70 restaurants.

The park's centerpiece is the gorgeous, tiered Buckingham Fountain (*between Columbus and Lake Shore Drives, east of Congress Plaza*), which has intricate pink-marble seashell designs, water-spouting fish, and bronze sculptures of sea horses. Built in 1927, it was patterned after one at Versailles but is about twice the size. See the fountain in all its glory between early May and mid-October, when it's elaborately illuminated at night and sprays colorfully lighted waters. Linger long enough to experience the spectacular display that takes place every hour on the hour, and you'll witness the center jet of water shoot 150 feet into the air. ✉ *Chicago Loop* ☎ *312/742–7529* ⊕ *www.chicagoparkdistrict.com/parks/clarence-f-buckingham-memorial-fountain.*

The lighting around Buckingham Fountain was designed to evoke soft moonlight.

Inland Steel Building

NOTABLE BUILDING | A runt compared to today's tall buildings, this sparkling 19-story high-rise from Skidmore, Owings & Merrill was a trailblazer when it was built in the late 1950s. It was the first skyscraper erected with external supports (allowing for wide-open, unobstructed floors within), the first to employ steel pilings (driven 85 feet down to bedrock), the first in the Loop to be fully air-conditioned, and the first to feature underground parking. ⊠ *30 W. Monroe St., Chicago Loop* ⊕ *www.inlandsteel-building.com.*

James M. Nederlander Theatre

PERFORMANCE VENUE | An opulent "hasheesh-dream decor" of Buddhas and elephant-type chairs made the erstwhile Eastern Theatre a popular spot for viewing first-run movies starting in 1926. Though listed on the National Register of Historic Places in 1978, the building continued to crumble for some time after. In 1998 it was restored to its past splendor and since then has had a second life as a home to Broadway shows; it was rechristened for the late patriarch of the Nederlander family of theater producers in 2019. ⊠ *24 W. Randolph St., Chicago Loop* ☏ *312/977–1702* ⊕ *broadwayinchicago.com/theatre/chicagos-james-m-nederlander-theatre/.*

James R. Thompson Center

GOVERNMENT BUILDING | People either hate or love this former state-government building. Former governor James Thompson, who selected the Helmut Jahn design, hailed it in his 1985 dedication speech as "the first building of the 21st century." For others, it's a case of postmodernism run amok. A bowl-like form topped by a truncated cylinder, the 17-story building's sky-blue-and-salmon color scheme screams 1980s. But the 17-story atrium, where exposed elevators zip up and down and sunlight casts dizzying patterns through the metal-and-glass skin, is one of the most animated interiors anywhere in the city. The state put the building up for sale in 2021; while preservationists are fighting to protect it,

Did You Know?

The BP Bridge is the first (and so far only) bridge to be designed by Frank Gehry. Pretty as the gently sloping, brushed steel structure is, the bridge also serves a practical purpose: it helps keep nearby traffic noise from interfering with concerts held at the Jay Pritzker Pavilion.

the Thompson Center's fate is unclear. ✉ *100 W. Randolph St., Chicago Loop* ☎ *312/814–2141* ⊕ *www2.illinois.gov/ cms/about/jrtc.*

Macy's

STORE/MALL | FAMILY | This neoclassical building, designed by Daniel Burnham, opened in 1907 as one of the world's earliest department stores, Marshall Field's. Macy's acquired the chain in 2005 and changed the store's name. An uproar ensued, and many Chicagoans still refer to the flagship as Marshall Field's. A visit is as much an architectural experience as a retail one. The building has distinct courtyards (one resembling an Italian palazzo), a striking Tiffany dome of mosaic glass, a calming fountain, and gilded pillars. Its green clock at the State and Randolph entrance is a Chicago landmark. For lunch, try the Walnut Room, and make sure to sample Frango mints—the store's specialty, they were once made on the 13th floor. ✉ *111 N. State St., Chicago Loop* ☎ *312/781–1000* ⊕ *macys.com.*

Maggie Daley Park

CITY PARK | FAMILY | Named after former Mayor Richard M. Daley's late wife, this park offers a place to play between Lake Michigan and the city's skyline. Opened in late 2014, it includes 40-foot-high rock-climbing sculptures, an Enchanted Forest with a kaleidoscope and mirrored maze, a Slide Crater, a Wave Lawn, and an area strictly for toddlers. A skating ribbon winds around the park, with ice skates available to rent in the winter months, and rollerblades and scooters in the summer. ✉ *337 E. Randolph St., at northeastern edge of Grant Park, Chicago Loop* ☎ *312/742–3918* ⊕ *maggiedaley-park.com.*

Marquette Building

NOTABLE BUILDING | Like a slipcover over a sofa, the clean, geometric facade of this 1895 building expresses what lies beneath: in this case, a structural steel frame. Sure, the base is marked with roughly cut stone and a fancy cornice crowns the top, but the bulk of the Marquette Building mirrors the cage around which it is built. Inside is another story. The intimate lobby is a jewel box of a space, where a single Doric column stands surrounded by a Tiffany glass mosaic depicting the exploits of French Jesuit missionary Jacques Marquette, an early explorer of Illinois and the Upper Midwest. From its steel skeleton to the terra-cotta ornamentation, this Holabird & Roche structure is a clear example of the Chicago style. ✉ *140 S. Dearborn St., Chicago Loop* ☎ *312/422–5500* ⊕ *marquette.macfound.org.*

★ Millennium Park

CITY PARK | FAMILY | With Anish Kapoor's giant, polished-steel *Cloud Gate* sculpture (affectionately known as "The Bean"), the fun fountains, and a Disney-esque music pavilion—all the pieces of this park quickly stole the hearts of Chicagoans and visitors alike when it opened 2004. The showstopper is Frank Gehry's stunning Jay Pritzker Pavilion. Dramatic ribbons of stainless steel stretching 40 feet into the sky look like petals wrapping the music stage. The 1,525-seat Harris Theater for Music and Dance provides an indoor alternative for fans of the performing arts.

In the park's southwest corner, the Crown Fountain features dozens of Chicagoans' faces rotating through on two 50-foot-high glass block–tower fountains. When a face purses its lips, water shoots out its "mouth." Kids love it, and adults feel like kids watching it. More conventional park perks include the lovely Lurie Garden (a four-season delight) and the seasonal McCormick Tribune Ice Rink, which opens for public skating each winter. ✉ *Between Michigan Ave. and Columbus Dr., Randolph and Monroe Sts., Chicago Loop* ☎ *312/742–1168* ⊕ *millenniumpark.org* 🎟 *Free.*

Monadnock Building

NOTABLE BUILDING | Built in two segments a few years apart, the Monadnock captures the turning point in high-rise construction. Its northern half, designed in 1891 by Burnham & Root, was erected with traditional load-bearing masonry walls (6-feet deep at the base). In 1893 Holabird & Roche designed its southern half, which rose around the soon-to-be-common steel skeleton. The building's stone-and-brick exterior, shockingly unornamented for its time, led one critic to liken it to a chimney. The lobby is equally spartan; lined on either side with windowed shops, it's essentially a corridor, but one well worth traveling. Walk it from end to end and you'll feel as if you're stepping back in time. ⊠ *53 W. Jackson Blvd., Chicago Loop* ☏ *312/922–1890* ⊕ *www.monadnockbuilding.com.*

150 North Michigan Avenue

NOTABLE BUILDING | Some wags have pointed out that this building, with its diamond-shape top, looks like a giant pencil sharpener. Built in 1984 as the Smurfit-Stone Building and later known as the Crain Communications Building, it has a slanted top that carves through the top 10 of its floors. In the plaza is Yaacov Agam's *Communication X9*, a painted, folded aluminum sculpture that was restored to some controversy and reinstalled in 2008. You'll see different patterns in the sculpture depending on your vantage point. ⊠ *150 N. Michigan Ave., Chicago Loop* ⊕ *150northmichigan. com.*

190 South LaSalle Street

NOTABLE BUILDING | This 40-story postmodern office building, resembling a supersized château, was designed by John Burgee and Philip Johnson in the mid-1980s. The grand, gold-leaf vaulted lobby is spectacular. ⊠ *190 S. LaSalle St., Chicago Loop* ⊕ *190southlasalle.com.*

Did You Know?

The Chicago Window, a popular window design used in buildings all over America (until air-conditioning made it obsolete), consists of a large fixed central pane with smaller movable windows on each side. The picture window offered light, and the double-hung windows let in the Lake Michigan breeze. Developed in Chicago by engineer and architect William Le Baron Jenney, who pioneered the use of metal-frame construction in the 1880s, the Chicago Window helps to define buildings across the city.

Prudential Plaza

NOTABLE BUILDING | There are two architecturally notable buildings at the plaza. Directly west of the Aon Center and across from Millennium Park is **One Prudential Plaza**. Designed by Alfonso Iannelli and completed in 1955, this limestone-and-ridged-aluminum structure was once the city's tallest building (barring the statue of Ceres atop the Board of Trade). At the time, it had the world's fastest elevators and an observation deck that became passé once some of the city's other behemoths were completed. Attached to One Prudential is its sibling **Two Prudential Plaza,** nicknamed "Two Pru," a towering glass-and-granite giant with an address of 180 North Stetson Avenue. Along with their neighbors they form a block-long business-oriented minicity. Two Prudential is the tallest reinforced concrete building in the city, and its blue detailing and beveled roof are instantly recognizable from afar. ⊠ *One Prudential, 130 E. Randolph St., Chicago Loop* ☏ *312/565–6700* ⊕ *onetwopru.com.*

Did You Know?

Much to locals' chagrin, the Sears Tower was rechristened the Willis Tower in 2009, after its new tenant, Willis Group Holdings, a London-based insurance broker. It joins Marshall Field's (now a Macy's), Carson, Pirie, Scott & Co. (now the Sullivan Center), and Comiskey Park (now Guaranteed Rate Field) as major Chicago institutions to be renamed.

Frank Lloyd Wright remodeled the lobby of the Rookery, originally designed by Burnham & Root.

Reliance Building

NOTABLE BUILDING | The clearly expressed, gleaming verticality that characterizes the modern skyscraper was first and most eloquently articulated in this trailblazing steel-frame tower, built by Burnham, Root, and Charles Atwood. Completed in 1895 and now home to the stylish Staypineapple hotel, the building was a crumbling eyesore until the late 1990s, when the city initiated a major restoration. In the early and mid-1900s, it was a mixed-use office building. Al Capone's dentist reportedly worked out of what's now Room 809. Don't be misled when you go looking for this masterpiece—a block away, at State and Randolph streets, a dormitory for the School of the Art Institute of Chicago shamelessly mimics it. Once you've found the real thing, admire the mosaic floor and ironwork in the reconstructed elevator lobby. The building boasts early examples of the Chicago Window, which define the entire facade by adding a shimmer and glimmer to the surrounding white terracotta. ⊠ *1 W. Washington St., Chicago Loop* ☎ *312/940–7997* ⊕ *staypineapple.com/the-loop-chicago*.

Richard J. Daley Center

NOTABLE BUILDING | Named for late mayor Richard J. Daley, this boldly plain high-rise is the headquarters of the Cook County court system, but it's best known as the site of a sculpture by Picasso. Simply dubbed the *Picasso,* this monumental piece provoked an outcry when it was installed in 1967; baffled Chicagoans tried to determine whether it represented a woman or an Afghan hound. In the end, they gave up guessing and simply embraced it as a unique symbol of the city. The building itself was constructed in 1965 of Cor-Ten steel, which weathers naturally to an attractive bronze. In summer, its plaza is the site of concerts, political rallies, and a Thursday farmers' market. In December, Christkindlmarket (a traditional German market selling food and gifts) takes over the area. ⊠ *50 W. Washington St., Chicago Loop* ☎ *312/603–7980* ⊕ *www.thedaleycenter. com*.

★ The Rookery

NOTABLE BUILDING | This 11-story structure, with its eclectically ornamented facade, got its name from the pigeons and politicians who roosted at the temporary city hall constructed on this site after the Great Chicago Fire of 1871; the structure didn't last long, and the Rookery replaced it. Designed in 1885 by Burnham & Root, who used both masonry and a more modern steel-frame construction, the Rookery was one of the first buildings in the country to feature a central court that brought sunlight into interior office spaces. Frank Lloyd Wright, who kept an office here for a short time, renovated the two-story lobby and light court, eliminating some of the ironwork and terracotta and adding marble scored with geometric patterns detailed in gold leaf. The interior endured some less tasteful alterations after that, but it has since been restored to the way it looked when Wright completed his work in 1907. ⊠ 209 S. LaSalle St., Chicago Loop ☎ 312/553–6100 ⊕ therookerybuilding. com.

71 S. Wacker

NOTABLE BUILDING | At 48 stories, this modern high-rise is no giant, but it more than makes its mark on South Wacker Drive with a bold elliptical shape, a glass-faced street-level lobby rising 36 feet, and a pedestrian-friendly plaza. It displays a noticeable tweaking of the unrelieved curtain wall that makes many city streets forbidding canyons. Designed by Pei Cobb Freed & Partners, the Hyatt Center was completed in 2004. ⊠ 71 S. Wacker Dr., Chicago Loop ⊕ www.irvinecompanyoffice.com/locations/chicago/west-loop/71-south-wacker.html.

Sullivan Center (Carson, Pirie, Scott & Co.)

NOTABLE BUILDING | From 1899 to 2007 this was the flagship location for the department store Carson, Pirie, Scott & Co. The work of one of Chicago's most renowned architects, it combines Louis H. Sullivan's visionary expression of modern design with intricate cast-iron ornamentation. The eye-catching rotunda and the 11 stories above it are actually an addition Sullivan made to his original building. In later years D.H. Burnham & Co. and Holabird & Root extended Sullivan's smooth, horizontal scheme farther down State Street. The ground floors now house a Target and a DSW, with office tenants occupying the floors above. ⊠ 1 S. State St., Chicago Loop.

Symphony Center

NOTABLE BUILDING | Now home to the acclaimed Chicago Symphony Orchestra (CSO), this complex includes Orchestra Hall, built in 1904 under the supervision of Daniel Burnham. The Georgian building has a symmetrical facade of pink brick with limestone quoins, lintels, and other decorative elements. An interior renovation, completed in 1997, added a seating area that is behind and above the stage, allowing patrons a unique vantage point. ⊠ 220 S. Michigan Ave., Chicago Loop ☎ 312/294–3000 ⊕ www.cso.org.

311 South Wacker Drive

NOTABLE BUILDING | The first of three towers intended for the site, this pale pink edifice is the work of Kohn Pedersen Fox, who also designed 333 West Wacker Drive, a few blocks away. The 1990 building's most distinctive feature is its Gothic crown, brightly lit at night. During migration season so many birds crashed into the illuminated tower that management was forced to tone down the lighting. An inviting atrium has palm trees and a splashy, romantic fountain. ⊠ 311 S. Wacker Dr., Chicago Loop ☎ 312/692–8200 ⊕ www.311southwacker.com.

333 West Wacker Drive

NOTABLE BUILDING | This green-glazed beauty doesn't follow the rules. Its riverside facade echoes the curve of the Chicago River just in front of it, while the other side is all business, conforming

Continued on page 77

A GUIDE TO THE ART INSTITUTE

The Art Institute of Chicago, nestled between the contemporary public art showplace of Millennium Park and the Paris-inspired walkways of Grant Park, is both intimate and grand, a place where the rooms are human-scale and the art is transcendent.

Come for the sterling collection of Old Masters and Impressionists (an entire room is dedicated to Monet), linger over the extraordinary and comprehensive photography collection, take in a number of fine American works, and discover paintings, drawings, sculpture, design, and photography spanning the ages.

The Art Institute is more than just a museum; in fact, it was originally founded by a small group of artists in 1866 as a school with an adjoining exhibition space. Famous alumni include political cartoonist Herblock and artists Grant Wood and Ed Paschke. Walt Disney and Georgia O'Keeffe both took classes, but didn't graduate. The School of the Art Institute of Chicago, one of the finest art schools in the country, is across the street from the museum; occasionally there are lectures and discussions that are open to the public.

Top: Pose with one of the two bronze lions; Bottom: Millefiori paperweight, French, 1845/55

BEST PAINTINGS

AMERICAN GOTHIC (1930). GALLERY 263
Grant Wood won $300 for his iconic painting of a solemn farmer and his wife (really his sister and his dentist). Wood saw the work as a celebration of solid, work-based Midwestern values, a statement that rural America would survive the Depression and the massive migration to cities.

American Gothic (1930).

NIGHTHAWKS (1942). GALLERY 262
Edward Hopper's painting of four figures in a diner on the corner of a deserted New York street is a noir portrait of isolated lives and is one of the most recognized images of 20th-century art. The red-haired woman is the artist's wife, Jo.

Nighthawks (1942).

THE CHILD'S BATH (1893). GALLERY 273
Mary Cassatt was the only American to become an established Impressionist and her work focused on the daily lives of women and children. In this, her most famous work, a woman gently bathes a child who is tucked up on her lap. The piece was unconventional when it was painted because the bold patterns and cropped forms it used were more often seen in Japanese prints at the time.

The Child's Bath (1893).

SKY ABOVE CLOUDS IV (1965). GALLERY 249
(not pictured) Georgia O'Keeffe's massive painting, the largest canvas of her career, is of clouds seen from an airplane. The rows of white rectangles stretching toward the horizon look both solid and ethereal, as if they are stepping stones for angels.

THE OLD GUITARIST (1903/04). MODERN WING GALLERY 391
(not pictured) One of the most important works of Pablo Picasso's Blue Period, this monochromatic painting is a study of the crooked figure of a blind and destitute street guitarist, singing sorrowfully. When he painted it, Picasso was feeling particularly empathetic toward the downtrodden—perhaps because of a friend's suicide—and the image of the guitarist is one of dignity amid poverty.

Grainstack (1890/91).

GRAINSTACK (1890/91). GALLERY 243
The Art Institute has the largest collection of Monet's Grainstacks in the world. The stacks rose 15 to 20 feet tall outside Monet's farmhouse in Giverny and were a symbol to the artist of sustenance and survival.

THE MODERN WING

The Modern Wing

In May 2009 the Art Institute unveiled its highly anticipated Modern Wing. Designed by Pritzker Prize–winning architect Renzo Piano, designer of Paris's Pompidou Center, the 264,000-square-foot addition is almost a separate museum unto itself, providing 65,000 square feet of display space for the museum's extensive collection of modern and contemporary art. With the addition, the Art Institute became the country's second largest art museum.

THE DESIGN
The rectangle of glass, steel, and limestone cost just under $300 million and took nearly four years to build. The airy, ultra-modern structure provides abundant natural light and dramatic views of Millennium Park through floor-to-ceiling windows. Green building features include a "flying carpet" canopy that filters sunlight through skylights in the third-floor galleries and a sophisticated lighting system that self-adjusts based on available light and temperature.

North facade of the Modern Wing

THE COLLECTION
View works from major art movements of the 20th and 21st centuries, ranging from painting and sculpture to video and installation art. Notable artists represented in the collection include Eva Hesse, David Hockney, Jasper Johns, Kerry James Marshall, Joan Mitchell, Jackson Pollock, Gerhard Richter, and Andy Warhol.

GRIFFIN COURT
The light-filled central corridor provides a dramatic passageway to the three-story pavilions flanking it on both sides and to the street-level Pritzker Garden. Griffin Court also houses a ticket area, gift shop, coat check, education center, garden café, and balcony café.

Griffin Court

NICHOLS BRIDGEWAY
A 625-foot pedestrian bridge soars over Monroe Street and the Lurie Gardens, connecting the third floor of the Modern Wing's West Pavilion to the southwest corner of Millennium Park—and providing stunning views of the park, skyline, and lake.

BLUHM FAMILY TERRACE
Rotating sculpture installations occupy the free, 3,400-square-foot outdoor space on the West Pavilion's third floor, adjacent to the seasonally focused restaurant Terzo Piano (reservations recommended).

A painting by Gerhard Richter

neatly to the straight lines of the street grid. The 1983 Kohn Pedersen Fox design, roughly contemporary to the James R. Thompson Center, enjoyed a much more positive public reception. It also had a small but important role in the 1986 movie *Ferris Bueller's Day Off* as the location of Ferris's dad's office. ✉ *333 W. Wacker Dr., between W. Lake St. and N. Orleans St., Chicago Loop* 🌐 *www.333westwackerdrive.com.*

Wabash Arts Corridor
PUBLIC ART | Running along both sides of Wabash Avenue from Ida B. Wells Drive south to 16th Street, this mile-long stretch is an outdoor gallery of murals and street art. There are nearly 40 permanent installations and an evolving set of temporary exhibitions. Chicago artists including Shepard Fairey, Hebru Brantley, and Sam Kirk have had work shown here. ✉ *635 Wabash Ave., Chicago Loop* 🌐 *wabashartscorridor.org.*

★ Willis Tower
NOTABLE BUILDING | **FAMILY** | Designed by Skidmore, Owings & Merrill in 1974, the former Sears Tower was the world's tallest building until 1996. The 110-story, 1,730-foot-tall structure may have lost its title and even changed its name, but it's still tough to top the Willis Tower's 103rd-floor **Skydeck**—on a clear day it offers views of Illinois, Michigan, Wisconsin, and Indiana. Enter on Jackson Boulevard to take the ear-popping ride up. **■ TIP→ Check the visibility ratings at the security desk before you decide to ascend.**

Video monitors turn the 70-second elevator ride into a thrilling trip. Interactive exhibits inside the observatory bring Chicago's dreamers, schemers, architects, musicians, and sports stars to life; and computer kiosks in six languages help international travelers key into Chicago hot spots. For many visitors, though, the highlight (literally) is stepping out on the Ledge, a glass box that extends 4.3 feet from the building, making you feel as if you're suspended 1,353 feet in the air. ✉ *233 S. Wacker Dr., Chicago Loop* ☎ *312/875–9447* 🌐 *www.willistower.com, www.theskydeck.com* 🎟 *Skydeck $35.*

🍴 Restaurants

Cherry Circle Room
$$$ | **AMERICAN** | Mid-century style reigns at this wood-paneled clublike restaurant, where the menu draws inspiration from the landmarked space's previous incarnation as a tony men's club. The sweeping bar is perfect for sipping historic and house cocktails over bar snacks or raw seafood, or settle into a comfortable leather booth for private conversations and all manner of meat perfectly prepared. **Known for:** lovely presentation of beef tartare; tableside cocktail service; old-world–focused wine list. [$] *Average main: $35* ✉ *Chicago Athletic Association, 12 S. Michigan Ave., Chicago Loop* ☎ *312/792–3515* 🌐 *www.lsdatcaa.com/cherry-circle-room* 🕒 *Closed Mon.-Tues. No lunch.*

The Grillroom Chophouse & Winebar
$$$ | **STEAKHOUSE** | If you're going to see a performance at the CIBC Theatre across the street, you're close enough to dash over here for a drink at intermission (there's a lengthy by-the-glass wine selection). Pre- and post-curtain, the clubby confines fill with showgoers big on beef, though there are also ample raw bar, seafood, and pasta choices. **Known for:** lunch deals; mac-and-cheese; happy hour specials. [$] *Average main: $29* ✉ *33 W. Monroe St., Chicago Loop* ☎ *312/960–0000* 🌐 *www.grillroom-chicago.com* 🕒 *Closed Sat.-Sun. unless there's a show at CIBC.*

Morton's, The Steakhouse
$$$$ | **STEAKHOUSE** | The specialty at the Loop location of Morton's, one of Chicago's premiere steak houses, is a 14-ounce (or more) taste of heaven for

meat lovers. Excellent service and a solid wine list add to the principal attraction: beautiful, hefty steaks cooked to perfection, though non–meat eaters aren't left out of the fun, thanks to notable seafood offerings and plenty of salads. **Known for:** over-the-top desserts; happy hour specials; mixed grills. $ Average main: $42 ⊠ 65 E. Wacker Pl., Chicago Loop ☎ 312/201–0410 ⊕ www.mortons.com ⊗ No lunch.

The Plaza

$ | **AMERICAN** | **FAMILY** | A seat outside at the summertime-only Plaza, shaded with a rainbow of umbrellas and in full view of Millennium Park, is one of most desired in the city. While service can be slow due to summer crowds, grin and bear it with another drink from the walk-up outdoor bar, snacks like hummus and nachos, and live music and other entertainment. **Known for:** picnic supplies to take to the park; perfect people-watching; burgers. $ Average main: $14 ⊠ Millennium Park, 11 N. Michigan Ave., Chicago Loop ☎ 312/521–7275 ⊕ www.parkgrillchicago.com ⊗ Closed Nov.–Apr.

Russian Tea Time

$$ | **RUSSIAN** | Russian culture is on the menu and in the air at this restaurant distinguished with mahogany trim, samovars, and balalaika music. The ambience sets the stage for dishes from Russia and neighboring republics (the owners hail from Uzbekistan), while chilled vodka flights lend a festive nature to any meal. **Known for:** the vodka; blinis with salmon caviar; afternoon tea service. $ Average main: $24 ⊠ 77 E. Adams St., Chicago Loop ☎ 312/360–0000 ⊕ www.russianteatime.com ⊗ Closed Mon.

312 Chicago

$$$ | **ITALIAN** | Part handy hotel restaurant, part Loop power diner, and all Italian down to its first-generation chef, Luca Corazzina, 312 Chicago earns its popularity with well-executed dishes that range from house-made pastas to thoughtful

seafood dishes. You'll be tempted to carbo-load on the house-baked bread alone, but save room for Italian-inspired desserts, including a spread of cookies, biscotti, and cannoli. **Known for:** fritto misto; prix-fixe lunch; extensive wine list. $ Average main: $28 ⊠ Hotel Allegro, 136 N. LaSalle St., Chicago Loop ☎ 312/696–2420 ⊕ www.312chicago.com.

Coffee and Quick Bites

Garrett Popcorn

$ | **FAST FOOD** | **FAMILY** | Lines form early and stay throughout the day. The popcorn is so popular that there are several other Chicago outlets plus branches in Dubai, Hong Kong, Singapore, Japan, South Korea, Thailand, and Malaysia. **Known for:** frango chocolates; Garrett mix (cheese and caramel); customizable tins. $ Average main: $5 ⊠ 26 W. Randolph St., Chicago Loop ☎ 888/476–7267 ⊕ www.garrettpopcorn.com.

Hotels

The Allegro Royal Sonesta Hotel Chicago Loop

$$ | **HOTEL** | **FAMILY** | Theater lovers will relish an opportunity to stay at this art deco–theme hot spot, with its plush banquettes, intimate candlelight spaces, and oversize works of modern art. **Pros:** complimentary 24/7 fitness center; great pretheater bar scene; bicycles available for complimentary checkout. **Cons:** there are better choices for those seeking an intimate atmosphere; no on-site spa; small bathrooms and closets. $ Rooms from: $229 ⊠ 171 W. Randolph St., Chicago Loop ☎ 312/236–0123 ⊕ www.allegrochicago.com ⤴ 483 rooms ⊗ No Meals.

★ Chicago Athletic Association

$$ | **HOTEL** | Hearkening to the city's golden age of architecture, this historic private men's club was converted to a

sprawling luxury hotel and boozy adult playground with distinctly Chicago flavor—amazing views of Millennium Park included. **Pros:** historical gem with thoughtful design; proximity to lake and parks; happening social scene. **Cons:** no on-site spa; hard to find a room in high season; bar and restaurants can get crowded, with lines to get in common. [$] *Rooms from: $269* ✉ *12 S. Michigan Ave., Chicago Loop* ☎ *312/940–3552* 🌐 *www.chicagoathletichotel.com* 🛏 *241 rooms* 🍴 *No Meals.*

Fairmont Chicago Millennium Park

$$ | **HOTEL** | On a quiet block between bustling Michigan Avenue and the Lake Michigan shoreline, this 45-story pink-granite building has suites with stunning views of Millennium Park. **Pros:** spacious rooms; short walk from the heart of the city; soothing spa facilities. **Cons:** could use some refreshing; not child-friendly; no swimming pool. [$] *Rooms from: $289* ✉ *200 N. Columbus Dr., Chicago Loop* ☎ *312/565–8000* 🌐 *www.fairmont.com* 🛏 *687 rooms* 🍴 *No Meals.*

Hampton Inn Majestic Chicago Theatre District

$ | **HOTEL** | The Hampton Inn Majestic is in one of the most high-traffic areas of town; it offers stunning, quiet guest rooms done up in designer tones. **Pros:** great complimentary breakfast; steps from the Art Institute and downtown theaters; unique style. **Cons:** no pets allowed; the lobby can get crowded; a hike to the Magnificent Mile. [$] *Rooms from: $199* ✉ *22 W. Monroe, Chicago Loop* ☎ *312/332–5052, 800/548–8690* 🌐 *www.hilton.com/en/hotels/chitdhx-hampton-majestic-chicago-theatre-district/* 🛏 *135 rooms* 🍴 *Free Breakfast.*

Hotel Monaco Chicago

$$ | **HOTEL** | **FAMILY** | A global-chic lobby featuring pops of color and texture (check out the high-gloss red alligator fabric on the registration desk) as well as rooms with steamer-trunk nightstands and Moroccan lamps inspire wanderlust. **Pros:** comfortable beds; inspiring aesthetic; no extra charge for pets. **Cons:** located on a often noisy corner of the Loop; no on-site spa; small gym for a hotel of this size. [$] *Rooms from: $269* ✉ *225 N. Wabash Ave., Chicago Loop* ☎ *312/960–8500, 866/610–0081* 🌐 *www.monaco-chicago.com* 🛏 *191 rooms* 🍴 *No Meals.*

Hyatt Regency Chicago

$$ | **HOTEL** | A massive, light-filled lobby—part of a $168-million renovation—is the centerpiece of the Hyatt Regency Chicago, the city's largest hotel with 2,032 rooms in a prime downtown locale. **Pros:** great winter rates; great loyalty program; excellent location. **Cons:** no on-site spa; not designed for families; there's always a lot of activity. [$] *Rooms from: $299* ✉ *151 E. Wacker Dr., Chicago Loop* ☎ *312/565–1234* 🌐 *www.hyatt.com/en-US/hotel/illinois/hyatt-regency-chicago/chirc* 🛏 *2032 rooms* 🍴 *No Meals.*

JW Marriott Chicago

$$$ | **HOTEL** | Mixing architectural elegance with a sleek modern style, this historic property has lots of gorgeous areas, from a bright and welcoming lobby bar to spacious guest rooms with high ceilings and marble baths. **Pros:** very friendly staff; blocks from Art Institute and Millennium Park; use of 24-hour fitness center and pool. **Cons:** immediate neighborhood is not lively on weekends or evenings; not a good option for families; lackluster views. [$] *Rooms from: $329* ✉ *151 W. Adams St., Chicago Loop* ☎ *312/660–8200, 888/238–2427* 🌐 *www.jwmarriottchicago.com* 🛏 *610 rooms* 🍴 *No Meals.*

The Palmer House Hilton

$$ | **HOTEL** | The epitome of a grande dame, this massive property in the center of the Loop has undergone a $215-million renovation, but the lobby—with its wow-worthy ceiling mural and lots of gold, marble, and

tapestry—preserves the original splendor. **Pros:** classy service; within walking distance of almost everything most visitors want to; beautiful Instagram-able lobby. **Cons:** you can hear the El train from some rooms; steep parking fees and daily charges for fitness center; some rooms are quite small. [$] *Rooms from: $229* ✉ *17 E. Monroe St., Chicago Loop* ☎ *312/726–7500, 800/445–8667* 🌐 *www.palmerhousehiltonhotel.com* 🛏 *1641 rooms* 🍴 *No Meals.*

Pendry Chicago

$$ | **HOTEL** | City history and contemporary design come together with stylish elegance at the Pendry Chicago, in the iconic 1929 art deco Carbide and Carbon Building. **Pros:** rooftop bar; great location; 24-hour fitness center. **Cons:** no fridge or microwave in rooms; standard rooms are small; some traffic noise in street-facing rooms. [$] *Rooms from: $225* ✉ *230 Michigan Ave., Chicago Loop* ☎ *312/777–9000* 🌐 *www.pendry.com/chicago/* 🍴 *No Meals* 🛏 *364 rooms.*

★ **Radisson Blu Aqua**

$$ | **HOTEL** | **FAMILY** | With design savvy inside as well as out, this gem breathes life into an 82-story skyscraper designed by revered architect Jeanne Gang. **Pros:** great location; unique design; friendly. **Cons:** hard to nab rooms in high season; no full-service spa; room keycards need to be swiped quickly in the elevator, or you're sent off to the lobby. [$] *Rooms from: $271* ✉ *221 N. Columbus Dr., Chicago Loop* ☎ *312/638–6686, 800/333–3333* 🌐 *www.radissonblu.com* 🛏 *334 rooms* 🍴 *No Meals.*

Renaissance Chicago Downtown Hotel

$$ | **HOTEL** | Perched on prime real estate on the south bank of the Chicago River, this cosmopolitan spot is shouldered by high-rises but you can enjoy still enjoy fantastic views of the Chicago skyline right from your room. **Pros:** great location; excellent service, even when the hotel is packed to capacity; spacious rooms are a good value. **Cons:** tends to be always-bustling; no full-service spa; can get pricey during high season. [$] *Rooms from: $299* ✉ *1 W. Wacker Dr., Chicago Loop* ☎ *312/372–7200* 🌐 *www.renaissancechicagodowntown.com* 🛏 *553 rooms* 🍴 *No Meals.*

The Silversmith Hotel

$$ | **HOTEL** | Don't be fooled by the tiny front entrance under the El; the Silversmith's oak-covered lobby is enormous and houses a sleek, chandelier-decked restaurant and lounge. **Pros:** historic charm; convenient to public transportation; window seats for prime city views. **Cons:** no on-site spa; some guests complain about outside noise; entrance can be hard to find. [$] *Rooms from: $279* ✉ *10 S. Wabash Ave., Chicago Loop* ☎ *312/372–7696, 833/970–2909* 🌐 *www.silversmithchicagohotel.com* 🛏 *144 rooms* 🍴 *No Meals.*

Staypineapple Chicago

$$ | **HOTEL** | The historic property, built in 1895 by D.H. Burnham & Co. as one of the first skyscrapers, retains ornate original details including Carrara marble and wrought-iron-trimmed elevators. **Pros:** excellent in-house dining; in the heart of the Theatre District; building on National Registry of Historic Places. **Cons:** limited lobby space for gathering and lounging; not many rooms big enough for larger families; room decor is rather plain. [$] *Rooms from: $229* ✉ *1 W. Washington St., Chicago Loop* ☎ *312/940–7997* 🌐 *staypineapple.com/the-loop-chicago* 🛏 *122 rooms* 🍴 *No Meals.*

Swissôtel Chicago

$$$ | **HOTEL** | The Swissôtel's triangular Harry Weese design allows for panoramic vistas of the city, lake, or river—and the comfortable, contemporary rooms feel like condos. **Pros:** amazing pool; great views; marble bathrooms. **Cons:** no full-service spa; room rates soar in high season; pricey parking. [$] *Rooms from: $399* ✉ *323 E. Wacker Dr., Chicago Loop* ☎ *312/565–0565, 888/737–9477* 🌐 *www.*

swissotel.com/hotels/chicago 🛏 *662 rooms* 🍴 *No Meals.*

theWit

$$ | **HOTEL** | The atmosphere at this sleek spot, topped by ROOF, one of the Loop's most happening bars, is fun and youthful; the same can be said of the guest rooms, which are moderately sized and modern, with hanging wall art meant to resemble puckered lips. **Pros:** close to theaters, shopping, and public transportation; bold, bright modern decor; excellent dining and drinking options. **Cons:** no pool; located on a very congested corner of the Loop; may be too cool for families. [$] *Rooms from: $230* ✉ *201 N. State St., Chicago Loop* ☎ *312/467–0200, 866/318–1514* 🌐 *www.thewithotel.com* 🛏 *310 rooms* 🍴 *No Meals.*

The Virgin Hotel

$$$ | **HOTEL** | The world's first Virgin Hotel offers loads of tech-age amenities: a custom app called "Lucy" lets guests check in or out remotely, order room service, control the thermostat, and more, plus there is free Wi-Fi at unlimited bandwidth, and outlets are everywhere—including in front of each stool at the sleek lobby bar. **Pros:** no delivery charge for room service; in the heart of downtown, close to major attractions; free Wi-Fi and lots of outlets. **Cons:** no full-service spa; pricey parking; no pool. [$] *Rooms from: $399* ✉ *203 N. Wabash Ave., Chicago Loop* ☎ *312/940-4400, 855/946–6600* 🌐 *virginhotels.com/chicago* 🛏 *250 rooms* 🍴 *No Meals.*

W Chicago–City Center

$$$ | **HOTEL** | With a clublike lobby and spacious high-tech rooms done up in graphite and cream, this financial district hotel attracts both business travelers and tourists. **Pros:** great location; sleek, modern design. **Cons:** you can hear the El from some rooms; no free in-room Wi-Fi. [$] *Rooms from: $399* ✉ *172 W. Adams St., Chicago Loop* ☎ *312/332–1200, 877/822–0000* 🌐 *www.marriott.com/chiwc* 🛏 *394 rooms* 🍴 *No Meals.*

Nightlife

BARS

Sleek and sexy wine bars and lounges like ROOF on theWit Hotel light up Chicago's core business district after work.

Château Carbide

COCKTAIL LOUNGES | The eye-catching Carbide and Carbon Building has its first rooftop bar. The Pendry Chicago Hotel, the skyscraper's latest occupant, turned a former private-event space on the 24th floor into a chic indoor-outdoor lounge overlooking the Chicago River. The wine list emphasizes rosés (there are even several rosé cocktails), the kitchen offers sushi and small bites, and after dark, DJ's spin French House. ✉ *230 N. Michigan Ave., Chicago Loop* ☎ *312/777–9000* 🕒 *Closed Nov.-Apr.*

ROOF on theWit

COCKTAIL LOUNGES | One of the city's hottest perches, ROOF occupies the 27th floor of theWit Hotel. The outdoor space entices with fire pits and panoramic city views; floor-to-ceiling glass windows make the indoor area equally breathtaking. DJs spinning eclectic beats and a menu of pricey cocktails and small plates complete the scene. ✉ *201 N. State St., Chicago Loop* ☎ *312/239–9502* 🌐 *www.roofonthewit.com* 🕒 *Closed Mon.*

Performing Arts

CLASSICAL MUSIC

Chicago Symphony Orchestra

MUSIC | **FAMILY** | Under the direction of internationally celebrated conductor Riccardo Muti, the Chicago Symphony Orchestra is a musical tour de force. It has two award-winning, in-house composers and an annual calendar with 150-plus performances. The impressive roster includes regular concerts as well as special themed series dedicated to classical, chamber, and children's concerts. The season runs from September through June. Tickets are sometimes

scarce, but they do become available; call or check the website for status updates. ✉ *Symphony Center, 220 S. Michigan Ave., Chicago Loop* ☎ *312/294–3000* ⊕ *www.cso.org.*

Music of the Baroque

MUSIC | Rewind time with one of the Midwest's leading music ensembles. Specializing in Baroque and early classical music, it mounts about eight programs a year, mostly at Millennium Park's Harris Theater. ☎ *312/551–1414* ⊕ *www. baroque.org.*

DANCE

Hubbard Street Dance Chicago

MODERN DANCE | Hubbard Street Dance Chicago exudes a jazzy vitality that has made it extremely popular. The style mixes classical-ballet techniques, theatrical jazz, and contemporary dance. Most performances take place at the Harris Theater in Millennium Park. ☎ *312/635–3799* ⊕ *www.hubbardstreetdance.com.*

★ Joffrey Ballet

BALLET | Fine-tuned performances, such as the glittering production of *The Nutcracker*, make this Chicago's premier classical-dance company. The Joffrey performed at the Auditorium Theatre of Roosevelt University for nearly two decades but took up residence with the Lyric Opera in 2021. ✉ *Civic Opera House, 20 N. Wacker Dr., Chicago Loop* ☎ *312/386–8905* ⊕ *joffrey.org.*

FILM

Gene Siskel Film Center

FILM | New releases from around the globe and revivals of cinematic classics are shown at the Gene Siskel Film Center; the best part is that filmmakers often make appearances at screenings. ✉ *164 N. State St., Chicago Loop* ☎ *312/846–2600, 312/846–2800 hotline* ⊕ *www.siskelfilmcenter.org.*

OPERA

Chicago Opera Theater

OPERA | This company shrugs off esoteric notions of opera, preferring to make productions that are accessible to aficionados and novices alike. From innovative versions of traditional favorites to important lesser-known works, the emphasis is on both theatrical and musical aspects. Fear not—performances are sung in English or in Italian with English supertitles projected above the stage. They alternate between the Harris Theater in Millennium Park and the Studebaker Theater in the Fine Arts Building on Michigan Avenue. ✉ *Studebaker Theater, 410 S. Michigan Ave., Chicago Loop* ☎ *312/704–8414* ⊕ *www.chicagooperatheater.org.*

Lyric Opera of Chicago

OPERA | At the Lyric Opera of Chicago, the big voices of the opera world star in top-flight productions September through May. This is one of the top two opera companies in America today. Don't worry about understanding German or Italian; English translations are projected above the stage. All of the superb performances have sold out for more than a dozen years, and close to 90% of all Lyric tickets go to subscribers. The key to getting in is to call the Lyric in early August, when individual tickets first go on sale. ✉ *Civic Opera House, 20 N. Wacker Dr., Chicago Loop* ☎ *312/827–5600* ⊕ *www. lyricopera.org.*

VENUES

Cadillac Palace Theatre

THEATER | Designed by famed theater architects the Rapp Brothers, the Cadillac Palace opened to much fanfare in 1926. The ornate, gilded interior was inspired by the palaces of Versailles and Fontainebleau; restored to its original opulence in 1999, the 2,500-seat space now hosts a wide range of traveling productions. ✉ *151 W. Randolph St., Chicago Loop* ☎ *312/977–1700, 800/775–2000* ⊕ *www.broadwayinchicago.com.*

Chicago Cultural Center

ARTS CENTERS | This block-long landmark building houses several performance spaces. The most magnificent is the top-floor Preston Bradley Hall, with its Tiffany glass dome and ornately detailed white marble walls. ⊠ *78 E. Washington St., Chicago Loop* ☎ *312/744–3316* ⊕ *www. chicagoculturalcenter.org.*

The Chicago Theatre

THEATER | Since 1921, visitors to the Chicago Theatre, which began as a Balaban and Katz movie palace, have marveled at its stunning Baroque interior. The 3,600-seat auditorium features crystal chandeliers, bronze light fixtures, and murals on the wall and ceiling. Lately it has hosted big-name music acts like Beyoncé and Arcade Fire. ⊠ *175 N. State St., Chicago Loop* ☎ *312/462–6300* ⊕ *www.thechicagotheatre.com.*

CIBC Theatre

THEATER | After debuting as the Majestic in 1906, this 1,800-seat theater became a major stop on the vaudeville circuit. Today, after a series of name changes (the current naming-rights holder is a Canadian bank), the plush, red-and-gold venue hosts Broadway in Chicago performances such as *Jersey Boys*, *The Book of Mormon*, and other traveling shows. ⊠ *18 W. Monroe St., Chicago Loop* ☎ *312/977–1700, 800/775–2000* ⊕ *www. broadwayinchicago.com.*

Goodman Theatre

THEATER | Founded in 1925, the city's oldest and largest nonprofit theater presents an exceptional repertoire of plays each year featuring local and national performers. Works by August Wilson and David Mamet have premiered here, and the Goodman's annual holiday staging of *A Christmas Carol* is a Chicago tradition. ⊠ *170 N. Dearborn St., Chicago Loop* ☎ *312/443–3800* ⊕ *www.goodmantheatre.org.*

James M. Nederlander Theatre

THEATER | Originally dubbed the Oriental Theatre, this former movie palace has a grand, over-the-top Far Eastern decor (think Buddha statues and huge mosaics of an Indian prince and princess). First opened in 1926, it reopened in 1998 after a period of disrepair to accommodate big-name Broadway hits, and received a welcome name change in 2019. ⊠ *24 W. Randolph St., Chicago Loop* ☎ *312/977–1700, 800/775–2000* ⊕ *www.broadway-inchicago.com.*

Joan W. and Irving B. Harris Theater for Music and Dance

THEATER | Located on the northwest corner of Millennium Park, this 1,500-seat, mostly belowground theater is a sleek, contemporary space where you can catch music and dance performances by the likes of Laurie Anderson, Magnetic Fields, and Hubbard Street Dance Chicago. ⊠ *205 E. Randolph St., Chicago Loop* ☎ *312/334–7777* ⊕ *www.harristheater-chicago.org.*

 ## Shopping

Named for the elevated train tracks encircling it, the Loop is the city's business and financial hub as well as a thriving shopping destination.

The Loop's main thoroughfare, State Street, has had its share of ups and downs. After serving as Chicago's retail corridor for much of the 20th century, the street lost its stature for a time, but these days "that great street" is once again on the ascent, with a multilevel shopping mall. One block east, Wabash Street's "Jewelers Row" is a series of high-rises and street-level shops where you're sure to find that perfect sparkly something.

ANTIQUES

Harlan J. Berk

ANTIQUES & COLLECTIBLES | Travel back to antiquity amid this wondrous trove of classical Greek, Roman, and Byzantine coins and artifacts. Don't miss the gallery rooms in the back. ⊠ *31 N. Clark St., Chicago Loop* ☎ *312/609–0016* ⊕ *www. hjbltd.com* ☺ *Closed weekends.*

CAMERAS AND ELECTRONICS
★ Central Camera
CAMERAS & PHOTOGRAPHY | This century-old store is a Loop institution. It's stacked to the rafters with cameras and dark-room equipment at competitive prices. ⊠ *230 S. Wabash Ave., Chicago Loop* ☎ *312/427–5580* ⊕ *www.centralcamera. com* ☺ *Closed Tues., Thurs., and Sun.*

CLOTHING
Florodora
WOMEN'S CLOTHING | This boutique's location in the historic Monadnock Building complements the vintage-inspired clothing and accessories it carries. Just down the hall, at 348 South Dearborn, you can browse the well-edited selection of footwear at sister shop Florodora Shoes; it stocks brands like Coclico and Chie Mihara. ⊠ *330 S. Dearborn St., Chicago Loop* ☎ *312/212–8860* ⊕ *florodora.com* ☺ *Closed weekends.*

Syd Jerome
MEN'S CLOTHING | Board of Trade types who like special attention and the perfect fit come to this legendary clothier for brands like Giorgio Armani and Ermenegildo Zegna. Home and office consultations are available. ⊠ *20 N. Clark St., Chicago Loop* ☎ *312/346–0333* ⊕ *www. sydjerome.com* ☺ *Closed Sun.*

FOOD AND TREATS
Iwan Ries and Co.
TOBACCO | Iwan Ries didn't just jump on the cigar bandwagon; the family-owned store has been around since 1857. Cigar smokers are welcome to light up in a designated area, which also displays antique pipes. ■**TIP**➔ **Almost 100 brands of cigars are available, along with 15,000 or so pipes, deluxe Elie Bleu humidors, and many other smoking accessories.** ⊠ *19 S. Wabash Ave., 2nd fl., Chicago Loop*

☎ *312/372–1306* ⊕ *www.iwanries.com* ☺ *Closed Sun.*

JEWELRY AND ACCESSORIES
Jewelers Center
JEWELRY & WATCHES | The largest concentration of wholesale and retail jewelers in the Midwest has been housed in this building since 1921, and it's open to the general public. Roughly 190 retailers span 13 floors, offering all kinds of jewelry, watches, and related repairs and services. ⊠ *5 S. Wabash Ave., Chicago Loop* ☎ *312/424–2664* ⊕ *www.jeweler-scenter.com.*

Legend of Time
JEWELRY & WATCHES | This family-owned business, the former Chicago Watch Center, has one of the city's most outstanding inventories of used luxury watches. ⊠ *5 S. Wabash Ave., 7th Floor, #708, Chicago Loop* ☎ *312/609–0003* ⊕ *www.legendoftime.com* ☺ *Closed Sun.*

Wabash Jewelers Mall
JEWELRY & WATCHES | Whether it's an engagement ring or tennis bracelet, you're primed to do great comparison shopping at the Wabash Jewelers Mall, which houses more than a dozen vendors under one roof. Looking for loose diamonds? They've got those, too. ⊠ *21 N. Wabash Ave., at Washington St.* ☎ *312/263–1757.*

MUSEUM STORES
Museum Shop at the Art Institute of Chicago
SOUVENIRS | Museum reproductions in the form of jewelry, posters, and Frank Lloyd Wright–inspired decorative accessories, as well as books and toys, fill the Art Institute's gift shop. If you're keen on one of the museum's current big exhibits, chances are you'll find some nifty souvenirs to take away. ⊠ *111 S. Michigan Ave., Chicago Loop* ⊕ *shop.artic.edu* ☺ *Closed Tues.-Wed.*

South Loop

The South Loop's main claim to fame is the Museum Campus—the Field Museum, Shedd Aquarium, and the Adler Planetarium, on Northerly Island. Jutting out into the lake, it affords amazing skyline views. To the north, giant gargoyles (actually stylized owls signifying wisdom) loom atop the Harold Washington Library. East on Congress at Michigan Avenue is the Romanesque Revival–style Auditorium Theatre, designed by architects Sullivan and Adler. Farther south at Printers Row, lofts that once clattered with Linotype machines now contain condos. The South Loop begins more or less where the Loop itself ends, starting south of Van Buren, extending down to Chinatown, and including everything between Lake Michigan and the Chicago River.

Sights

★ Adler Planetarium and Astronomy Museum

OBSERVATORY | FAMILY | Taking you on a journey through the stars to unlock the mysteries of our galaxy and beyond, the Adler tells amazing stories of space exploration through high-tech exhibits and immersive theater experiences. Artifacts and interactive elements bring these fascinating tales of space and its pioneers down to earth. The Grainger Sky Theater gives an up-close view of stunning space phenomena, and the magnificent imagery is so realistic that it might only be surpassed by actual space travel. The newest permanent exhibit is "The Universe: A Walk Through Space and Time." A spectacular projection showcases the enormity of the universe, and touch screens let you investigate diverse and beautiful objects from deep space. Journey through space in the Definiti Space Theater, or don 3-D glasses to view celestial phenomena in the Samuel C. Johnson Family Star Theater. ⊠ 1300 S. Lake Shore Dr., South Loop

Chicago Theater District

On State, north of Randolph Street, is Chicago's old theater district. The ornate 1921 Beaux-Arts **Chicago Theatre**, a former movie palace, now hosts live performances. Across the street is the **Gene Siskel Film Center**, which screens art, foreign, and classic flicks. The glitzy neon sign of the **James M. Nederlander Theatre** shines and the **Goodman Theatre**, on Dearborn, has new productions in a 1925 art deco landmark. One block west is the **Cadillac Palace Theatre**, built as a vaudeville venue in 1926.

☎ 312/922–7827 ⊕ www.adlerplanetarium.org ⊠ $19, $50 all-access pass.

★ Auditorium Theatre

NOTABLE BUILDING | Hunkered down across from Grant Park, this 110,000-ton granite-and-limestone behemoth was an instant star when it debuted in 1899, and it didn't hurt the careers of its designers, Dankmar Adler and Louis H. Sullivan, either. Inside were offices, a 400-room hotel, and a 4,300-seat state-of-the-art theater with electric lighting and an air-cooling system that used 15 tons of ice per day. Adler managed the engineering—the theater's acoustics are renowned—and Sullivan ornamented the space using mosaics, cast iron, art glass, wood, and plaster. During World War II the building was used as a Servicemen's Center. Then Roosevelt University moved in and, thanks to the school's Herculean restoration efforts, the theater is again one of the city's premiere performance venues. Tours are offered on Monday, Tuesday, and Thursday. ⊠ 50 E. Ida B. Wells Dr., South Loop ☎ 312/341–2100 ⊕ www.auditoriumtheatre.org ⊠ Tours $15.

The exhibits in Field Museum's main lobby are a taste of what you'll see elsewhere in the museum.

Dearborn Station

NOTABLE BUILDING | Part of Printers Row, this is Chicago's oldest-standing passenger train station, designed in the Romanesque Revival style in 1885 by New York architect Cyrus L.W. Eidlitz. Now filled with offices and stores, it has a wonderful 12-story clock tower and a red-sandstone and redbrick facade ornamented with terra-cotta. Striking features inside are the marble floor, wraparound brass walkway, and arching wood-frame doorways. ✉ *47 W. Polk St., South Loop* ☎ *312/554–8100* ⊕ *www.dearbornstation.com.*

★ Field Museum

HISTORY MUSEUM | **FAMILY** | More than 400,000 square feet of exhibit space fill this gigantic museum, which explores cultures and environments from around the world. Interactive displays examine such topics as the secrets of Egyptian mummies, the art and innovations of people living in the Ancient Americas, and the evolution of life on Earth. Originally funded by Chicago retailer Marshall Field, the museum was founded in 1893 to hold material gathered for the World's Columbian Exposition; its current neoclassical home opened in 1921. The museum holds the world's best dinosaur collections but the star of the show is 65-million-year-old "Sue," the largest and most complete Tyrannosaurus rex fossil ever found. ■**TIP**➜ **Don't hesitate to take toddlers to the Field. In the Crown Family PlayLab, kids two to six years old can play house in a re-created pueblo and compare their footprints with a dinosaur's.** ✉ *1400 S. Lake Shore Dr., South Loop* ☎ *312/922–9410* ⊕ *www.fieldmuseum.org* ✉ *$26, $40 all-access pass.*

Franklin Building

NOTABLE BUILDING | Built in 1888 as the home of the Franklin Company, one of the largest printers at the time, this building has intricate decoration. The tile work on the facade leads up to *The First Impression*—a medieval scene illustrating the first application of the printer's craft. Above the entryway is a motto: "The excellence of every art must consist

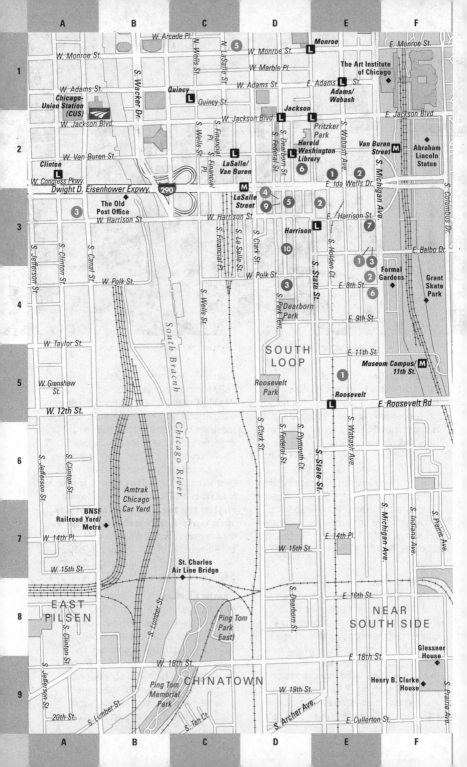

South Loop

KEY

- **1** Exploring Sights
- **1** Restaurants
- **1** Quick Bites
- **1** Hotels
- **L** CTA Lines
- **M** Metra Lines

Museum Campus Tips

The parklike, pedestrian-friendly Museum Campus is home to the Big Three—the **Field Museum,** the **John G. Shedd Aquarium,** and the **Adler Planetarium and Astronomy Museum**. If you're driving, park in one of the lots just past the Field Museum on McFetridge Drive; alternately, you can arrive via the **Chicago Trolley HOP ON HOP OFF Tour** (773/648–5000), which connects sites on the 57-acre campus with other downtown tourist attractions and train stations. Just east of the Field Museum is the Shedd Aquarium, on the lakefront; farther still, at the end of a peninsula jutting into Lake Michigan on the man-made Northerly Island, is the Adler. Look north from here for a fantastic view of the city skyline.

If you're visiting all three museums plus other major attractions, consider a Chicago CityPASS ($109, valid for nine consecutive days). You'll avoid long lines and get access to the Field, the Shedd, and the Willis Tower Skydeck, plus any two of the Adler, the Art Institute, 360 Chicago (formerly the John Hancock Center Observatory) or the Museum of Science and Industry.

in the complete accomplishment of its purpose." The building was turned into condos in 1989. ⊠ *720 S. Dearborn St., South Loop* ⊕ *www.thefranklinbuilding.com.*

Harold Washington Library Center

LIBRARY | FAMILY | Opened in 1991 and named for Chicago's first African American mayor, this library was primarily designed by architect Thomas Beeby, of Hammond, Beeby & Babka. Gargantuan and almost goofy, the granite-and-brick edifice is a uniquely postmodern homage to Chicago's great architectural past. The heavy, rusticated ground level recalls the Rookery; the stepped-back, arched windows are a reference to the great arches in the Auditorium Theatre; the swirling terra-cotta design is pinched from the Marquette Building; and the glass curtain wall on the west side is a nod to 1950s modernism. The huge, gargoyle-like sculptures atop the building include owls, a symbol of wisdom. The excellent Children's Library, an 18,000-square-foot haven on the second floor, has vibrant wall-mounted figures by Chicago Imagist Karl Wirsum. Works by noted Chicago artists are displayed along a second-floor walkway above the main lobby. There's also an impressive Winter Garden with skylights on the ninth floor. Free programs and performances are offered regularly. ⊠ *400 S. State St., South Loop* ☎ *312/747–4300* ⊕ *www.chipublic.org/locations/34.*

Museum of Contemporary Photography at Columbia College Chicago

ART MUSEUM | "Contemporary" is generally defined here as work made in the past two or three decades. Curators constantly seek out new talent and underappreciated established photographers, which means that there are artists here you probably won't see elsewhere. Rotating exhibits have included explorations of infrastructure, crime, and American identity. ⊠ *600 S. Michigan Ave., South Loop* ☎ *312/663–5554* ⊕ *www.mocp.org* ☜ *Free.*

Northerly Island

CITY PARK | Part of the Museum Campus, Northerly Island is a man-made peninsula in Lake Michigan. It's home to the Adler Planetarium as well as a 40-acre park, with walking and biking trails and the

12th Street Beach. ⊠ *1521 S. Linn White Dr., South Loop.*

Pontiac Building

NOTABLE BUILDING | Built in 1891, the simple, redbrick Pontiac is an early Chicago School skyscraper—note the classic rectangular shape and flat roof. It is the city's oldest existing Holabird & Roche building. ⊠ *542 S. Dearborn St., South Loop.*

Printers Row

HISTORIC DISTRICT | Bounded by Ida B. Wells Drive on the north, Polk Street on the south, Plymouth Court to the east, and the Chicago River to the west, this district fell into disrepair in the 1960s, but a neighborhood resurgence began in the late 1970s. Bibliophiles flock in for the Printers Row Lit Fest, a weekend-long literary celebration held each June. But, at any time of year, you can admire examples of buildings by the group that represented the First Chicago School of Architecture (including Louis Sullivan). ⊠ *Between Ida B. Wells Dr. and Polk St., Plymouth Ct. and the Chicago River, South Loop.*

★ Shedd Aquarium

AQUARIUM | **FAMILY** | One of the most popular aquariums in the country, the Shedd houses more than 32,500 creatures from around the world. "Amazon Rising" houses piranhas, snakes, and stingrays in an 8,600-square-foot exhibit that resembles a flooded forest and re-creates the rise and fall of floodwaters. A shark-filled 400,000-gallon tank is part of "Wild Reef," which explores marine biodiversity in the Indo-Pacific. The exhibit also has colorful corals, stingrays that slide by under your feet, and other surprising creatures, all from the waters around the Philippines. Whales and dolphins live in the spectacular Oceanarium, which has pools that seem to blend into Lake Michigan. The aquatic show here stars dancing belugas, leaping dolphins, and comical penguins. Be sure to get an underwater glimpse of the dolphins and whales through the viewing windows on the lower level, where you can also find a bunch of information-packed, hands-on activities. ■TIP➔ **Lines for the Shedd often extend all the way down the neoclassical steps. Buy a ticket in advance to avoid the interminable wait, or spring for a CityPASS.** ⊠ *1200 S. Lake Shore Dr., South Loop* ☎ *312/939–2438* ⊕ *www.sheddaquarium.org* 🖃 *$40.*

Soldier Field

SPORTS VENUE | **FAMILY** | Opened in 1924 as the Municipal Grant Park Stadium, the facility was renamed in 1925 to commemorate American soldiers who died during World War I. Just south of the Museum Campus, the building and its massive columns are reminiscent of ancient Greece. It's the home field for the NFL's Chicago Bears and Major League Soccer's Chicago Fire FC, as well as a venue for college games and concerts. A controversial modern glass expansion, which looks like a spaceship that landed on the arena, was completed in 2003. Behind-the-scenes tours feature the Doughboy Statue, Colonnades, field, South Courtyard, visitors' locker room, the suites, and the United Club. ⊠ *1410 S. Museum Campus Dr., South Loop* ☎ *312/235–7000* ⊕ *www.soldierfield.net* 🖃 *Tours $15 (check website for times).*

🍽 Restaurants

Eleven City Diner

$ | **AMERICAN** | **FAMILY** | For all its great food, Chicago is not much of a deli town, which endears the old-school Eleven City Diner to locals looking for all-day breakfast and deli staples. There are also plenty of classic diner options including burgers and soda-fountain floats and malts, though breaking from the deli tradition, Eleven City also serves beer, wine, and cocktails. **Known for:** latkes; candy counter; pastrami sandwiches. **$** *Average main: $12* ⊠ *1112 S. Wabash Ave., South Loop* ☎ *312/212–1112* ⊕ *www.elevencitydiner.com* ⊗ *No dinner.*

Epic Burger

$ | **BURGER** | **FAMILY** | After walking through exhibits at the Art Institute, follow the local college crowd to this order-at-the-counter eatery, where the ambience is kitschy but the food is, as owner David Friedman describes it, "more mindful." Friedman serves hand-shaped, natural beef burgers, as well as a plant-based Beyond Burger, all served atop a soft bun with add-ons like Wisconsin cheese, nitrate-free bacon, or an organic fried egg. **Known for:** chicken sandwich; milk shakes; Epic Burger classic. $ *Average main: $7* ⊠ *517 S. State St., South Loop* ☎ *312/913–1373* ⊕ *www.epicburger.com.*

Mercat a la Planxa

$$$$ | **SPANISH** | Catalan-inspired restaurant Mercat offers a stylish respite from Michigan Avenue with a view of Grant Park and a menu of small to midsize plates, all of which are great for sharing. To get more bang for your buck, try the chef's tasting menu, with prices starting at $55. **Known for:** create-your-own gin and tonic; paella; tasting menus. $ *Average main: $38* ⊠ *Blackstone Hotel, 638 S. Michigan Ave., South Loop* ☎ *312/765–0524* ⊕ *www.mercatchicago. com* ☽ *Closed Sun. and Mon., No lunch.*

☕ Coffee and Quick Bites

Cafecito

$ | **CUBAN** | At this local chain of Cuban coffee houses, you can get the eponymous espresso drink or a café con leche, as well as a variety of pressed sandwiches including what might be the city's best Cubano. The South Loop location, attached to a hostel popular with young international travelers, makes for a lively atmosphere. **Known for:** cubano sandwich; ropa vieja with sweet plantains; cuban espresso. $ *Average main: $8* ⊠ *26 E. Ida B. Wells Dr., South Loop* ☎ *312/922–2233* ⊕ *cafecitochicago.com* ☽ *Closed Sun.*

Hotels

The Blackstone Hotel

$$$ | **HOTEL** | The lobby here is a crown jewel in Chicago's architecture scene; guest rooms are simple and elegant, with enough flair to feel updated yet still give a sense of the rich past. **Pros:** Chicago icon; great location; close to Museum Campus and theater district. **Cons:** prices soar during high season; no full-service spa; lobby can be a bit dark, and its decor a bit too ornate. $ *Rooms from: $339* ⊠ *636 S. Michigan Ave., South Loop* ☎ *312/447–0955* ⊕ *theblackstonehotel. com* ☞ *335 rooms* �‖ *No Meals.*

Hilton Chicago

$ | **HOTEL** | On a busy day the lobby of this Hilton might be mistaken for a terminal at O'Hare Airport; it's a bustling convention hotel, but one that retains its distinguished 1920s heritage in a Renaissance-inspired entrance hall and gold-and-gilt grand ballroom. **Pros:** a city icon; close to the museum district; well-appointed public spaces. **Cons:** not the best choice for people seeking quiet and calm; steep parking fees; fee for use of fitness area. $ *Rooms from: $199* ⊠ *720 S. Michigan Ave., South Loop* ☎ *312/922–4400* ⊕ *www.hiltonchicago-hotel.com* ☞ *1593 rooms* ❘‖ *No Meals.*

Holiday Inn & Suites Chicago-Downtown

$ | **HOTEL** | **FAMILY** | Not only is this Holiday Inn close to Chicago's main attractions, it's also within steps of CTA trains that go directly to either O'Hare or Midway airports. **Pros:** great for budget-conscious families; staff goes out of their way to be helpful; convenient on-site washing machines and dryers. **Cons:** no spa; bathrooms are on the small side; the lobby can get quite crowded. $ *Rooms from: $179* ⊠ *506 W. Harrison St., South Loop* ☎ *800/972–2494* ⊕ *ihg.com/holidayinn/ hotels/us/en/chicago/chiwh/hoteldetail* ☞ *145 rooms* ❘‖ *No Meals.*

Hotel Blake

$$ | HOTEL | A multimillion-dollar reno-vation a few years back updated this spacious landmark in Chicago's historic Printers Row neighborhood; the lobby is dark but welcoming, and the rooms, in a mix of browns, reds, and creams, are very large considering the location. **Pros:** enticing South Loop location; friendly staff; well-appointed rooms. **Cons:** the hotel spans three connected buildings, so the layout can be tricky; no full-service spa; no pool. $ *Rooms from: $309* ✉ *500 S. Dearborn, South Loop* ☎ *312/986–1234* ⊕ *www.hotelblake.com* ⇆ *162 rooms* ❄ *No Meals.*

Kimpton Gray Hotel

$$ | HOTEL | Prominently centered on the financial district, this handsome historical landmark (formerly home to the New York Life insurance building) received a sleek, bespoke redesign appealing to young professionals with discerning tastes. **Pros:** daily hosted happy hour; comfort-able beds; complimentary bike rentals. **Cons:** no spa; neighborhood isn't lively at night or on weekends; a bit of a walk to nightlife and attractions. $ *Rooms from: $299* ✉ *122 W. Monroe St., Chicago Loop* ☎ *312/750–9012* ⊕ *www.grayhotelchica-go.com* ⇆ *293 rooms* ❄ *No Meals.*

★ Le Meridien Essex Chicago

$ | HOTEL | FAMILY | Don't judge this place on appearance alone: the nondescript tower is actually one of the city's most family-friendly hotels, and its location—just five minutes by foot from the Muse-um Campus—is one reason why. **Pros:** good value; big pool; nice location. **Cons:** bathrooms on the small side; the Wi-Fi is free but slow; no spa. $ *Rooms from: $149* ✉ *800 S. Michigan Ave., South Loop* ☎ *312/939–2800* ⊕ *marriott.com/hotels/travel/child-le-meridien-essex-chicago/* ⇆ *274 rooms* ❄ *No Meals.*

Nightlife

BARS

Kitty O'Sheas

PUBS | This handsome spot in the Hilton Chicago is an authentic Emerald Isle pub with all things Irish, including live music Thursday through Sunday, beer, food, and bar staff. ✉ *Hilton Chicago, 720 S. Michi-gan Ave., South Loop* ☎ *312/294–6860.*

MUSIC VENUES
BLUES

★ Buddy Guy's Legends

LIVE MUSIC | Relocated from its original location a few doors down, Buddy Guy's Legends has a superb sound system, excellent sightlines, and more space to showcase Grammy Award–winning blues performer/owner Buddy Guy's collection of blues memorabilia. Look for local blues acts during the week and larger-scale touring acts on weekends. Don't miss Buddy Guy in January, when he performs a monthlong home stand of shows (tick-ets go on sale one month in advance). There's also a substantial menu of Cajun and Creole favorites. ✉ *700 S. Wabash Ave., South Loop* ☎ *312/427–1190* ⊕ *www.buddyguy.com* ☾ *Closed Mon. and Tues.*

Performing Arts

DANCE

Dance Center of Columbia College Chicago

MODERN DANCE | Thought-provoking fare with leading national and international contemporary-dance artists is presented by the Dance Center of Columbia College Chicago. ✉ *1306 S. Michigan Ave., South Loop* ☎ *312/369–8330* ⊕ *dance.colum.edu.*

Shopping

CLOTHING

Optimo Fine Hats

OTHER SPECIALTY STORE | One of the last establishments of its kind, Optimo makes high-end custom straw and felt hats for men in an atmosphere that evokes 1930s and '40s haberdashery. It also offers a complete line of related services, including cleaning, blocking, and repairs. ⊠ *51 W. Jackson Blvd., South Loop* ☎ *312/922–2999* ⊕ *www.optimo-hats.com* ☽ *Closed Sun. and Mon.*

West Loop

For an especially good meal, head to the West Loop, along the Chicago River. What was once skid row and meatpacking warehouses is now a vibrant community with trendy restaurants. Greektown, a five-block stretch of Halsted Street, serves up authentic *saganaki* (appetizers). A thriving art and restaurant scene has emerged around Fulton Market.

 Sights

Fulton Market

BUSINESS DISTRICT | A bustling center for food processing and distribution as recently as the 2000s, this former industrial district transformed into an upscale stretch of gleaming corporate offices, luxury condos, and Michelin-star restaurants with remarkable speed. The last of the seafood, produce, and meatpacking plants were gone by the end of the 2010s; Fulton Market is now a full-on dining and nightlife destination. ⊠ *Along Fulton Market and Lake St. between Desplaines St. and Ashland Ave., West Loop.*

★ **Garfield Park Conservatory**

GARDEN | FAMILY | Escape winter's cold or revel in summer sunshine inside this huge "landscape art under glass" structure, which houses tropical palms, spiny cacti, and showy blooms. A children's garden has climbable leaf sculptures and a tube slide that winds through trees. The "Sugar from the Sun" exhibit focuses on the elements of photosynthesis—sunlight, air, water, and sugar—in a full-sensory environment filled with spewing steam, trickling water, and chirping sounds. Don't miss the historic Jens Jensen–designed Fern Room with its lagoon, waterfalls, and profusion of ferns. On-site events include botanical-theme fashion shows, seasonal flower shows, and great educational programing. ⊠ *300 N. Central Park Ave., Garfield Park* ☎ *773/638–1766* ⊕ *garfieldconservatory.org* ⧉ *Free* ☽ *Closed Mon. and Tues.*

Greektown

NEIGHBORHOOD | This small strip may as well be half a world away from the rest of the West Loop. Greek restaurants are the main draw here. Continue west on Madison, past the slew of new condo developments and vintage conversions in progress, and you'll come to one of Chicago's popular dining and nightlife destinations. On a stretch of Madison roughly between Sangamon and Elizabeth streets, you'll find boutiques, trendy bars and lounges, and popular restaurants. The National Hellenic Museum, at 333 South Halsted, explores the Greek immigrant experience and the influence of Greek culture. ⊠ *Halsted St. between Madison and W. Van Buren Sts., West Loop* ⊕ *www.greektownchicago.org* ⧉ *Free.*

🍴 **Restaurants**

★ **Au Cheval**

$ | DINER | A menu packed with burgers, fries, and chopped liver might sound like a classic dive, but Au Cheval is no greasy spoon—exposed brick, dim lighting, and antique-inspired fixtures give a sultry feel, and rich takes on classic American diner dishes satisfy cravings. There's a perennial wait, but sneak in on weekends from 3 pm to 5 pm or Monday–Saturday

Did You Know?

Garfield Park Conservatory occasionally hosts installation art projects that blend sculpture with nature. On permanent display are a set of pieces from its 2001–2002 Dale Chihuly "A Garden of Glass" exhibit; find them in the Aroid House pond. If you have kids in tow, head to the Children's Garden to help them (and possibly you) learn about plants through giant seeds, roots, flowers, and vines.

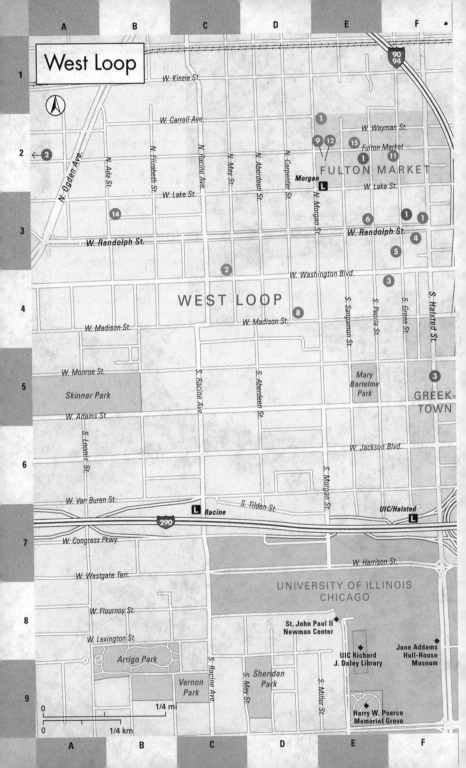

Sights ▼

Restaurants ▼

Quick Bites ▼

Hotels ▼

from midnight to 1 am for a limited menu consisting of the crowd-favorite cheeseburger and fries. **Known for:** chilaquiles; crispy fries with Mornay sauce; notable craft beer and cocktail list. S *Average main: $16 ⊠ 800 W. Randolph St., West Loop* ☎ *312/929–4580* ⊕ *http://auchevaldiner.com/chicago/.*

★ Avec

$$ | MEDITERRANEAN | Head to this Euro-style wine bar when you're feeling gregarious; the warm, intimate space has seating for only 55 people, and the results are loud and lively, with shareable fare—a mix of small and large Mediterranean plates—that's reasonably priced. **Known for:** summer late-night menu; chorizo-stuffed dates; savory wood-fired flatbread. S *Average main: $24 ⊠ 615 W. Randolph St., West Loop* ☎ *312/377–2002* ⊕ *www.avecrestaurant.com* ☾ *No lunch.*

El Che Steakhouse & Bar

$$$$ | ARGENTINE | The 12-foot blazing hearth at the back of this restaurant is the centerpiece of chef John Manion's ode to the Argentinian grilling tradition, and the steak-heavy menu is a worthy homage to the style. Manion draws on his extensive travels to South America for the shareable small plates and sizeable meat offerings, and there are cocktails perfect for pairing. **Known for:** fireside chef's table seating; Argentinian grilling; deep list of Argentinian wines. S *Average main: $48 ⊠ 845 W. Washington Blvd., West Loop* ☎ *312/265–1130* ⊕ *elchechicago.com* ☾ *Closed Sun. and Mon. No lunch.*

★ Girl & the Goat

$$ | ECLECTIC | Bravo's *Top Chef* Season 4 champion Stephanie Izard's always-packed restaurant lives up to the hype, serving her personal brand of sharable, eclectic plates with seasonal flair amid rustic decor with communal butcher tables and an open kitchen. Dishes are grouped into straightforward categories,

like vegetable, fish, and meat—with an array of offerings made with goat, naturally. **Known for:** wood-oven-roasted pig face; goat liver mousse; inventive desserts. S *Average main: $19 ⊠ 809 W. Randolph St., West Loop* ☎ *312/492–6262* ⊕ *www.girlandthegoat.com* ☾ *No lunch.*

Green Street Smoked Meats

$ | BARBECUE | Taking a cue from the barbecue kings of Texas, this cool smoke joint is a little bit Southern, a little bit hipster, and has a line that snakes through the cavernous space. It's best to queue up for counter service as soon as you walk in, then let the black-gloved carvers slice your meat by the half-pound; sides, like Frito pie, are about as American as you can get. **Known for:** barbecue sandwiches; craft beer and cocktail pitchers; smoked salmon. S *Average main: $13 ⊠ 112 N. Green St., West Loop* ☎ *312/754–0431* ⊕ *www.greenstreetmeats.com.*

Leña Brava

$$$ | MEXICAN | This Baja-inspired spot first opened in 2016 as the latest venture in chef Rick Bayless's exploration of Mexican cuisine. Bayless has since divested, but Leña Brava's all-wood-fired menu abides. **Known for:** desserts; whole fish presented with a variety of sauces; cocktail tasting of notable drinks. S *Average main: $34 ⊠ 900 W. Randolph St., West Loop* ☎ *312/733–1975* ⊕ *www.lenabrava.com* ☾ *No lunch.*

Lou Mitchell's

$ | DINER | Shelve your calorie and cholesterol concerns because Lou Mitchell's heeds no modern health warnings—the bustling old-school diner, a dining destination close to Union Station since 1923, specializes in filling breakfasts and comfort-food lunches. Though you'll almost certainly have to deal with out-the-door waits, especially at breakfast, staffers dole out doughnut holes and Milk Duds to pacify hunger pangs. **Known for:** Belgian waffles; soft-serve desserts;

meat loaf. $ *Average main: $10 ✉ 565 W. Jackson Blvd., West Loop ☎ 312/939–3111 🌐 www.loumitchells.com ⏲ Closed Mon. and Tues. No dinner.*

★ Monteverde Restaurant & Pastificio

$$ | ITALIAN | Classic meets innovative at chef Sarah Grueneberg's forward-thinking Italian restaurant, where a strategically placed mirror grants diners a view of pasta makers rolling and filling select pastas to order. The West Loop location means the restaurant gets busy before Blackhawks games, but *Top Chef* finalist Grueneberg's dishes, designed for sharing, are always a game changer. **Known for:** gluten-free offerings, including pasta options; burrata and ham; seasonal tortelli. $ *Average main: $21 ✉ 1020 W. Madison St., West Loop ☎ 312/888–3041 🌐 www.monteverdechicago.com ⏲ Closed Sun., Mon., and Tues. No lunch.*

Next Restaurant

$$$$ | ECLECTIC | Grant Achatz's buzzworthy sophomore effort is big on concept: the restaurant completely transforms its menu, tableware, decor, and beverage program every three months to focus on a unique theme, whether that's an homage to famed chef Auguste Escoffier's tenure at the Ritz Paris or Ancient Rome. Tickets for the one-of-a-kind meal from Executive Chef Ed Tinoco are paid for in advance, nonrefundable, and only available online. **Known for:** creative drink pairings; chef's table seating; excellent service. $ *Average main: $202 ✉ 953 W. Fulton Market, West Loop ☎ 312/226–0858 🌐 www.nextrestaurant.com ⏲ Closed Mon. and Tues. No lunch.*

★ Oriole

$$$$ | AMERICAN | There aren't many restaurant dinners that start by entering through an alley and into a freight elevator, but nothing about Oriole is typical, from the secretive entrance to the warm, impeccable service to the hit parade of bites on Noah Sandoval's $285 tasting menu. Wine pairings are a must, since the old-world, white-wine focus makes the flavors on the forward-thinking tasting menu truly sing. **Known for:** oyster and mangalica (a type of ham) course; nonalcoholic drink pairings; fun take-home treats. $ *Average main: $285 ✉ 661 W. Walnut St., West Loop ☎ 312/877–5339 🌐 www.oriolechicago.com ⏲ Closed Sun. and Mon. No lunch.*

★ The Publican Restaurant

$$ | AMERICAN | Don't call this beer-focused hot spot a gastropub—chef Paul Kahan prefers "beer hall" (though wine is available, too) and with the long communal tables, at which beer connoisseurs sample from a selection hovering above 50 brews, the bustling space has the air of an Oktoberfest celebration. The seafood- and pork-focused menu gives an elevated nod to pub fare, though there are plenty of veggie-friendly dishes as well. **Known for:** barbecue carrots; creative brunch menu; spicy pork rinds. $ *Average main: $27 ✉ 837 W. Fulton Market, West Loop ☎ 312/733–9555 🌐 www.thepublicanrestaurant.com ⏲ No lunch weekdays.*

Roister

$$$ | AMERICAN | Grant Achatz's and the Alinea Group's most casual, affordable restaurant is a rollicking good time, where the flavors of are as bold as the soundtrack. Snag a seat by the roaring fire, which assists the chef with capturing smoky flavors, or squeeze into the tables that overlook a busy West Loop corner; either way, you'll want to order a big meaty dish to share with the table, and some of the excellent cocktails. **Known for:** bonito-topped Yukon fries; fried chicken sandwich with chamomile mayo; peppercorn-crusted smoked rib eye. $ *Average main: $35 ✉ 951 W. Fulton Market, West Loop 🌐 www.roisterrestaurant.com ⏲ Closed Mon. and Tues. No lunch on weekdays.*

★ Sepia

$$$$ | MODERN AMERICAN | The name may evoke nostalgia for the building's gritty past as a print shop, but Sepia is thoroughly forward-thinking in both its design, which features glassed-in chandeliers and leather-topped tables, and chef Andrew Zimmerman's elegant, seasonal four-course prix-fixe menu. A well-chosen, international wine list and thoughtfully prepared cocktails satisfy oenophiles and cocktail-lovers alike; grab a spot on the lounge side for a predinner drink with a side of people-watching. **Known for:** extensive wine list; excellent desserts; vintage-tinged decor. $ *Average main: $75* ✉ *123 N. Jefferson St., West Loop* ☎ *312/441–1920* ⊕ *www.sepiachicago.com* ⊗ *Closed Sun. and Mon. No lunch.*

Smyth + The Loyalist

$$$$ | AMERICAN | Named 2020's Restaurant of the Year by Chicago's annual Jean Banchet Awards, Smyth features a 15-course tasting menu that's tweaked daily by husband-and-wife chefs John B. and Karen Urie Shields. The dishes are ever-changing and depend on what the kitchen can get from The Farm, just outside the city, which provides ingredients grown to the chefs' specifications; for a more casual meal—including the *Chicago Tribune*'s pick for the city's best burger—head downstairs to the Loyalist bar. **Known for:** warm surroundings and service; "dirty burg" cheeseburger; creative wine pairings. $ *Average main: $265* ✉ *177 N. Ada St., Suite 101, West Loop* ☎ *773/913–3773* ⊕ *www.smythandtheloyalist.com* ⊗ *Closed Sun. and Mon. No lunch.*

Time Out Market Chicago

$$ | ECLECTIC | This 50,000-square-foot food hall sports a rotating roster of counter-service stalls, representing 18 hand-picked Chicago eateries. Collected under one roof along with three bars, an outdoor terrace, and a working demo kitchen for chef-driven classes, it's a sort of EPCOT Center of Chicago food for those who don't have time to visit many different neighborhoods. $ *Average main: $25* ✉ *916 W. Fulton Market, West Loop* ☎ *312/637–3888* ⊕ *timeoutmarket.com/chicago.*

☕ Coffee and Quick Bites

★ Little Goat

$ | ECLECTIC | FAMILY | Following the wild success of her flagship restaurant, Girl & the Goat, *Top Chef* alum Stephanie Izard switched gears with this all-day counterpart. The diner/bakery/bar is open from morning to evening, serving comfort food that's heavy on Americana nostalgia, though with a splash of Izard's eclectic touches in the pastries, soups and sandwiches, burgers, and classic supper entrées. **Known for:** great coffee; saltado-style burger; sugargoat desserts. $ *Average main: $14* ✉ *820 W. Randolph St., West Loop* ☎ *312/888–3455* ⊕ *www.littlegoatchicago.com* ⊗ *Closed Mon. No dinner.*

Meddle Coffee Bar

$ | CAFÉ | This small but stylish café operated by local roastery Dark Matter Coffee serves up all kinds of joe, from drip to draft to canned varieties, amid playfully psychedelic decor. On the food side, look for savory breakfast tacos and empanadas, Do-Rite Donuts, and pastries from West Town Bakery. **Known for:** draft cold brews; small batch chocolates; beans to go. $ *Average main: $5* ✉ *601 W. Jackson Blvd., West Loop* ☎ *312/631–3553* ⊕ *www.darkmattercoffee.com* ⊗ *No dinner.*

Hotels

Ace Hotel Chicago

$$ | HOTEL | In a former life, this building was a cheesemaking company. **Pros:** rooms truly feel like an apartment; great nightlife scene; easy access to West

Loop galleries and restaurants. **Cons:** no full-service spa; no pool; a bit on the fringe of the Loop action. $ *Rooms from: $289* ✉ *311 N. Morgan St., West Loop* 🖀 *312/764–1919* ⊕ *www.acehotel.com/chicago* ⇥ *159 rooms* ❌ *No Meals.*

Publishing House Bed & Breakfast

$$ | **B&B/INN** | Spanning four stories, this labor of love features all en-suite rooms and a bevy of communal spaces—an industrial-chic reimagination of the traditional bed-and-breakfast. **Pros:** city's best restaurants within walking distance; intimate; affordable parking. **Cons:** not ideally suited to families; no spa; must cab or Uber to get to the Loop or Mag Mile. $ *Rooms from: $249* ✉ *108 N. May St., West Loop* 🖀 *312/554–5857* ⊕ *publishinghousebnb.com* ⇥ *11 rooms* ❌ *Free Breakfast.*

Nightlife

On weekends and late nights the action shifts to the West Loop—centered on Fulton, Lake, and Randolph streets—which is home to a diverse array of nightspots, from midsize music clubs like Bottom Lounge to upmarket drinking establishments like the Aviary.

■TIP→ **If you're sticking to downtown and North Side bars, it's relatively safe to rely on public transportation. But if you're planning on staying out past midnight, we suggest taking a cab home.**

BARS

The Aviary

COCKTAIL LOUNGES | Chef Grant Achatz applies his cutting-edge culinary style to cocktails at this West Loop bar, adjacent to his high-concept restaurant Next. Your newfangled old-fashioned might arrive injected into an egg of ice, or your drink's flavor might change subtly as its flavored ice melts. Inventive bar bites are on offer as well. It's strongly advised to book your seating in advance (⊕ *www.exploretock. com/theaviary*). ✉ *955 W. Fulton Market,*

West Loop 🖀 *312/226–0868* ⊕ *www. theaviary.com* ⊗ *Closed Mon. and Tues.*

Lone Wolf

BARS | This inviting cocktail and beer bar in the West Loop is the perfect spot to wait out the long lines at nearby restaurants Au Cheval or Girl & the Goat. The tiny but mighty menu of bar snacks (house-made corn dogs, grilled cheese, spicy fries) will tide you over nicely; solid takes on classic cocktails and a healthy rotating draft list make it a welcome addition to the restaurant-heavy 'hood. ✉ *806 W. Randolph St., West Loop* 🖀 *312/600–9391* ⊕ *www.lonewolftavern.com.*

DANCE CLUBS

Bottom Lounge

LIVE MUSIC | Once an metal factory and later a taxi cab repair shop, this 18,000-square-foot industrial conversion has an invitingly funky restaurant and bar up front. But the main draw is the midsize music room that accommodates 700 concertgoers—good for an up-and-coming underground act, or a higher-profile touring band looking for an intimate feel. ✉ *1375 W. Lake St., West Loop* 🖀 *312/666–6775* ⊕ *bottomlounge. com* ⊗ *Closed Sun.–Wed.*

Shopping

ANTIQUES

Salvage One

ANTIQUES & COLLECTIBLES | An enormous warehouse chock-full of leaded glass, garden ornaments, fireplace mantels, bathtubs, bars, and other architectural artifacts draws creative home remodelers and restaurant designers from around the country. ✉ *1840 W. Hubbard St., West Loop* 🖀 *312/733–0098* ⊕ *www. salvageone.com* ⊗ *Closed Mon.–Thurs.*

ART GALLERIES

Primitive

ART GALLERIES | Find ethnic and tribal art, including textiles, furniture, and jewelry, at this longtime Chicago favorite. ✉ *130*

N. Jefferson St., West Loop ☎ 312/575–9600 ⊕ www.beprimitive.com ⊙ Closed Sun.

MARKETS
Maxwell Street Market

MARKET | This legendary outdoor bazaar, which operates every first and third Sunday from 9 to 3, is part of Chicago's cultural landscape. Closed by the city amid much controversy in the 1990s, it reopened soon after in its current location and remains a popular spot, particularly for Latinx immigrants, to buy and sell wares year-round. The finds aren't so fabulous, but the atmosphere sure is fun, with live blues and stalls peddling Mexican street food. ✉ 800 S. Desplaines St., West Loop ☎ 312/745–4676 ⊕ www.cityofchicago.org/city/en/depts/dca/supp_info/maxwell_street_market.html.

★ Randolph Street Market

MARKET | March through December, usually on the last weekend of the month, 200-odd stalls selling clothing, furniture, jewelry, books, and more get treasure seekers' adrenaline flowing. The top-rated event also includes an Indie Designer Fashion Market, showcasing one-of-a-kind wearables by up-and-coming local designers. Weekend admission is $12 at the gate ($10 in advance), and children under 12 get in free. ✉ 1341 W. Randolph St., West Loop ☎ 312/666–1200 ⊕ www.randolphstreetmarket.com.

Activities
SPAS
Spa Space

SPAS | Serious pampering includes massages specifically geared to runners and golfers and a pedicure suite where bottles of wine are welcome. All facials are dermatologist approved, and body treatments include grapeseed scrubs, seaweed wraps, and waxing. ✉ 161 N. Canal St., West Loop ☎ 312/466–9585 ⊕ spaspacechicago.com ⌖ $120 60-min facial. Services: aromatherapy, facials, massages, nail treatments, scrubs, waxing, acupuncture.

Chapter 4

NEAR NORTH AND RIVER NORTH

Updated by
Matt Beardmore

4

⊙ Sights	🍴 Restaurants	🛏 Hotels	❸ Shopping	🍸 Nightlife
★★★★★	★★★★☆	★★★★☆	★★★★☆	★★★★☆

NEIGHBORHOOD SPOTLIGHT

GETTING HERE

Near North: If you're arriving from the north by car, take Lake Shore Drive south to the Michigan Avenue exit. From the south, exit at Grand Avenue for Navy Pier. The prepaid parking apps SpotHero and ParkWhiz can save you money.

The 2, 3, 10, 26, 125, 143, 146, 147, 148, 151, and 157 buses run along Michigan Avenue. Buses 2, 29, 65, 66, and 124 all service Navy Pier. If you're using the El, take the Red Line to Chicago Avenue or Clark and Division.

River North: The Merchandise Mart has its own stop on the El's Brown and Purple lines. If you're driving, there's a parking lot at 437 North Orleans Street. If you're heading to the northern tip of the neighborhood, take Wells Street to Chicago Avenue. You can also walk west from the Mag Mile a few blocks to get to the area.

MAKING THE MOST OF YOUR TIME

If you have kids, factor in at least a day for Navy Pier's family-friendly attractions. If you're into art, you could spend a day at the Museum of Contemporary Art and assorted galleries, while dedicated shoppers can easily spend the same amount of time flexing their wallets on the Magnificent Mile, *the* Chicago shopping spot. Along the way, get a bird's-eye view of Chicago, including the Tribune Tower and Marina City, from the State Street Bridge.

FESTIVAL OF LIGHTS

Chicago's holiday season officially gets under way every year at the end of November with The Magnificent Mile Lights Festival, a weekend-long event consisting of family-friendly activities that pack the shopping strip and neighboring streets. Music, a thoroughfare of festive shopping and food booths, and stage shows kick off the celebration, which culminates in a parade and the illumination of more than a million lights along Michigan Avenue. Neighborhood stores keep late hours to accommodate the crowds. For more information, check out *www. themagnificentmile.com/lights-festival/*.

TOP REASONS TO GO

■ **Enjoy the views:** Have a drink at the Signature Lounge at 875 North Michigan Avenue (formerly called the John Hancock Center), or just drink in the vista at 360 Chicago.

■ **Kick back with the kids:** The engaging Chicago Children's Museum is just one reason why families flock to Navy Pier.

■ **Get your retail fix:** Browse the shops of the Magnificent Mile, pausing for world-class people-watching en route.

■ **Dine at one of chef Rick Bayless's restaurants:** The celebrated restaurateur has several top-notch spots here, including Frontera Grill, Xoco, and Topolobampo.

River North, the Magnificent Mile, the Gold Coast: this area holds some of the city's greatest attractions. Navy Pier and the Chicago Children's Museum are top stops for families, and serious shoppers can seriously exercise their credit cards along Michigan Avenue's most famous stretch. Impressive architecture, compelling art, and top-notch restaurants also await.

Near North

The Near North Side is north of the Chicago River and includes the neighborhoods of River North, Streeterville, and the Gold Coast. It extends all the way up to North Avenue and the verdant green of Lincoln Park.

Near North has some of the city's best shopping and most crowd-pleasing restaurants, as well as some of its most distinctive buildings. To get a taste, start at the beginning of the Mag Mile and check out the architecture of the Tribune Tower. Then browse the shops on Michigan Avenue as well as the chichi boutiques on Oak and many other side streets. 875 North Michigan Avenue, formerly the John Hancock Center, offers one of the best sky-high views of Chicago. Instead of shelling out bucks at the observatory, though, you can get a drink at the Signature Lounge, on the 96th floor, for about the same price; the view comes free.

Hugging the lakeshore north of Oak Street and east of Clark Street is the Gold Coast. Potter Palmer (the principal developer of State Street and the Palmer House Hotel) built a mansion here, and his social-climbing friends followed suit, transforming the area. The less fortunate residents thought the new arrivals must have pockets lined with gold.

To the east of the Mag Mile on Grand Avenue, Navy Pier stretches more than a half mile (3,040 feet, to be exact) into Lake Michigan. Packed with restaurants, souvenir stalls, and folks out for a stroll, this perpetually busy wonderland is adored by kids and adults alike. You'll find the Chicago Children's Museum, a 196-foot Ferris wheel, and the Chicago Shakespeare Theatre here. It's also the starting point for many lake cruises. Make sure to dedicate an evening to seeing and being seen at one of the chic local restaurants.

Sights

Charnley-Persky House Museum
HISTORIC HOME | Designed by Louis Sullivan and his protégé Frank Lloyd Wright, this almost austere residence is one of

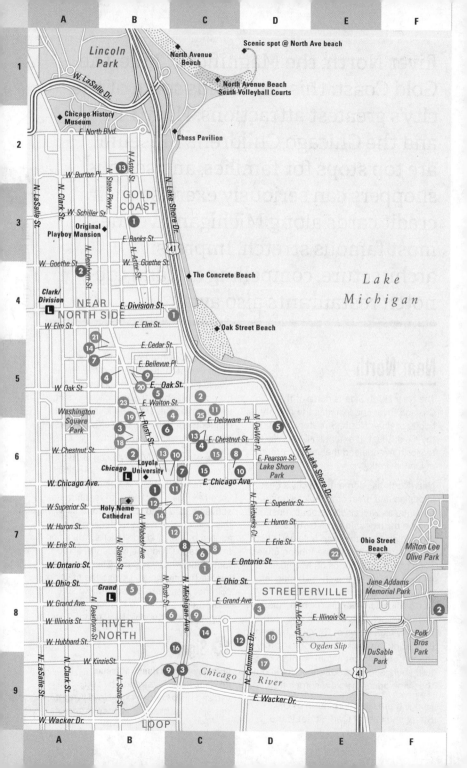

Near North

KEY

1 Exploring Sights

1 Restaurants

1 Quick Bites

1 Hotels

L CTA Lines

Sights ▼

1 Charnley-Persky
House Museum **B3**

2 Chicago Children's
Museum **F8**

3 DuSable Bridge
(Michigan Avenue
Bridge) **C9**

4 875 N. Michigan
Avenue (formerly the John
Hancock Center) and
360° Chicago **C6**

5 860–880 N. Lake Shore
Drive...................... **D6**

6 Fourth Presbyterian
Church **C6**

7 Historic Water Tower ... **C6**

8 Magnificent Mile **C7**

9 McCormick
Bridgehouse &
Chicago River
Museum **C9**

10 Museum of
Contemporary Art
Chicago **D6**

11 Navy Pier **G8**

12 NBC Tower **D8**

13 Patterson-McCormick
Mansion **B2**

14 Tribune Tower **C8**

15 Water Works
Pumping Station **C6**

16 Wrigley Building **C8**

Restaurants ▼

1 Adorn Bar
& Restaurant **C4**

2 Bistronomic **B6**

3 CDA....................... **B6**

4 Gibsons Bar
& Steakhouse **B5**

5 Le Colonial............... **B5**

6 Les Nomades............. **C7**

7 Maple & Ash **B5**

8 Marisol.................... **C6**

9 Nico Osteria **B5**

10 NoMI Kitchen **C6**

11 RL......................... **C6**

12 Shanghai Terrace........ **C7**

13 Signature Room
at the 95th **C6**

14 Somerset **B5**

Quick Bites ▼

1 Leonidas Chocolate
Cafe **B6**

2 3rd Coast
Cafe & Wine Bar........ **A4**

Hotels ▼

1 Courtyard by Marriott
Chicago/
Magnificent Mile **C7**

2 The Drake................. **C5**

3 Embassy Suites
by Hilton Chicago
Downtown
Magnificent Mile.......... **D8**

4 Four Seasons Hotel
Chicago **C5**

5 Freehand Chicago **B8**

6 The Gwen,
a Luxury Collection
Hotel...................... **C8**

7 Homewood Suites
by Hilton Chicago-
Downtown.............. **B8**

8 Hotel EMC2, Autograph
Collection................. **C7**

9 InterContinental Chicago
Magnificent Mile **C8**

10 Loews Chicago Hotel... **D8**

11 Millennium
Knickerbocker Hotel **C5**

12 Omni Chicago Hotel **C7**

13 Park Hyatt Chicago...... **C6**

14 The Peninsula
Chicago **C7**

15 The Ritz-Carlton,
Chicago **C6**

16 The Sable Hotel **H8**

17 Sheraton Grand
Chicago **D9**

18 Sofitel Chicago
Magnificent Mile **B6**

19 The Talbott Hotel **B5**

20 Thompson Chicago..... **B5**

21 Viceroy Chicago **B5**

22 W Chicago–
Lakeshore **E7**

23 Waldorf Astoria
Chicago **B5**

24 Warwick Allerton
Chicago................... **C7**

25 The Westin
Michigan Avenue
Chicago **C5**

E. Ohio St.

Jardine Water
Purification Plant

*Chicago
Harbor*

Navy Pier

Navy Pier
Observation
Deck

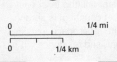

0 _____ 1/4 mi

0 _____ 1/4 km

A Revered School

The **Chicago School** had no classrooms and no curriculum, nor did it confer degrees. In fact, the Chicago School wasn't an institution at all but rather a name given to the collection of architects whose work, beginning in the 1880s, helped free American architecture from the often rigid styles of the past. Nonetheless, a number of their buildings echoed a classical column, the lower floors functioning as the base, the middle floors as the shaft, and the cornice on top being the equivalent of a capital. In pioneering the "tall building," these architects used steel-frame construction; they also reduced ornamentation. Alumni include Daniel Burnham, William Le Baron Jenney, Louis Sullivan, Dankmar Adler, John Root, William Holabird, and Martin Roche.

the few extant buildings that displays the combined talents of these two architectural innovators. Historians still squabble about who contributed what here, but it's easy to imagine that the young go-getter had a hand in the cleanly rendered interior. Note how the geometric exterior looks unmistakably modern next to its traditional neighbors. Public tours of both the interior and exterior are available and last about one hour. The complimentary Wednesday tours are less comprehensive than the paid ones on Saturday; reservations are required for all tours. Check the website for reservations and pricing. ⊠ *1365 N. Astor St., Gold Coast* ☎ *312/573–1365* ⊕ *www.sah.org/about-sah/charnley-persky-house* ⌚ *Tours free Wed., $10 Sat.* ⌚ *Advance reservations required.*

★ **Chicago Children's Museum**
CHILDREN'S MUSEUM | FAMILY | "Hands-on" is the operative concept at this brightly colored Navy Pier anchor. Kids can tinker with tools, climb through three stories of tunnels, play at being a firefighter, dig for dinosaur fossils, and create a masterpiece in the Art Studio. ⊠ *Navy Pier, 700 E. Grand Ave., Near North Side* ☎ *312/527–1000* ⊕ *www.chicagochildrensmuseum.org* ⌚ *$15* ⏱ *Closed Mon.-Thurs.*

DuSable Bridge (Michigan Avenue Bridge)
BRIDGE | Chicago is a city of bridges—and this one, completed in 1920, is among the most graceful. The structure's four pylons are decorated with impressive sculptures representing major Chicago events: its exploration by Marquette and Joliet, its settlement by trader Jean Baptiste Point du Sable, the Fort Dearborn Massacre of 1812, and the rebuilding of the city after the Great Chicago Fire of 1871. The site of the fort, at the south end of the bridge, is marked by a commemorative plaque. As you stroll Michigan Avenue, be prepared for a possible delay; the bridge rises about 50 times a year between April and November to allow boat traffic to pass underneath. ⊠ *River North.*

★ **875 N. Michigan Avenue (formerly the John Hancock Center) and 360 Chicago**
NOTABLE BUILDING | FAMILY | Designed by Skidmore, Owings & Merrill, this multipurpose skyscraper is distinguished by its tapering shape and enormous X braces, which help stabilize its 100 stories. Soon after it went up in 1970, it earned the nickname "Big John." No wonder: it's 1,127 feet tall (the taller east tower is 1,506 feet counting its antennae). Packed with retail space, parking, offices, a restaurant, and residences, it has been

875 N. Michigan Avenue, formerly the John Hancock Center, offers phenomenal views of the city.

likened to a city within a city. Like the Willis Tower, which was designed by the same architectural team, this skyscraper offers views of four states on clear days. To see them, ascend to the 94th-floor observatory—now dubbed 360 Chicago ($30). While there, visitors can grab a cocktail, beer, wine, hot drink or nonalcoholic beverage at Bar 94, which can only be accessed with a General Admission ticket. Thrill seekers can pay an additional fee to **take advantage of the tower's most exciting feature,** The Tilt ($8), which has eight windows that tilt downward to a 30-degree angle, giving you a unique perspective on the city below. Those with vertigo might prefer a seat in the bar of the 96th-floor Signature Lounge; the tab will be steep, but you don't pay the observatory fee and you'll be steady on your feet. ⊠ *875 N. Michigan Ave., Near North Side* ☎ *888/875–8439* ⊕ *875northmichiganavenue.com, www.360chicago. com* ⊠ *Observatory $30.*

860–880 N. Lake Shore Drive

NOTABLE BUILDING | These 26-story twin apartment towers overlooking Lake Michigan were an early and eloquent realization of Mies van der Rohe's "less is more" credo, expressed in high-rise form. I-beams running up the facade underscore their verticality; inside, mechanical systems are housed in the center so as to leave the rest of each floor free and open to the spectacular views. Completed in 1951, the buildings, called "flat-chested architecture" by Frank Lloyd Wright, are a prominent example of the International Style, which played a key role in transforming the look of American cities. ⊠ *860–880 N. Lake Shore Dr., at E. Chestnut St., Near North Side.*

Fourth Presbyterian Church

CHURCH | A welcome visual and physical oasis amid the high-rise hubbub of North Michigan Avenue, this Gothic Revival house of worship is the oldest building on North Michigan Avenue apart from the Old Water Tower complex (which

Did You Know?

You can book a sunset boat tour on the Chicago River to see the city's downtown buildings in their best light.

survived the Chicago Fire of 1871). Designed by Ralph Adams Cram, the church drew many of its congregants from the city's elite but now reflects the city's diversity. Local architect Howard Van Doren Shaw devised the cloister and companion buildings. ■TIP→ In July and August, free concerts are staged every Friday at 12:10 beside the courtyard fountain off Michigan Avenue; other months they're performed in the sanctuary. ✉ 126 E. Chestnut St., Near North Side ☎ 312/787–4570 ⊕ www.fourthchurch.org.

Historic Water Tower

NOTABLE BUILDING | This famous Michigan Avenue structure, designed by William W. Boyington (who also designed the Pumping Station to the East) and completed in 1869, was originally built to house a 135-foot iron standpipe that equalized the pressure of the water pumped by the similar pumping station across the street. Oscar Wilde uncharitably called it "a castellated monstrosity" studded with pepper shakers. One of the few buildings that survived the Great Chicago Fire, it remains a civic landmark and a symbol of the city's spirit. The small gallery inside hosts rotating art exhibitions of local interest. ✉ 806 N. Michigan Ave., at Pearson St., Near North Side ☎ 312/744–3315 ⌐ Free.

★ Magnificent Mile

BUSINESS DISTRICT | FAMILY | Michigan Avenue, or Mag Mile as some call it, is a potpourri of historic buildings, upscale boutiques, department stores, and posh hotels. (It is also the city's most popular place for people-watching.) Among its jewels are the Tribune Tower, the Wrigley Building, 875 North Michigan Avenue (formerly the John Hancock Center), the Drake Hotel, and the Historic Water Tower. ✉ Michigan Ave., between Chicago Ave. and Lake Shore Dr., Near North Side ☎ 312/642–3570 ⊕ www.themagnificentmile.com.

Did You Know?

The base of Tribune Tower is studded with pieces from approximately 150 famous sites and structures around the world, including the Parthenon, the Taj Mahal, Westminster Abbey, the Alamo, St. Peter's Basilica, the Great Wall of China, and Bunker Hill.

McCormick Bridgehouse & Chicago River Museum

OTHER MUSEUM | Located in the southwest tower of the DuSable (Michigan Avenue Bridge), this engaging museum provides a glimpse into the complicated history of the Chicago River System and its movable bridges—and has some great city views, too. The Chicago River has undergone an incredible transformation over the past 40 years, from a polluted waterway to a thriving, living river full of wildlife. On lift days visitors can see the gears that still raise the bridge put to work. This is the only bridge house in Chicago that is open to the public. See the website for a lift schedule; reservations are recommended on lift days. ✉ 376 N. Michigan Ave., at Wacker Dr. ☎ 312/977–0277 ⊕ www.bridgehouse-museum.org ⌐ $6, $12 on lift days ⊘ Closed Nov.-May.

★ Museum of Contemporary Art Chicago

ART MUSEUM | A group of art patrons who felt the great Art Institute was unresponsive to modern work founded the MCA in 1967, and it has remained a renegade art museum ever since. It doesn't have any permanent exhibits; this lends a feeling of freshness but also makes it impossible to predict what will be on display at any given time. Special exhibits are devoted mostly to original shows you can't see anywhere else. ✉ 220 E. Chicago Ave., Near North Side ☎ 312/280–2660 ⊕ www.mcachicago.org

The Navy Pier has attractions to entertain the family all year round.

✉ *$15 suggested donation; free Tues. for Illinois residents* ⊘ *Closed Mon.*

Navy Pier

PEDESTRIAN MALL | FAMILY | No matter the season, Navy Pier is a fun place to spend a few hours, especially with kids in tow. Opened in 1916 as a commercial-shipping pier and part of Daniel Burnham's Master Plan of Chicago, it stretches more than a half a mile into Lake Michigan. Redesigned and reopened in 1995, Navy Pier underwent another major transformation for its 100th anniversary in 2016, which included the opening of the Polk Bros Park, the Fifth Third Bank Family Pavilion, and the Peoples Energy Welcome Pavilion. Other popular activities and venues on the pier include tour boats and cruises, the Centennial Wheel, the Chicago Children's Museum, and the Chicago Shakespeare Theatre. ✉ *600 E. Grand Ave., Near North Side* ☎ *312/595–7437* ⊕ *www.navypier.org.*

NBC Tower

NOTABLE BUILDING | This 1989 limestone-and-granite edifice by Skidmore, Owings & Merrill looks back to the art deco days without becoming a victim of fashion's past. Four floors of the 38-story tower are dedicated to a radio and television broadcasting facility. ✉ *455 N. Cityfront Plaza Dr., Near North Side* ☎ *312/222–9611* ⊕ *www.nbc-tower.com.*

Patterson-McCormick Mansion

NOTABLE BUILDING | On the northwest corner of Astor and Burton places in the swanky Gold Coast, you'll find this Georgian building. It was commissioned in 1891 by *Chicago Tribune* chief Joseph Medill and built by Stanford White. You can't go inside, though, because it's been converted into condos. ✉ *20 E. Burton Pl., Gold Coast.*

★ Tribune Tower

NOTABLE BUILDING | Big changes have arrived at this iconic tower, which opened in 1925 to house the *Chicago Tribune.* Sold by the Tribune Company to CIM Group and Golub & Company for $240 million in 2016, the neo-gothic structure is no longer home to the newspaper, and WGN's final broadcast there took place in

2018. Now the interior is 162 luxury residences with more than 55,000 square feet of indoor amenities. Visitors can still see fragments from famous sites, including the Taj Mahal and the Alamo, embedded in the building's façade. ⊠ *435 N. Michigan Ave., Near North Side.*

Water Works Pumping Station
NOTABLE BUILDING | Water is still pumped to some city residents at a rate of about 250 million gallons per day from this Gothic-style structure, which, along with the Water Tower across the street, survived the 1871 conflagration. **Lookingglass Theatre,** located in the same complex, has called this place home since 2013. ⊠ *163 E. Pearson St., at Michigan Ave., Near North Side* ☎ *312/337–0665* ⊕ *lookingglasstheatre.org.*

★ Wrigley Building
NOTABLE BUILDING | The gleaming white landmark—designed by Graham, Anderson, Probst & White and the former headquarters of the chewing-gum company—was instrumental in transforming Michigan Avenue from an area of warehouses to one of the most desirable spots in the city. Its two structures were built several years apart and later connected, and its clock tower was inspired by the bell tower of the Giralda Tower in Seville, Spain. Be sure to check it out at night, when lamps bounce light off the 1920s terracotta facade. ⊠ *400–410 N. Michigan Ave., Near North Side* ⊕ *www. thewrigleybuilding.com.*

🍴 Restaurants

The Near North district, home to shopping's Magnificent Mile and the residential Gold Coast, specializes in upscale restaurants that suit the clientele like a bespoke suit. The Magnificent Mile is the land of posh hotels and their sleek dining rooms, as well as many stand-alone stars.

Adorn Bar & Restaurant
$$$ | CONTEMPORARY | James Beard–award-winning chef Jonathon Sawyer explores the use of ingredients from close to home while preparing global cuisine at this sleek restaurant on the seventh floor of the Four Seasons Chicago. Signature dishes include an appetizer size crispy confit of chicken wings and a rich lobster and spaghetti dish inspired by the Montreal restaurant Joe Beef. **Known for:** fancy and delicious desserts; top-quality meat; sitting at the bar. Ⓢ *Average main: $35* ⊠ *120 E. Delaware Pl., Near North Side* ⊕ *www.adornrestaurant. com.*

Bistronomic
$$ | FRENCH | Classic French dishes using local and sustainable ingredients have been the ethos of Bistronomic (Bistro-Economic) since it opened in 2011. Escargots, onion soup, and mains like a braised lamb shank served with French lentils are highlights at this cozy but elegant neighborhood favorite. **Known for:** family-owned; modern approach to French cooking; long-term, friendly waitstaff. Ⓢ *Average main: $25* ⊠ *840 N. Wabash, Near North Side* ☎ *312/944–8400* ⊕ *www.bistronomic.net* ⊗ *Closed Mon. No lunch Tues.*

CDA
$$$ | FRENCH | French cuisine sometimes gets knocked for being too rich, too heavy, and too expensive, but that's an image that French-Canadian-born chef Cliff Crawford is doing his best to prove wrong at this stylish restaurant on the ground floor of the Sofitel. The menu features Le Burger, seasonal salads, and a decadent brioche French toast. **Known for:** gluten-free options; notable desserts, like salted caramel praline crunch with lemon madeleine and fresh berries; Mediterranean fare. Ⓢ *Average main: $32* ⊠ *Sofitel Chicago, 20 E. Chestnut St., Near North Side* ☎ *312/324–4000* ⊕ *www.cafedesarchitectes.com* ⊗ *No dinner.*

Continued on page 120

tHE SKY'S THE LIMIT

Talk about baptism by fire. Although Chicago was incorporated in 1837, it wasn't until after the Great Fire of 1871 that the city really started to take shape. With four square miles gone up in flames, the town was a clean slate. The opportunity to make a mark on this metropolis drew a slew of architects, from Adler & Sullivan to H. H. Richardson and Daniel H. Burnham—names renowned in the annals of American architecture. A Windy City tradition was born: the city's continuously morphing skyline is graced with tall wonders designed by architecture's heavy hitters, including Mies van der Rohe; Skidmore, Owings & Merrill; and, most recently, Santiago Calatrava. In the next four pages, you'll find an eye-popping sampling of Chicago's great buildings and how they've pushed—and continue to push—the definition of even such a lofty term as "skyscraper."

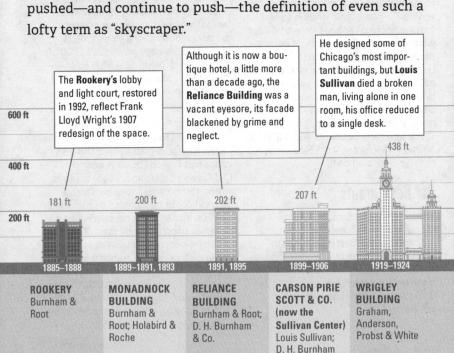

The **Rookery's** lobby and light court, restored in 1992, reflect Frank Lloyd Wright's 1907 redesign of the space.

Although it is now a boutique hotel, a little more than a decade ago, the **Reliance Building** was a vacant eyesore, its facade blackened by grime and neglect.

He designed some of Chicago's most important buildings, but **Louis Sullivan** died a broken man, living alone in one room, his office reduced to a single desk.

600 ft

400 ft

200 ft

438 ft

181 ft — 1885–1888 — **ROOKERY** Burnham & Root

200 ft — 1889–1891, 1893 — **MONADNOCK BUILDING** Burnham & Root; Holabird & Roche

202 ft — 1891, 1895 — **RELIANCE BUILDING** Burnham & Root; D. H. Burnham & Co.

207 ft — 1899–1906 — **CARSON PIRIE SCOTT & CO. (now the Sullivan Center)** Louis Sullivan; D. H. Burnham & Co.

1919–1924 — **WRIGLEY BUILDING** Graham, Anderson, Probst & White

THE BIRTH OF THE SKYSCRAPER

Houses, churches, and commercial buildings of all sorts rose from the ashes after the blaze of 1871, but what truly put Chicago on the architectural map was the tall building. The earliest of these barely scrape the sky—especially when compared to what towers over us today—but in the late 19th century, structures such as William Le Baron Jenney's ten-story Home Insurance Building (1884) represented a bold push upward. Until then, the sheer weight of stone and cast-iron construction had limited how high a building could soar. But by using a lighter yet stronger steel frame and simply sheathing his building in a thin skin of masonry, Jenney blazed the way for ever taller buildings. And with only so much land available in the central business district, up was the way to go.

Although the Home Insurance Building was razed in 1931, Chicago's Loop remains a rich trove of early skyscraper design. Some of these survivors stand severe and solid as fortresses, while others manifest an almost ethereal quality. They—and their descendants along Wacker Drive, North Michigan Avenue, and Lake Shore Drive—reflect the technological, economic, and aesthetic forces that have made this city on the prairie one of the most dramatically vertical communities in the country.

Bits and bobs of famous sites are embedded in the exterior of the building and are easy to spot. Check out the Taj Mahal.

Soul Train, the wildly popular dance program, first aired from WCIU–TV studios atop the **Chicago Board of Trade**.

With its restaurants and other amenities—and initially reasonable rents—**Marina City** was designed to help stem the flood of urbanites to the suburbs.

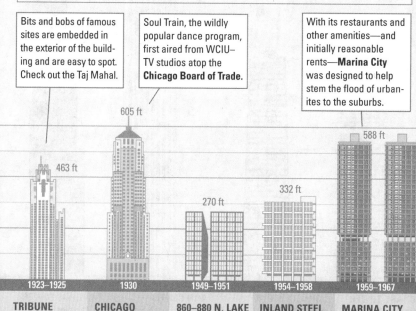

605 ft			588 ft
463 ft		332 ft	
	270 ft		

1923–1925	1930	1949–1951	1954–1958	1959–1967
TRIBUNE TOWER Howells & Hood	**CHICAGO BOARD OF TRADE** Holabird & Root	**860–880 N. LAKE SHORE DRIVE** Ludwig Mies van der Rohe	**INLAND STEEL BUILDING** Skidmore, Owings & Merrill	**MARINA CITY** Bertrand Goldberg Associates

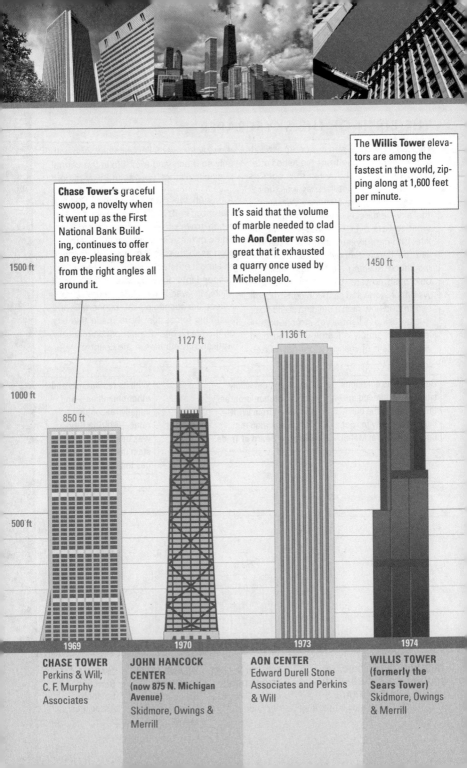

The **Willis Tower** elevators are among the fastest in the world, zipping along at 1,600 feet per minute.

Chase Tower's graceful swoop, a novelty when it went up as the First National Bank Building, continues to offer an eye-pleasing break from the right angles all around it.

It's said that the volume of marble needed to clad the **Aon Center** was so great that it exhausted a quarry once used by Michelangelo.

1500 ft

1450 ft

1000 ft

1127 ft

1136 ft

850 ft

500 ft

1969
CHASE TOWER
Perkins & Will;
C. F. Murphy
Associates

1970
JOHN HANCOCK CENTER
(now 875 N. Michigan Avenue)
Skidmore, Owings & Merrill

1973
AON CENTER
Edward Durell Stone Associates and Perkins & Will

1974
WILLIS TOWER
(formerly the Sears Tower)
Skidmore, Owings & Merrill

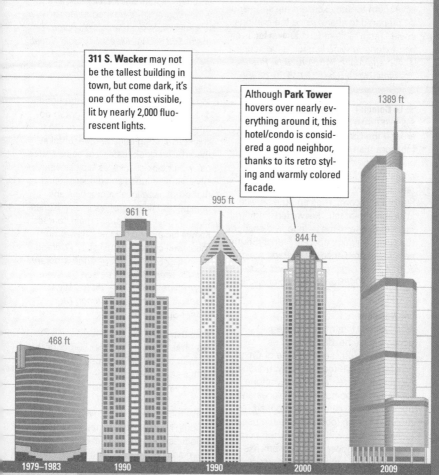

311 S. Wacker may not be the tallest building in town, but come dark, it's one of the most visible, lit by nearly 2,000 fluorescent lights.

Although **Park Tower** hovers over nearly everything around it, this hotel/condo is considered a good neighbor, thanks to its retro styling and warmly colored facade.

1389 ft

995 ft

961 ft

844 ft

468 ft

1979–1983	1990	1990	2000	2009
333 W. WACKER DRIVE Kohn Pedersen Fox and Perkins & Will	**311 S. WACKER DRIVE** Kohn Pedersen Fox	**2 PRUDENTIAL PLAZA** Loebl, Schlossman & Hackl	**PARK TOWER** Lucien LaGrange Architects	**TRUMP TOWER** Skidmore, Owens, and Merrill

Gibsons Bar & Steakhouse

$$$$ | **STEAKHOUSE** | Chicago movers and shakers mingle with conventioneers at Gibsons, a lively, homegrown, Gold Coast steak house renowned for overwhelming portions, good service, and celebrity spotting. Generous prime steaks and chops are the focus of the menu, but there are plenty of fish options, too; just save room for the excellent desserts and be prepared to share, since the portions could feed a table of four. **Known for:** lively bar; extensive wine list; fun patio scene. [$] *Average main: $45* ✉ *1028 N. Rush St., Near North Side* ☎ *312/266–8999* 🌐 *www.gibsonssteakhouse.com.*

★ **Le Colonial**

$$$ | **VIETNAMESE** | Formerly located around the corner on North Rush Street for more than two decades, Le Colonial continues to deliver delicate and sophisticated and French-Vietnamese fare in its new location. The ambience is relaxed and comforting and the service is simply top-notch. **Known for:** long-time favorite for Vietnamese food; red snapper (Ca Chien Saigon); upscale French/Southeast Asian ambience. [$] *Average main: $30* ✉ *57 E. Oak St., Near North Side* ☎ *312/255–0088* 🌐 *www.lecolonialchicago.com.*

Les Nomades

$$$$ | **FRENCH** | Intimate and elegant doesn't make headlines, but Les Nomades quietly serves some of Chicago's best French food in the warm dining room of this Streeterville brownstone, which has wood-burning fireplaces and original art. The carefully composed menu of French food includes the usual suspects along with more contemporary fare—you compose your own prix-fixe dinner from the menu; four courses cost $135; five courses are $150. **Known for:** extensive French-leaning wine list; house-made pâtés; caviar surprise. [$] *Average main: $138* ✉ *222 E. Ontario St., Near North Side* ☎ *312/649–9010* 🌐 *www.lesnomades.net* 🕒 *Closed Sun.-Wed. No lunch* 👔 *Jacket required.*

Maple & Ash

$$$$ | **STEAKHOUSE** | This high-end, innovative take on the traditional steak house is a natural fit for the Gold Coast. Chef Danny Grant serves decadent dishes that appeal to high rollers, groups of friends, and date nights. **Known for:** cocktail and wine program; fire-roasted seafood tower; wood-fire steaks. [$] *Average main: $63* ✉ *8 W. Maple St., Gold Coast* ☎ *312/944–8888* 🌐 *www.mapleandash.com* 🕒 *No lunch Mon.–Sat.*

Marisol

$$ | **AMERICAN** | After winding through the galleries at the Museum of Contemporary Art, head downstairs where the food is just as cutting-edge and beautiful as the art. The sleek restaurant has a coffee bar with quick snacks, as well as seasonally changing lunch and dinner menus that emphasize local vegetables and unexpected flavor profiles in salads, pasta, and meat and seafood main courses. **Known for:** artsy crowd; sunflower hummus; well-curated wine list. [$] *Average main: $27* ✉ *Museum of Contemporary Art, Chicago, 205 E. Pearson St., Near North Side* ☎ *312/799–3599* 🌐 *www.marisolchicago.com* 🕒 *Closed Mon. No dinner Sun.*

Nico Osteria

$$$ | **ITALIAN** | On a premier corner of the Gold Coast, in The Thompson Chicago, is this seafood-focused gem helmed by award-winning chef Jacob Verstegen. Go here for elevated seafood dishes, a well-stocked raw bar with oysters and crudos, house-made pastas like the lamb bolognese, an exceptional cocktail program and people-watching galore on the wraparound patio. **Known for:** excellent breakfast; creative cocktails; fabulous pastries. [$] *Average main: $31* ✉ *Thompson Hotel, 1015 N. Rush St., Gold Coast* ☎ *312/994–7100* 🌐 *www.nicoosteria.com.*

The views from the tables at the 95th floor Signature Room are pretty spectacular.

NoMI Kitchen

$$$$ | **MODERN AMERICAN** | The views of Michigan Avenue from the floor-to-ceiling windows are breathtaking at the Park Hyatt's NoMI Kitchen, a seventh-floor lifestyle-focused concept that goes along with NoMI Lounge, NoMI Garden, and NoMI Spa. The open kitchen features a locally sourced menu rooted in French techniques, though the sushi is some of the city's best (with fresh wasabi grated on the side). **Known for:** rooftop dining; desserts; bar scene. [$] *Average main: $39* ✉ *Park Hyatt Hotel, 800 N. Michigan Ave., Near North Side* ☎ *312/239–4030* 🌐 *www.hyatt.com/corporate/restaurants/nomi/en/home.html.*

RL

$$$$ | **AMERICAN** | Power brokers, moneyed locals, and Michigan Avenue shoppers keep the revolving doors spinning at RL, the initials of designer Ralph Lauren, whose signature soigné style is infused into the eatery that adjoins the Ralph Lauren flagship store. Inside, cozy leather banquettes are clustered under hunt-club-style art hung on wood-paneled walls, while the menu of American classics perfectly suits the setting. **Known for:** Dover sole; RL Burger; lobster roll. [$] *Average main: $40* ✉ *115 E. Chicago Ave., Near North Side* ☎ *312/475–1100* 🌐 *www.rlrestaurant.com.*

Shanghai Terrace

$$$ | **CANTONESE** | As precious as a jewel box, this red, lacquer-trimmed 80-seat restaurant hidden away in the Peninsula Hotel reveals the hotelier's Asian roots. Come for stylishly presented upscale dim sum, stay for the outdoor terrace that seats up to 70 during warmer months and lets you revel in a relaxing Cantonese and Shanghainese meal four stories above the madding crowds of Michigan Avenue. **Known for:** noteworthy cocktail list; Peking duck with mandarin pancakes; dim sum. [$] *Average main: $32* ✉ *Peninsula Hotel, 108 E. Superior St., 4th fl., Near North Side* ☎ *312/573–6744* 🌐 *https://www.peninsula.com/en/chicago/hotel-fine-dining/*

shanghai-terrace-cantonese ⊘ *No lunch in winter. Closed Mon. and Tues.*

Signature Room at the 95th

$$$$ | AMERICAN | When you've got the best view in town and a lock on special-occasion dining, do you need to be daring with the food? The Signature Room keeps it simple but crowd-pleasing, making a formal affair of classic American dishes while everyone ogles the skyline and lake views from 95 stories high; head to the lounge on the 96th floor for a nightcap. **Known for:** raw bar; rack of lamb; brunch buffet. Ⓢ *Average main: $40* ✉ *875 N. Michigan Ave., 95th fl., Near North Side* ☎ *312/787–9596* ⊕ *www.signatureroom.com* ⊘ *Closed Mon.-Tues.*

Somerset

$$$ | AMERICAN | Sleek and elegant, this all-day restaurant, with two bars and views of the open kitchen, is an ideal spot for Gold Coast see-and-be-seen drinks and sampling thoughtful new American cuisine. Chef Stephen Gillanders, says he has taken a "simple and chic approach" to developing the breakfast, lunch, and dinner menus. **Known for:** relaxed daytime vibes; spicy crab on crispy rice; excellent classic cocktails. Ⓢ *Average main: $27* ✉ *Viceroy Hotel, 1112 N. State St., Gold Coast* ☎ *312/586–2150* ⊕ *www.somersetchicago.com.*

☕ Coffee and Quick Bites

Leonidas Chocolate Cafe

$ | CAFÉ | FAMILY | This chocolate café just off Michigan Avenue is a chocolate lover's dream, where Belgian chocolate and hot chocolate are the stars. You can also order sandwiches, quiche, waffles, French pastries, and build-your-own crepes (sweet and savory). **Known for:** chocolate display; heavenly aroma; gift boxes. Ⓢ *Average main: $9* ✉ *59 E. Chicago Ave., Near North Side* ☎ *312/929–2323* ⊕ *www.Leonidas-Cafe.com* ⊘ *No dinner.*

3rd Coast Cafe & Wine Bar

$ | AMERICAN | The oldest coffeehouse in the Gold Coast pleases just about everyone with breakfast all day, a nightly dinner specials. They stay open until 9 pm seven nights a week. **Known for:** neighborhood institution; the scones; everything breakfast. Ⓢ *Average main: $12* ✉ *1260 N. Dearborn St., Near North Side* ☎ *312/649–0730* ⊕ *www.3rdcoast-cafe.com.*

Hotels

Courtyard by Marriott Chicago/Magnificent Mile

$ | HOTEL | FAMILY | Fully renovated in 2017, this modern hotel has a convenient location and bubbly vibe that visitors will love; the modest accommodations, with their art deco–inspired decor, white linens, and splashes of red, are also appealing. **Pros:** nice loyalty program; great location in the heart of the shopping district; fabulous for families. **Cons:** no spa; some guests complain of noise problems; pool is small. Ⓢ *Rooms from: $211* ✉ *165 E. Ontario St., Near North Side* ☎ *312/573–0800, 800/321–2211* ⊕ *www.courtyardchicago.com* ⇄ *306 rooms* ⊙ *No Meals.*

The Drake

$$ | HOTEL | Built in 1920, the grande dame of Chicago hotels stands tall where Michigan Avenue and Lake Shore Drive intersect in the city's swanky Gold Coast. **Pros:** a piece of living history; lovely, walkable neighborhood; steps from Oak Street Beach and high-end boutiques. **Cons:** no full-service spa; some rooms are tiny; no swimming pool. Ⓢ *Rooms from: $299* ✉ *140 E. Walton Pl., Gold Coast* ☎ *312/787–2200, 800/553–7253* ⊕ *www.thedrakehotel.com* ⇄ *609 rooms* ⊙ *No Meals.*

Embassy Suites by Hilton Chicago Downtown Magnificent Mile

$$ | HOTEL | FAMILY | Every room here features a separate bedroom and living area, as well as a view of either Lake Michigan or the Chicago skyline. **Pros:** complimentary snack time and breakfast; fitness center with a view of the city; heated indoor pool. **Cons:** parking is pricey; noise levels known to rise; pool and lounge areas can get congested. $ *Rooms from: $259* ⊠ *511 N. Columbus Dr., Near North Side* ☎ *312/836–5900, 800/362–2779* ⊕ *www.embassysuitesmagmile.com* ⇄ *455 rooms* ❑ *Free Breakfast.*

★ Four Seasons Hotel Chicago

$$$ | **HOTEL** | At the refined Four Seasons, guest rooms begin on the 30th floor (the hotel sits atop the tony 900 North Michigan Shops), so there's a distinct feeling of seclusion—and great views to boot. **Pros:** indoor pool; in the middle of high-end shopping; 24-hour fitness room. **Cons:** atmosphere can be overly formal at times; being so high up means that rooms can get a little noisy on windy days; very expensive. $ *Rooms from: $405* ⊠ *120 E. Delaware Pl., Near North Side* ☎ *312/280–8800, 800/332–3442* ⊕ *www.fourseasons.com/chicagofs* ⇄ *343 rooms* ❑ *No Meals.*

Freehand Chicago

$ | **HOTEL** | This 1927 building got a fresh new life as a combination upmarket hostel/traditional hotel that attracts the young and free spirited with a hot nightlife scene and city-apartment-style rooms. **Pros:** walk to great shops and restaurants; locally loved bar scene; affordable for the area. **Cons:** targeted for a young crowd; better for social butterflies; no on-site spa. $ *Rooms from: $149* ⊠ *19 E. Ohio St., River North* ☎ *312/940–3699* ⊕ *www.freehandhotels. com/chicago* ⇄ *217 rooms* ❑ *No Meals.*

The Gwen, a Luxury Collection Hotel

$$ | **HOTEL** | Named for the late sculptor Gwen Lux, this central hot spot recalls the 1930s, from its rooftop bar to its restaurant, to its monochromatic-glam guest rooms. **Pros:** walk to most central restuaurants and shops; chic design; lively rooftop dining. **Cons:** prices soar in high season; may be too precious for families; no on-site spa. $ *Rooms from: $229* ⊠ *521 N. Rush St., Magnificent Mile* ☎ *312/645–1500* ⊕ *www.thegwenchicago.com* ❑ *No Meals* ⇄ *311 rooms.*

Homewood Suites by Hilton Chicago-Downtown

$ | **HOTEL** | **FAMILY** | The suites here seem custom-designed for families, with sleeper sofas, separate bedrooms, and fully equipped kitchens that feature full-size refrigerators and granite countertops. **Pros:** free, hot breakfast; great view of skyline; heated pool. **Cons:** bathrooms feel cramped. $ *Rooms from: $159* ⊠ *40 E. Grand Ave., Near North Side* ☎ *312/644–2222, 800/225–5466* ⊕ *www. homewoodsuiteschicago.com* ⇄ *233 rooms* ❑ *Free Breakfast.*

Hotel EMC2, Autograph Collection

$$ | **HOTEL** | Eclectic design meets high-tech details in this daring boutique newbie, which has robots delivering room service to your small, mid-century modern-inspired quarters. **Pros:** center of the action; high-tech amenities; fab fitness center. **Cons:** no full-service spa; charges for in-room Wi-Fi; average-size guest rooms. $ *Rooms from: $295* ⊠ *228 E. Ontario St., River North* ☎ *312/915–0000* ⊕ *hotelemc2.com* ⇄ *195 rooms* ❑ *No Meals.*

★ InterContinental Chicago Magnificent Mile

$$ | **HOTEL** | Blessed with the double threat of sumptuous historic architecture and an enviable location on the Mag Mile, it's no shocker that this hotel has been going strong for around a century. **Pros:** view of the Magnificent Mile; historic feel; jaw-dropping pool. **Cons:** enormity of the property can be overwhelming; concierge service is spotty; parking is pricey. $ *Rooms from: $299* ⊠ *505 N. Michigan Ave., Near North Side* ☎ *312/944–4100, 800/628–2112* ⊕ *www.icchicagohotel. com* ❑ *No Meals* ⇄ *792 rooms.*

The Magnificent Mile, aka Michigan Avenue, is ground zero for power shopping and classy hotels.

Loews Chicago Hotel

$$ | **HOTEL** | **FAMILY** | Nestled between Michigan Avenue and the lakefront, this hotel is loved by families for the suitelike accommodations and other offerings (game library, indoor pool, amenities for teens, tweens, and kids) that make boredom impossible. **Pros:** cool amenities like texting for anything you want; goes all out for kids and families; pets are welcome. **Cons:** on a side street that is a bit hard to find; lobby can be busy at times; spa is small with not much room to chill. [$] *Rooms from: $230* ✉ *455 N. Park Dr., Magnificent Mile* ☎ *312/840–6600* 🌐 *www.loewshotels.com/chicagodowntown* 🛏 *300 rooms* 🍴 *No Meals.*

Millennium Knickerbocker Hotel

$$ | **HOTEL** | This 1927 hotel has had a number of identities—including the Speak Easy for Ralph Capone to a 1970s stint as the Playboy Hotel and Towers under owner Hugh Hefner; these days the guest rooms sport a gold, beige, plum, and espresso color palette. **Pros:** classic Chicago glamour; location can't be beat; generously sized rooms. **Cons:** vibe can be overly formal; no on-site spa; quality of rooms is inconsistent. [$] *Rooms from: $249* ✉ *163 E. Walton Pl., Near North Side* ☎ *312/751–8100, 800/621–8140* 🌐 *www.knickerbockerchicago.com* 🛏 *306 rooms* 🍴 *No Meals.*

Omni Chicago Hotel

$$ | **HOTEL** | **FAMILY** | The only all-suites hotel on Michigan Avenue has a lot going for it: every room is a good size, and French doors separate the living room from the bedroom, making them feel more like apartments. **Pros:** family-friendly; modern, comfortable rooms with spacious sitting area, desk, and bar; easy access to top shopping. **Cons:** no on-site spa; hotel can be too noisy for some; hard to find a room in high season. [$] *Rooms from: $225* ✉ *676 N. Michigan Ave., Near North Side* ☎ *312/944–6664, 800/843–6664* 🌐 *www.omnichicago.com* 🍴 *No Meals* 🛏 *347 suites.*

★ **Park Hyatt Chicago**
$$$ | **HOTEL** | This Gold Coast star still dominates the skyline above the old Water Tower and the views are as spectacular as ever following a $60-million renovation to all of its guestrooms and suites in early 2022. **Pros:** known as a foodie destination; updated, modern rooms; baths and soaking tubs that open up to the rest of the guestroom/suite. **Cons:** can be too formal for some; some people complain of street noise and slow elevators; hard to nab a room in high season. [$] *Rooms from: $475* ✉ *800 N. Michigan Ave., Near North Side* ☎ *312/335–1234, 800/633–7313* 🌐 *www.hyatt.com/en-US/hotel/illinois/park-hyatt-chicago/chiph* 🍴 *No Meals* 🛏 *182 rooms.*

★ **The Peninsula Chicago**
$$$$ | **HOTEL** | One of several American branches of the venerable Hong Kong–based chain, Chicago's Peninsula features a rooftop lap pool enclosed in a Zen aerie with stunning views. **Pros:** amazing tea service; top-notch bath products; separate shower and bath. **Cons:** rates are sky-high; in-house dining options aren't the best for families; vibe lacks spontaneity that some travelers love. [$] *Rooms from: $625* ✉ *108 E. Superior St., Near North Side* ☎ *312/337–2888, 866/288–8889* 🌐 *www.peninsula.com* 🍴 *No Meals* 🛏 *422 rooms.*

★ **The Ritz-Carlton, Chicago**
$$$ | **HOTEL** | **FAMILY** | Sophisticated yet comfortable, the Ritz-Carlton has indoor access to the Water Tower Place shopping mall and is close to many high-end boutiques. **Pros:** excellent spa; guests feel pampered; great stay for families with children. **Cons:** vibe can be too formal for some; adjoining Water Tower Place has been hit hard by exiting retailers; expensive. [$] *Rooms from: $395* ✉ *160 E. Pearson St., Near North Side* ☎ *312/266–1000, 800/332–3442 outside Illinois* 🌐 *www.ritzcarlton.com/en/hotels/chicago* 🛏 *435 rooms* 🍴 *No Meals.*

Gold Coast

North of Oak Street, hugging Lake Shore Drive, is the Gold Coast neighborhood. Astor Street is the grande dame of Gold Coast promenades, and homes like the Patterson-McCormick Mansion and the Charnley-Persky House still impress. Where Rush Street meets Oak Street is the Gold Coast's famous shopping district. A walk past the former **Playboy Mansion** (1340 N. State St.), all the way to North Avenue, is lovely on a sunny summer afternoon.

The Sable Hotel
$$ | **HOTEL** | Opened in early 2021, the Sable is the first hotel located right on Navy Pier in the latter's 100-plus year history. **Pros:** excellent on-site dining; floor-to-ceiling windows in all guest rooms provide unmatched Lake Michigan and Chicago views; only hotel on Navy Pier. **Cons:** it's a bit of walk to the front of Navy Pier; expensive valet parking; no swimming pool. [$] *Rooms from: $269* ✉ *900 E. Grand St., Navy Pier, Near North Side* ☎ *872/710–5700* 🌐 *https://sablehotel.com* 🍴 *No Meals* 🛏 *223 rooms.*

Sheraton Grand Chicago
$$ | **HOTEL** | **FAMILY** | An urban sanctuary amid iconic attractions, this hotel calls out to families with its generously sized rooms and indoor pool. **Pros:** great for families; a short walk from Michigan Avenue, Navy Pier, and Millennium Park; a reasonable cab ride away from major museums. **Cons:** fees for all FedEx business center usage; parking is pricey; a bit too bustling for those seeking an intimate escape. [$] *Rooms from: $229* ✉ *301 E. N. Water St., Near North Side* ☎ *312/464–1000* 🌐 *www.sheratonchicago.com* 🛏 *1218 rooms* 🍴 *No Meals.*

★ Sofitel Chicago Magnificent Mile

$$ | HOTEL | A wonder of modern architecture, this French-owned gem is a prism-shape structure that juts over the street and widens as it rises; design sensibility also shines in the guest rooms, thanks to honey maple–wood furnishings, Barcelona chairs, and marble bathrooms. **Pros:** corner room views are amazing; modern decor; great ambience. **Cons:** lobby is small; the place is so sleek that some guests have a hard time finding the light switches; pricey. $ *Rooms from: $285* ✉ *20 E. Chestnut St., Near North Side* ☎ *312/324–4000, 877/813–7700* ⊕ *www.sofitel.com/Chicago* ⦿ *No Meals* ⇌ *448 rooms.*

The Talbott Hotel

$$ | HOTEL | Built in 1927, this classic boutique hotel has an elegant and inviting lobby and guestroom accommodations that mix classic and contemporary. **Pros:** residential vibe; a hotel where the guest comes first; pet-friendly property. **Cons:** no pool; not overly family-friendly; a hike from Millennium Park and Museum Campus. $ *Rooms from: $309* ✉ *20 E. Delaware Pl., Gold Coast* ☎ *312/944–4970* ⊕ *www.talbotthotel.com* ⇌ *178 rooms* ⦿ *No Meals.*

Thompson Chicago

$$$ | HOTEL | Contemporary and design-centric, this gallery-like hotel (with unique art in each room and fabulous lobby art) is known for its homey, wired rooms geared toward the business traveler. **Pros:** C.O. Bigelow products in the bathrooms; centrally located; Salone Nico is one of the best bars in the neighborhood. **Cons:** pricey parking; no pool; better suited to business travelers than families. $ *Rooms from: $329* ✉ *21 E. Bellevue Pl., Gold Coast* ☎ *312/266-2100* ⊕ *www.thompsonhotels.com* ⇌ *247 rooms* ⦿ *No Meals.*

★ Viceroy Chicago

$$ | HOTEL | Channeling the old-school glamour of its Gold Coast neighborhood, this completely rehabbed 1920s property is draped in luxury; think generously sized gold-and-black-adorned guest rooms, a dazzling rooftop pool that overlooks the Gold Coast Triangle, and a happening dining room and bar. **Pros:** buzzed-about restaurant; gorgeous mid-century modern design; in classic-chic neighborhood. **Cons:** pricey valet; could be too formal in feel for kids and families; no spa. $ *Rooms from: $275* ✉ *1118 N. State St., Gold Coast* ☎ *312/586–2000* ⊕ *www.viceroyhotelsandresorts.com/en/chicago* ⦿ *No Meals* ⇌ *180 rooms.*

W Chicago–Lakeshore

$$$ | HOTEL | Overlooking Lake Michigan on a prime spot on *Lake Shore Drive*, this hotel is a sleek, contemporary escape with easy access to the Mag Mile, Navy Pier, and the rest of the city's cultural and business landscape. **Pros:** lakefront views; cool, hip vibe; indoor pool. **Cons:** rooms could use an upgrade; no refrigerators in the room; service isn't as high as the price would lead you to expect. $ *Rooms from: $369* ✉ *644 N. Lake Shore Dr., Near North Side* ☎ *312/943–9200, 877/946–8357* ⊕ *www.whotels.com/lakeshore* ⇌ *520 rooms* ⦿ *No Meals.*

★ Waldorf Astoria Chicago

$$$ | HOTEL | Just steps from the Mag Mile, the Waldorf Astoria Chicago is a haven of exclusivity, located near the some of the city's best shops, dining, and nightlife. **Pros:** fabulous spa and dining; intimate courtyard arrival experience; spacious suites with terraces and fireplaces. **Cons:** no outdoor pool; limited views in some guest rooms; valet parking only. $ *Rooms from: $335* ✉ *11 E. Walton St., Near North Side* ☎ *312/646–1300, 888/370–1938* ⊕ *www.waldorfastoriachicagohotel.com* ⇌ *189 rooms* ⦿ *No Meals.*

Warwick Allerton Chicago

$$ | HOTEL | Named a National Historic Landmark in 1999, the Allerton was a residential, 12-story "club hotel" for men when it opened in 1924; the hotel added

14 more floors in 1930, making it the tallest building on Michigan Avenue at the time. **Pros:** delightful concierge and doormen; lovely neighborhood; close to Mag Mile shopping, Rush Street nightlife, and Navy Pier. **Cons:** no restaurant; no pool; no full-service spa. [$] *Rooms from: $229* ✉ *701 N. Michigan Ave., Near North Side* ☎ *312/440–1500* 🌐 *www.theallertonhotel.com* 🛏 *497 rooms* 🍴 *No Meals.*

The Westin Michigan Avenue Chicago

$$ | HOTEL | Location-wise, this hotel scores big because major malls and flagship shops are steps from the front door; though once inside, the lobby seems a bit like an airport terminal—long, narrow, and full of folks tapping away on laptops. **Pros:** executive lounge for elite members; "heavenly" beds; proximity to area attractions. **Cons:** no on-site restaurant; steep parking fees; guests have complained of poor water pressure. [$] *Rooms from: $279* ✉ *909 N. Michigan Ave., Near North Side* ☎ *312/943–7200, 800/937–8461* 🌐 *www.westin.com/michiganavenue* 🛏 *775 rooms* 🍴 *No Meals.*

Nightlife

BARS

Coq d'Or

BARS | A dark, wood-paneled room in the Drake Hotel, Coq d'Or has red-leather booths where Chicago legend Buddy Charles held court before retiring. Fine music and cocktails served in blown-glass goblets draw hotel guests as well as neighborhood regulars. ✉ *Drake Hotel, 140 E. Walton St., Near North Side* ☎ *312/932–4623* 🌐 *www.thedrakehotel.com/dining/coq-d-or.*

Original Mother's

LIVE MUSIC | Since the 1960s, Original Mother's has been a local favorite for cutting-edge music and dance-'til-you-drop partying. The subterranean destination was immortalized by Demi Moore, Jim Belushi, and Rob Lowe in the '80s rom-com *About Last Night.* ✉ *26 W. Division St., Near North Side* ☎ *312/642–7251* 🌐 *www.originalmothers.com.*

★ **Signature Lounge**

BARS | When it comes to views, the Signature Lounge has no competition. Perched on the 96th floor of the building formerly known as the John Hancock Center—above even the tower's observation deck—it offers stunning vistas of the skyline and lake for only the cost of a pricey drink. The ladies' room has an incredible south-facing view through floor-to-ceiling windows. ✉ *875 N. Michigan Ave., Near North Side* ☎ *312/787–9596* 🌐 *www.signatureroom.com/lounge* ⏲ *Closed Mon.-Tues.*

Zebra Lounge

PIANO BARS | Small and funky with zebra-stripe lamps and other kitschy accoutrements, this lounge attracts an interesting crowd of dressed-up and dressed-down regulars who come to sing along with the pianist on duty. ✉ *1220 N. State St., Near North Side* ☎ *312/642–5140* 🌐 *www.thezebralounge.net.*

LIVE MUSIC

Howl at the Moon

LIVE MUSIC | Among the performers at this fun spot are dueling pianists who encourage the crowd to belt out popular songs. Walk-ins are welcome, but weekend table reservations can be purchased in advance. Pricing begins at $175 for a table of four ($40 of which can be applied to your bill); semi-private and private party packages for bigger groups also available. ✉ *26 W. Hubbard St., Near North Side* ☎ *312/863–7427* 🌐 *www.howlatthemoon.com/chicago.*

Performing Arts

THEATER

Chicago Shakespeare Theater

THEATER | FAMILY | The Chicago Shakespeare Theater devotes its considerable talents to keeping the Bard's flame alive, and also showcases new international dramas and musicals. It has three theaters of varying sizes in its Navy Pier complex, so there's almost always something on. ✉ *800 E. Grand Ave., Near North Side* ☎ *312/595–5600* ⊕ *www. chicagoshakes.com.*

Lookingglass Theatre Company

THEATER | Staged in the belly of the historic Chicago Water Works building, the Lookingglass Theatre Company's physically and artistically daring works incorporate theater, dance, music, and circus arts. ✉ *821 N. Michigan Ave., Near North Side* ☎ *312/337–0665* ⊕ *www. lookingglasstheatre.org.*

 # Shopping

If you haven't done Chicago's Magnificent Mile, you simply haven't shopped. With more than 450 stores along the stretch of Michigan Avenue that runs from the Chicago River to Oak Street, the "Mag Mile" is one of the best retail strips in the world. There are plenty of fashion houses with over-the-top boutiques, though shoppers with more modest budgets will find there's plenty to be had as well, with national chains making an extra effort at their multilevel megastores here. Cozying up against the Mag Mile is the Gold Coast, an area that's as moneyed as it sounds. The streets teem with luxury hotels, upscale restaurants, and designer boutiques, mainly concentrated on Oak and Rush streets. Many consider swanky Oak Street part of the Mag Mile, though neighboring streets technically are not.

ART GALLERIES

Gray

ART GALLERIES | Previously the Richard Gray Gallery, this location of Gray (there's also one in West Town) in the John Hancock Center lures serious collectors with work by modern artists ranging from Pablo Picasso and David Hockney to Alex Katz and local artist Theaster Gates. ✉ *875 N. Michigan Ave., 38th fl., Near North Side* ☎ *312/642–8877* ⊕ *www.rich- ardgraygallery.com* ☾ *Closed weekends.*

R. S. Johnson Fine Art

ART GALLERIES | More than 50 museums are among the clients of R. S. Johnson Fine Art, established on the Mag Mile more than 65 years ago. The family-run gallery sells Old Master Prints alongside art by Picasso, Barnabe, and Goya to the public and to private collectors. ✉ *645 N. Michigan Ave., 9th fl., entrance on Erie St., Near North Side* ☎ *312/943–1661* ⊕ *www.rsjohnsonfineart.com.*

BEAUTY

Bravco Beauty Centre

COSMETICS | Need a hard-to-find shampoo, an ionic hair dryer, or simply a jar of Vaseline? Bravco—family-owned and -operated for more than 45 years—is the place for all this and more, with an expert staff and a huge inventory. ✉ *43 E. Oak St., Near North Side* ☎ *312/943–4305* ⊕ *www.bravco.com/Instagram* @ *bravcobeautyboutique.*

Ulta Beauty

A massive retail store, a skin bar, a salon; this Chicago-born, nationwide chain carries a savvy mix of high and low, all the fave brands at all price points. The Salon does express services, should you want to squeeze a blowout or facial into your day. ✉ *430 N. Michigan Ave., Magnificent Mile* ☎ *312/527–9045* ⊕ *ulta.com.*

CLOTHING

Ikram

MIXED CLOTHING | The striking red facade of this flagship is unique and stylish, as is the merchandise inside, selected by fashion maven Ikram Goldman, known as the informal stylist to Michelle Obama. There are clothing and accessories from well-known designers names like Azzedine Alaïa, Comme des Garcons, Gucci, and Valentino as well as lesser-known brands like Muveil and Undercover. The Ikram sales staff is welcoming and knowledgeable, and skilled at helping customers develop their style. ✉ *15 E. Huron St., Near North Side* ☎ *312/587–1000* ⊕ *ikram.com.*

Mighty Vertical Malls

Forget all those notions about malls being suburban wastelands. Three decidedly posh ones dot the Mag Mile, and another holds court on State Street. The toniest of the four is 900 North Michigan Shops, which promises a dazzling list of tenants and fine dining. A more casual but no less entertaining shopping mecca is just blocks away at Water Tower Place. The newer kids on the block, although certainly established by now, are The Shops at North Bridge and Block 37.

The elegant deco design of **900 North Michigan Shops** (*900 N. Michigan Ave.,312/915–3916*) matches the upscale ambience of the stores it houses. Inside you'll find the Chicago branches of Bloomingdale's and L.K. Bennett as well as dozens of boutiques, including Gucci, Psycho Bunny, and J. Crew.

Water Tower Place (*835 N. Michigan Ave.,312/440–3165*) has seven floors of retail, and spots like the flagship American Girl store, the LEGO Store, and the Chicago Sports Museum gift shop make it popular with the younger set.

The Shops at North Bridge (*520 N. Michigan Ave.,312/222–1622*) is home to a wide variety of stores like Nordstrom, Hugo Boss, APM Monaco, MCM Worldwide, and MAC Cosmetics. There are also plenty of food options, including Eataly, Joe's Seafood Prime Steak & Stone Crab, Eddie V's Prime Seafood, Doc B's Fresh Kitchen, and Shake Shack.

The modern glass-enclosed **Block 37** (*108 N. State St.,312/361-4700*) occupies a full city block—bordered by Randolph, Washington, Dearborn, and State streets (number 37 of the city's original 58 blocks). Big-name retailers like Zara and Sephora share space with local favorites such as Akira.

Londo Mondo

MIXED CLOTHING | There's a great selection of swimwear, workout clothes, and yoga gear here. ✉ *1100 N. Dearborn St., Near North Side* ☎ *312/751–2794* ⊕ *www.londomondo.com.*

SPACE 519

MIXED CLOTHING | This is a truly curated local shopping and dining experience, created by guys-in-the-know Jim Wetzel and Lance Lawson. The clothing selection (focused on new and emerging brands) is the big draw but there are also wonderful home items, apothecary goods, inspired coffee table books, and all kinds of gifty items. While you're here, you can grab a bite at The Lunchroom, the 40-seat breakfast, lunch, and weekend brunch restaurant. The Lunchbox features take-away sandwiches, baked goods, and quiches, along with a coffee bar, cold drinks, and curated wine bottles. In the warmer months, The Lunchroom has a 24-seat dog-friendly patio. ✉ *200 E. Chestnut St., Magnificent Mile* ☎ *312/751–1519* ⊕ *space519.com.*

DEPARTMENT STORES

Bloomingdale's

DEPARTMENT STORE | Chicago's Bloomie's is built in a clean, airy style that is part Prairie School, part postmodern (and quite unlike its New York City sibling), giving you plenty of elbow room to sift through its selection of designer labels. ✉ *900 North Michigan Shops, 900 N. Michigan Ave., Near North Side* ☎ *312/440–4460* ⊕ *bloomingdales.com.*

Macy's

DEPARTMENT STORE | The Chicago flagship on State Street, formerly Marshall Field's, is known for the beloved Walnut Room and iconic holiday traditions like the Great Tree and their magnificent holiday windows as well as for its position as a National Historic Landmark. Macy's State Street is well known for its architecture and ornamentation; it has a Louis Comfort Tiffany vaulted ceiling, two "Great Clocks" on State Street at Randolph and Washington, the Burnham Fountain, and more. ⊠ *111 N. State St., Chicago Loop* ☎ *312/781–1000* ⊕ *macys.com.*

Nordstrom

DEPARTMENT STORE | This is a lovely department store with a killer shoe department, a vast juniors' section, great petites and menswear departments, and outstanding customer service. Leave yourself time to linger at Café Nordstrom on the fourth floor. ⊠ *The Shops at North Bridge, 520 N. Michigan Ave., Near North Side* ☎ *312/327–2300* ⊕ *shop.nordstrom.com.*

FOOD AND TREATS
★ Eataly Chicago

FOOD | Opened since 2013, Chicago's sprawling Eataly location has a little bit of everything. Part market, part upscale food court, part microbrewery, with multiple cafés, and a gelato shop thrown in for good measure, it is a foodie's paradise. ⊠ *43 E. Ohio St., Near North Side* ☎ *312/521–8700* ⊕ *www.eataly.com/ us_en/stores/chicago.*

Garrett Popcorn

FOOD | Bring home a tin of Chicago's famous popcorn and you'll score major points. Lines can be long, but this stuff is worth the wait. To avoid lines, you can place an order in advance on the website, then go to the pickup window at certain Garrett's locations, including the one on the Mag Mile. ⊠ *625 N. Michigan Ave., Near North Side* ☎ *888/476–7267* ⊕ *www.garrettpopcorn.com.*

MUSEUM STORES
Museum of Contemporary Art Chicago Store

MUSEUM SHOP | This fabulous museum gift shop has out-of-the-ordinary accessories, tableware, and jewelry, as well as a wide collection of books on modern and contemporary art. Some of the items you'll find here are truly one of a kind, as the museum has collaborated with artists and designer to develop exclusive/limited-edition products. ⊠ *220 E. Chicago Ave., Near North Side* ☎ *312/397–4000* ⊕ *www.mcachicagostore.org* ⊘ *Closed Mon.*

SHOES, HANDBAGS, AND LEATHER GOODS
Hanig's Footwear

SHOES | This family-owned store in the Hancock Building stocks a well-chosen selection of stylish and comfortable brands, including Thierry Rabotin, On Running, Mephisto, Birkenstock, Hoka One One, and more. ⊠ *875 N. Michigan Ave., Delaware Entrance, Near North Side* ☎ *312/787–6800* ⊕ *www.hanigs. com.*

★ Nike Chicago

SPORTING GOODS | Although maybe not as popular as it was during its Nike Town days, this five-story store in the heart of Michigan Avenue is still a tourist attraction. Many visitors—including professional athletes—stop here to take in the sports memorabilia, road test a pair of sneakers, or watch the inspirational videos. The shop includes a Nike Lab, where you can design your own kicks. ⊠ *669 N. Michigan Ave., Near North Side* ☎ *312/642–6363* ⊕ *store.nike.com.*

SHOPPING MALLS
Water Tower Place

MALL | **FAMILY** | Long considered the pinnacle of Chicago shopping, this multistory mall is so much more than a gathering of great retailers; it's also home to Broadway Playhouse (where you can see Broadway quality touring shows), The Ritz-Carlton Hotel Chicago (known for amazing tea service), and a few restaurant and snack options. Regardless of these extras, you're going to want to shop. If you have kids, the LEGO Store is a must, as is the flagship American Girl Place store (it has a café and theater all its own). Fashion seekers can go to the usual faves: Aeropostale, Express, Forever 21, and Hollister California. ⊠ *835 N. Michigan Ave., Magnificent Mile* ☎ *312/440–3165* ⊕ *shopwatertower.com.*

TOYS
American Girl Place

TOYS | Kiddos from just about everywhere arrive here with their signature dolls in tow. There's easily a day's worth of activities offered at American Girl Place—you can shop the doll boutiques, browse in the bookstore, get some pampering in the salon, and have lunch or afternoon tea at the café, where dolls can partake in the meal from their own "treat seats." Brace yourself for long lines just to get into the store during high shopping seasons. ⊠ *Water Tower Place, 835 N. Michigan Ave., Near North Side* ☎ *877/247–5223* ⊕ *www.americangirl. com.*

 ## Activities

SPAS
NoMi Spa at Park Hyatt

SPAS | This elegant, full-service spa offers ultimate relaxation within its treatment rooms. Spa-goers have access to the hotel's swimming pool and fitness center, both with downtown cityscape views. ⊠ *Park Hyatt, 800 N. Michigan Ave., Near North Side* ☎ *312/335–1234* ⊕ *www.hyatt.com/corporate/spas/ Nomi-Spa/en/home.html* ☞ *$160 60-min massage, $180 45-min facial.*

Spa at Four Seasons Hotel Chicago

SPAS | This 8,000 square-foot spa includes a Roman-columned pool with sky-lit dome, eucalyptus steam rooms, and four private treatment rooms that are soundproofed for maximum serenity. A variety of massage, pedicure, and facial treatments are available, and if you're ready to splurge, go for the Magnificent Mile Massage (50–80 minutes), which is customizable to your needs and your choice of Signature Four Seasons

Essential Oil Blends. There are even customized treatments designed for teens. ⊠ *Four Seasons Hotel, 120 E. Delaware Pl., Near North Side* ☎ *312/280–8800* ⊕ *www.fourseasons.com/chicagofs.*

The Spa by Asha

SPAS | Arrive early for a complimentary preservice aromatherapy foot bath in the darkened lounge. It may feel like a shame to leave for the actual treatments, which may include Aveda plant-based facials, body wraps, and massages. Don't miss the Himalayan rejuvenation treatment that claims to boost your immune system during the change of seasons. ⊠ *James Hotel, 55 E. Ontario St., Near North Side* ☎ *312/664–0200* ⊕ *www.ashasalonspa. com.*

River North

Chicago's warehouse district is known for its sleek restaurants, art galleries, and design and furniture stores, as well as the enormous theMART (formerly the Merchandise Mart) complex, which still serves as a neighborhood landmark. River North is part of Chicago's Near North Side, directly north of the Loop and the Chicago River, south of Chicago Avenue, and west of the Mag Mile.

 ## Sights

Driehaus Museum

HISTORIC HOME | Curious about how the wealthy built their urban palaces during America's Gilded Age? Steps away from the Magnificent Mile, the former Samuel Mayo Nickerson mansion has lavish interiors with 19th-century furniture and objets d'art, including pieces by Louis Comfort Tiffany and George Schastey. ⊠ *40 E. Erie St., River North* ☎ *312/482–8933* ⊕ *www.driehausmuseum.org* ⊠ *$20; $5 for tour* ⊗ *Closed Mon.-Thurs.* ⚲ *Reservations encouraged.*

Did You Know?

The twin buildings known as Marina City have served as a backdrop for many films, including *The Blues Brothers*, *Batman Begins*, *The Dark Knight*, and Steve McQueen's final flick, *The Hunter*.

Marina City

NOTABLE BUILDING | Likened to everything from corncobs to the spires of Antonio Gaudí's Sagrada Familia in Barcelona, these twin towers were a bold departure from the severity of the International Style, which began to dominate high-rise architecture beginning in the 1950s. Designed by Bertrand Goldberg and completed in between 1964 and 1968, they contain condominiums (all pie-shape, with curving balconies); the bottom 19 stories of each tower are given over to exposed spiral parking garages. The complex is also home to six restaurants, including the House of Blues, plus Hotel Chicago, a huge bowling alley, and the marina. ✉ *300 N. State St., River North* 🌐 *www.marinacity.org.*

River North Gallery District

NEIGHBORHOOD | North of the Merchandise Mart and south of Chicago Avenue, between Orleans and Dearborn, is a concentration of art galleries carrying just about every kind of work imaginable. Virtually every building on Superior Street between Wells and Orleans houses at least one gallery, and visitors are welcome to stop in.

Free tours leave from Addington Gallery at 704 N. Wells on the second Saturday of the month at 11; galleries also coordinate their exhibitions to showcase new works typically on "First Fridays" (check the *Chicago Gallery News* for dates). Although many artists have left this high-rent district for the less expensive, more industrial West Town, there is still a lot to see here, just a 10-minute walk from Michigan Avenue. ✉ *River North* ☎ *312/649–0064 Chicago Gallery News* 🌐 *www.chicagogallerynews.com.*

TheMART

NOTABLE BUILDING | This massive art deco building takes up nearly two square blocks and was the world's largest building when it opened in 1930. These days the neighborhood landmark is known as ground zero for home-design shopping, with the first floor given over to LuxeHome, a vast collection of high-end kitchen, bath, and building showrooms open to the public. The upper floors are lined with trade-only showrooms. ✉ *222 Merchandise Mart Plaza, River North* ☎ *800/677–6278* 🌐 *www.mmart.com.*

Tree Studios

OTHER ATTRACTION | Built in 1894 with a courtyard and annexes constructed in 1911 and 1912, the nation's oldest surviving artist studios have been restored and designated a Chicago landmark. Shops, galleries, and event spaces now fill the studios. ✉ *4 E. Ohio St., at State St., River North.*

🍴 Restaurants

A couple of decades ago, when Rick Bayless and his wife, Deann, opened Frontera Grill, River North was still seen as a dicey part of town. In fact, anything west of Michigan Avenue was suspect. How times change. Now the neighborhood draws art and design lovers who patronize the area's dining hot spots.

Beatrix

$$ | **AMERICAN** | **FAMILY** | If you're finding it difficult to accommodate everyone's cravings, Beatrix is the ultimate crowd-pleaser. The restaurant offers comfort food with a healthy twist for breakfast, lunch, dinner, and weekend brunch: options include salads and burgers as well as larger entrées. **Known for:** parmesan-crusted Chicken Bebe; gluten-free menu; caramel pie. [$] *Average main: $19* ✉ *519 N. Clark St., River North* ☎ *312/284–1377* 🌐 *www.beatrixrestaurants.com.*

Billy Goat Tavern

$ | **AMERICAN** | The late comedian John Belushi immortalized the Goat's short-order cooks on *Saturday Night Live,* barking their signature, "No Pepsi, Coke!" and "No fries, cheeps!" at customers, and you can still hear the shtick at this subterranean spot. The diner food is cheap

River North

KEY

- **1** Exploring Sights
- **1** Restaurants
- **1** Quick Bites
- **1** Hotels
- **L** CTA Lines

RIVER NORTH

Merchandise Mart

The Wrigley Building

DuSable Bridge

Chicago River

LOOP

and tasty, the staff is super friendly, and people-watching is a favorite sport—pop by during a break in sight-seeing or head by late-night to check out the bar. **Known for:** late-night dining; the "cheezborgers"; breakfast. [$] *Average main: $5* ✉ *430 N. Michigan Ave., lower level, River North* ☎ *312/222–1525* 🌐 *www.billygoattavern.com.*

★ Chicago Cut Steakhouse

$$$$ | STEAKHOUSE | As if steak houses don't offer enough luxury already, Chicago Cut takes decadence to the next level with sumptuous red banquettes, floor-to-ceiling windows, and prime views of the Chicago River. Steak is clearly the star, and there are more than a dozen different cuts of prime beef and sauces and spices to enhance the meat, but the rest of the menu, including a full raw bar, is just as opulent. **Known for:** "lobsterscargot" appetizer; notable wine list; rare spirits. [$] *Average main: $54* ✉ *300 N. LaSalle St., River North* ☎ *312/329–1800* 🌐 *www.chicagocutsteakhouse.com.*

Coco Pazzo

$$$$ | TUSCAN | There are a lot of good things to come when you enter this Tuscan-inspired restaurant, namely lusty, richly flavored pastas, an antipasto table, impeccable seafood, and meats from the wood-fired oven. The discreet, professional service softens the rustic, open-loft setting of exposed-brick walls and wood floors, while the seasonal menus keeps customers coming back again and again. **Known for:** Italian desserts; all-Italian wine list; lunch pizzas. [$] *Average main: $40* ✉ *300 W. Hubbard St., River North* ☎ *312/836–0900* 🌐 *www.cocopazzochicago.com* ⏲ *Closed Sun. No lunch.*

Fogo de Chão

$$$$ | BRAZILIAN | Gaucho-clad servers parade through the dining room brandishing carved-to-order fire-roasted meats at this Brazilian churrascaria. The Full Churrasco Experience starts at $57.95 and the first stop should be the lavish Market Table with an array of seasonal salads, antipasti, and charcuterie; then, using a plate-side poker-chip-like disc, you signal green for "go" to bring on the selection of meats, stopped only by flipping your chip to red, for "stop" though you can restart as often as you like. **Known for:** South American wines; lively weekend scene; Brazilian side dishes. [$] *Average main: $40* ✉ *661 N. LaSalle Blvd., River North* ☎ *312/932–9330* 🌐 *www.fogo.com.*

★ Frontera Grill

$$ | MEXICAN | Devotees of Chef Rick Bayless queue up for the bold flavors of his distinct fare at this casual restaurant brightly trimmed in Mexican folk art, where the menu changes monthly. Bayless visits Mexico frequently, updating his already extensive knowledge of regional food and cooking techniques, and he frequently takes his staff with him, ensuring that even the servers have an encyclopedic knowledge about the food. **Known for:** Bar Sótano in the basement for bar food and mezcal; mole sauce; margaritas. [$] *Average main: $26* ✉ *445 N. Clark St., River North* ☎ *312/661–1434* 🌐 *www.rickbayless.com/restaurants/frontera-grill* ⏲ *Closed Mon.*

Gene & Georgetti

$$$$ | STEAKHOUSE | This old-school steak house, in business since 1941, is a Chicago institution that attracts high-powered regulars and celebrities who pop in for lunch or dinner. The walls in the always-packed dining room are lined with vintage photos and the menu features massive steaks, quality chops, and Italian-American classics—the vibe is absolutely Chicago to the core. **Known for:** chicken alla Joe; garbage salad; prime rib. [$] *Average main: $40* ✉ *500 N. Franklin St., River North* ☎ *312/527–3718* 🌐 *www.geneandgeorgetti.com* ⏲ *Closed Mon.*

★ GT Fish & Oyster

$$ | SEAFOOD | The "GT" here stands for chef-partner Giuseppe Tentori, who has reinterpreted the classic seafood shack as a refined, contemporary eatery, decorated with a few well-placed nautical details: think mounted shark jaws and rope buoy chandeliers. With an oyster bar spanning East and West coasts and pristine seafood featured in salads, tacos, and pasta, GT Fish & Oyster proves that Chicago can tackle seafood as well as any coastal city. **Known for:** clam chowder; oysters; lobster roll. $ *Average main: $25* ⊠ *531 N. Wells St., River North* ☎ *312/929–3501* ⊕ *www.gtoyster.com* ⊗ *Closed Sun.-Mon. No lunch.*

Harry Caray's Italian Steakhouse

$$$ | STEAKHOUSE | Famed Cubs announcer Harry Caray died in 1998, but his legend lives on as fans continue to pour into the namesake restaurant—where Harry frequently held court—for Italian-American specialties, prime steaks and chops, and ice-cold martinis. If you're looking for a classic Chicago spot to catch a game, the generally thronged bar serves items off the restaurant menu; you can also follow the summer crowds to Navy Pier and the Harry Caray's outpost there. **Known for:** Nitti's Vault, a former mob hideout; chicken vesuvio; "Breaking Ball" chocolate cake dessert. $ *Average main: $30* ⊠ *33 W. Kinzie St., River North* ☎ *312/828–0966* ⊕ *www.harrycarays. com.*

Joe's Seafood, Prime Steaks & Stone Crab

$$$$ | SEAFOOD | Joe's may be far from the ocean, but the winning combination of stone crabs (in season October to May, and served chilled with mustard sauce for dipping) and other seafood, as well as prime steaks, has made this outpost of the original South Florida restaurant a continued success. There's plenty else on the menu all year-round, too, including sandwiches and lunch salads, perfect fuel during shopping and sight-seeing breaks. **Known for:** extensive wine list; those stone crab claws; fried chicken. $ *Average main: $40* ☎ *60 E. Grand Ave., River North* ☎ *312/379–5637* ⊕ *www. joes.net/chicago* ⊗ *Closed Mon.–Wed.*

The Lobby at the Peninsula

$$$ | AMERICAN | While many contemporary restaurants lean toward the avant-garde, The Lobby continues the tradition of classic upscale hotel dining with all the frills. During the day, sunlight pours through the expansive floor-to-ceiling windows overlooking the terrace while diners take in elevated breakfast staples; later, the space transforms into a romantic dinner spot with a menu of elegant seasonal takes on New American cuisine. **Known for:** afternoon tea service; majestic 20-foot floor-to-ceiling windows; intimate feel in a large space. $ *Average main: $35* ⊠ *108 E. Superior St., River North* ☎ *312/573–6695* ⊕ *www.peninsula.com/chicago.*

Mr. Beef

$ | AMERICAN | FAMILY | A Chicago institution for two-fisted Italian beef sandwiches piled with green peppers and provolone cheese, Mr. Beef garners citywide fans from area hard hats to restaurateurs and TV personalities. Service and setting—two indoor picnic tables and a dining rail—are fast-food no-nonsense, and the fare is inexpensive; it's a workingman's favorite, though located near River North's art galleries. **Known for:** chili; Italian sausage; barbecue beef. $ *Average main: $7* ⊠ *666 N. Orleans St., River North* ☎ *312/337–8500* ⊗ *Closed Sun.*

Osteria via Stato

$$ | ITALIAN | It's easy, crowd-pleasing Italian here, with an array of classic pasta, salads, meat, and seafood dishes. If you opt for the $39.95 prix-fixe, you pick an entrée and servers do the rest, working the room with several rounds of communal platters of antipasti followed by your entrée, and dessert—the results are tasty, but Osteria shines brightest at making you feel comfortable. **Known for:** Italian wine list; pizza bar; chicken Mario. $ *Average main: $26* ⊠ *620 N. State St., River North* ☎ *312/642–8450* ⊕ *www. osteriaviastato.com* ⊗ *No lunch.*

Pizzeria Due

$$ | PIZZA | FAMILY | Serving inch-thick pizzas in a comfortable, well-worn dining room, Pizzeria Due is where everyone goes when they've found out that Uno, the original home of Chicago's deep-dish pizza up the street, has an hour-plus wait. Both restaurants serve deep-dish, but Due also offers thin-crust pizzas (and is easier to get into). **Known for:** southside sausage thin-crust pizza; Numero Uno pizza; weekday express lunch. $ *Average main: $20* ✉ *619 N. Wabash Ave., River North* ☎ *312/943–2400* ⊕ *www.pizzeriaunodue.com* ⊘ *Closed Mon.-Tues.*

Pizzeria Uno

$$ | PIZZA | FAMILY | Chicago deep-dish pizza got its start here in 1943, and both local and out-of-town fans continue to pack this Victorian brownstone for the filling pies, while the dim paneled rooms with reproduction light fixtures make the setting a slice of Old Chicago. Plan on two thick, cheesy slices or less as a full meal; this is no quick-to-your-table pie so also order salads and be prepared to entertain the kids during the inevitable wait. **Known for:** deep-dish sundae; Numero Uno pizza; weekday express lunch. $ *Average main: $20* ✉ *29 E. Ohio St., River North* ☎ *312/321–1000* ⊕ *www.pizzeriaunodue.com.*

★ The Purple Pig

$$ | MEDITERRANEAN | The Magnificent Mile isn't usually known for dining, but locals and tourists alike love the Purple Pig, a Mediterranean wine bar with a deep wine list and many affordable wines by the glass. Adventurous eaters will revel in chef Jimmy Bannos Jr.'s offal-centric dishes, though there's plenty for tamer palates and vegetarians here as well, along with an array of notable Mediterranean-styled desserts. **Known for:** milk-braised pork shoulder; cured meats and cheeses; roasted bone marrow. $ *Average main: $18* ✉ *444 N. Michigan Ave., River North* ☎ *312/464–1744* ⊕ *www.thepurplepigchicago.com.*

Shaw's Crab House

$$$$ | SEAFOOD | Shaw's is, hands down, one of the city's best seafood spots, and though it's held an exalted position for years, the restaurant doesn't rest on its laurels. The kitchen turns out classics along with sushi, maki, and fresh sashimi, and the menu is available in both the main dining room and the lively Oyster Bar, where you can watch the shell shuckers hard at work. **Known for:** Key lime pie; live music in the oyster bar; weekend brunch buffet. $ *Average main: $44* ✉ *21 E. Hubbard St., River North* ☎ *527–2722* ⊕ *www.shawscrabhouse.com.*

Sunda New Asian

$$ | ASIAN | Named for the Sunda Shelf, an ancient Southeast Asian landmass, this trendy spot scours Asia for riotously flavorful fare, including dim sum, rice, and noodle dishes and signature sushi offerings, while well-executed cocktails and Asian beer selections complement the sweet, sour, and spicy dishes. The buzzing and expansive space cobbles together communal and traditional tables and lounge seating alongside Asian antiques. **Known for:** oxtail pot stickers; well-crafted cocktails; gluten-free and vegetarian options. $ *Average main: $27* ✉ *110 W. Illinois St., River North* ☎ *312/644–0500* ⊕ *www.sundanewasian.com.*

Tanta

$$$ | PERUVIAN | World-renowned Peruvian chef Gastón Acurio makes his foray into the Chicago dining scene with this sleek homage to the cuisine of his homeland. Small format dishes make it easy to try everything, and the pisco-based cocktails are unmatched; just be wary of your wallet as prices tend to add up quickly. **Known for:** ceviches; the Japanese/Peruvian dish wagyu nigiri; rooftop bar. $ *Average main: $29* ✉ *118 W. Grand Ave., River North* ☎ *312/222–9700* ⊕ *www.tantachicago.com* ⊘ *No lunch weekdays.*

★ Topolobampo

$$$$ | MEXICAN | Chef-owner Rick Bayless wrote the book on regional Mexican cuisine—several books, actually—and here he takes his faithfully prepared regional food upscale. Next door to the more casual Frontera Grill, Topolobampo shares Frontera's address, phone, and dedication to quality, though it's a higher-end room, with a more subdued mood and a menu of tasting options. **Known for:** agave spirits pairings; themed tasting menus; wine pairings. $ *Average main: $115* ✉ *445 N. Clark St., River North* ☎ *312/661–1434* ⊕ *www.rickbayless. com/restaurants/topolobampo* ☉ *Closed Sun.-Tues. No lunch.*

Travelle at The Langham

$$$ | AMERICAN | The luxurious Langham Hotel doesn't disappoint with this elegant American restaurant located on the second floor, where cushy white leather seats pamper guests gaping at the glittering city lights through the floor-to-ceiling windows. The menu offers an array of shareable snacks along with entrées and salads; the dishes have global touches that keep them interesting while still remaining approachable. **Known for:** "charred-tar" (tenderloin with aioli and fried quail eggs); $29 three-course express lunch menu; classic cocktails. $ *Average main: $36* ✉ *330 N. Wabash Ave., 2nd fl., River North* ☎ *312/923–7705* ⊕ *www.travellechicago.com.*

Vermilion

$$ | ECLECTIC | Vermilion's focus on creative, high-end Latin–Indian fusion fare sets it apart on a busy stretch in River North, and lots of small-plate options, including takes on classic Indian street food for both brunch and dinner, encourage sampling. Despite cool fashion photography on the walls and techno music in the air, the vibe is warm and welcoming. **Known for:** lobster or "gobi" Portuguese; blackened tamarind ribs; late-night weekend dining hours. $ *Average main: $24* ✉ *10 W. Hubbard St., River North* ☎ *312/527–4060* ⊕ *www. thevermilionrestaurant.com* ☉ *Closed Mon. and Tues., no lunch.*

Wildfire

$$$ | AMERICAN | The Wildfire kitchen's wood-burning oven is visible from the dining room at this cozy supper club–style steak house that plays a sound track of vintage jazz. No culinary innovations here, just exceptional cuts of meat and top quality seafood. **Known for:** bread basket; roasted prime rib; clubby atmosphere. $ *Average main: $30* ✉ *159 W. Erie St., River North* ☎ *312/787–9000* ⊕ *www.wildfirerestaurant.com* ☉ *No lunch.*

Xoco

$ | MEXICAN | By opening a third restaurant next door to perennial favorites Frontera Grill and Topolobampo, celeb chef Rick Bayless has taken control of this River North block. With Xoco, he's given the city the ultimate place for tortas (Mexican sandwiches) served at breakfast, lunch, and dinner; caldos, generous bowls of pozole, and other Latin-inspired soups; and hot chocolate made from cacao beans that are roasted and ground on the premises. **Known for:** Saturday brunch; pepito torta; happy hour drinks and snacks. $ *Average main: $11* ✉ *449 N. Clark St., River North* ☎ *312/334–3688* ⊕ *www.rickbayless.com* ☉ *Closed Sun. and Mon.*

☕ Coffee and Quick Bites

Brett's Kitchen

$ | AMERICAN | FAMILY | Under the El at Superior and Franklin, Brett's Kitchen is an excellent spot for a quick pastry, sandwich, or omelet. It's super casual: order at the counter and grab a seat. **Known for:** tuna melt; turkey club; black bean burger. $ *Average main: $8* ✉ *233 W. Superior St., River North* ☎ *312/664–6354* ⊕ *www. brettskitchen.com* ☉ *Closed Sun.*

Portillo's

$ | **AMERICAN** | **FAMILY** | Started in 1963 as a hot dog stand called "The Dog House" in the Chicago suburbs, this River North restaurant is a favorite among locals and tourists alike (usually with a drive-thru line to prove it). A "Chicago Style" hot dog (mustard, relish, onions, tomatoes, pickle, celery salt, and peppers) is the obvious quick bite, but what about an Italian beef sandwich—yum! **Known for:** malts and shakes; memorabilia on the walls; Italian Beef sandwich. [$] *Average main: $7* ✉ *100 W. Ontario, River North* ☎ *312/587–8910* 🌐 *www.portillos.com.*

Hotels

Embassy Suites by Hilton Chicago Downtown

$$ | **HOTEL** | **FAMILY** | Suites here are arranged around an 11-story, plant-filled atrium lobby where bubbling fountains keep noise levels relatively high; making efficient use of space, all have separate living rooms with a pullout sofa, four-person dining table, and an extra TV. **Pros:** hotel is just three blocks away from the Magnificent Mile; great cocktail hour; family friendly. **Cons:** rooms could use some updating; external noise can be distracting; pricey valet. [$] *Rooms from: $250* ✉ *600 N. State St., River North* ☎ *312/943–3800* 🌐 *www.embassysuiteschicago.com* 🛏 *368 suites* 🍴 *Free Breakfast.*

The Godfrey Hotel Chicago

$$ | **HOTEL** | Tech-minded travelers who like to mix business with pleasure will feel right at home at this hotel, which has what worker bees need (generously sized in-room desks with multiple outlets) and what party animals want (a sizzling rooftop bar, I|O Godfrey). **Pros:** small on-site spa; windows open in rooms; great bar. **Cons:** too hip for some; no pool; not ideal for kids. [$] *Rooms from: $309* ✉ *127 W. Huron St., River North* ☎ *312/649–2000* 🌐 *www.godfreyhotelchicago.com* 🛏 *221 rooms* 🍴 *No Meals.*

★ **The Langham, Chicago**

$$$ | **HOTEL** | A Mies van der Rohe–designed skyscraper is now home to the city's hottest stay. **Pros:** location can't be beat; attentive and friendly service; gorgeous facilities. **Cons:** opulent design may be too formal for some; quite pricey; street noise may be heard on lower floors. [$] *Rooms from: $500* ✉ *330 N. Wabash Ave., River North* ☎ *312/923–9988* 🌐 *chicago.langhamhotels.com* 🛏 *316 rooms* 🍴 *No Meals.*

Royal Sonesta Chicago Downtown

$ | **HOTEL** | Steps from iconic Chicago attractions, the Royal Sonesta has some of the largest standard guest rooms in Chicago, many with a river or city view. **Pros:** large guest rooms; many rooms feature river views; walkable to many major Chicago attractions. **Cons:** no on-site spa; parking can be a challenge; no pool. [$] *Rooms from: $309* ✉ *505 N. State Street, River North* 🌐 *https://www.sonesta.com/us/illinois/chicago/royal-sonesta-chicago-downtown* 🍴 *No Meals* 🛏 *381 rooms.*

Nightlife

BARS

The Berkshire Room

BARS | The bartenders at this swanky but unfussy cocktail bar on the ground floor of the hip ACME Hotel specialize in improvisation—name a spirit, flavor profile, and type of glassware from the "Dealer's Choice" menu and they'll craft a drink for you on the spot. ✉ *15 E. Ohio St., River North* ☎ *312/894–0945* 🌐 *www.theberkshireroom.com.*

Broken Shaker

Like its siblings in Miami, NYC, and elsewhere, Chicago's Broken Shaker specializes in highly creative cocktails, with a rotating menu that leans to the savory side. On one visit, we sampled a "Log Cabin Old Fashioned," with a hint of

Did You Know?

Chicago's House of Blues, located in the Marina City complex, is one of the city's premier live music venues, showcasing all types of music, including jazz, gospel, rock, hip-hop, and R&B.

maple and garnished with a slice of toasted waffle; also look out for the Daiquiri of the Month. The bar itself is on the small side, but seating and service spill out into the Freehand hotel lobby. ⊠ *Freehand Chicago, 19 E. Ohio St., River North* ☎ *312/940–3699* ⊕ *freehandhotels.com/chicago/broken-shaker*.

Castaways

BARS | This breezy, seasonal, casual bar and grill puts you so close to Lake Michigan that you might consider wearing a swimsuit. Perched atop the North Avenue Beach Boathouse, Castaways creates the perfect setup for lazy summertime sipping. ⊠ *1603 N. Lake Shore Dr., River North* ☎ *773/281–1200* ⊕ *www.castawayschicago.com* ⊙ *Closed Oct.–May*.

Celeste

BARS | This ambitious bar and lounge, open till the early morning hours, offers a different environment on each of the four levels and high-quality cocktails throughout. Highlights include the fourth-floor Roof Garden, a year-round escapist experience under a fully retractable glass rooftop, and DISCO, on the third floor, which captures the energy, glamour, and sexiness of the 1970s in NYC, Paris, and Rome. DJs spin classics, deep cuts and disco that evoke Studio 54 and Paradise Garage. ⊠ *111 W. Hubbard St., River North* ☎ *312/828–9000* ⊕ *www.celeste-chicago.com*.

Fado

BARS | Imported wood, stone, and glass are used to create Fado's Irish look. The second floor—with a bar brought in from Dublin—feels more like the real thing than the first. Expect expertly drawn Guinness, a fine selection of whiskeys, a menu of traditional dishes, and live music on weekends. ⊠ *100 W. Grand Ave., River North* ☎ *312/836–0066* ⊕ *www.fadoirishpub.com/chicago*.

★ Gilt Bar

BARS | Vintage furnishings, upholstered walls, and intriguing details set the 1920s speakeasy scene at this low-lighted lounge. Downstairs, The Library has velvet booths and vintage art surrounding a handsome book-lined bar. ⊠ *230 W. Kinzie St., River North* ☎ *312/464–9544* ⊕ *www.giltbarchicago.com*.

Hub 51

BARS | Sip cocktails with the after-work crowd in Hub 51's vaulted, loftlike industrial space, and then linger for inventive light bites or more substantial fare. The downstairs lounge, **Sub 51**, has DJ-driven beats, but get there early or reserve a table. ⊠ *51 W. Hubbard St., River North* ☎ *312/828–0051* ⊕ *www.hub51chicago.com*.

Hubbard Inn

BARS | Billing itself as a "Continental tavern," this two-story River North hot spot pays homage to Ernest Hemingway's travels with classic cocktails and eclectic, globetrotting decor—think Moroccan tiled walls, vintage books, dramatic oil paintings, brass light fixtures, and tables made from reclaimed wood. Small plates are designed with communal dining in mind, though you may want to keep your perfectly balanced Sazerac all to yourself. ⊠ *110 W. Hubbard St., River North* ☎ *312/273-6207* ⊕ *www.hubbardinn.com*.

Pops for Champagne

BARS | Pops got its start almost 40 years ago and it's Chicago's only Champagne bar. These days there's a focus on small grower producers. The basement is home to Watershed, a cozy spot with limestone walls focused on Great Lakes regional craft beers and spirits. ⊠ *601 N. State St., River North* ☎ *312/266–7677* ⊕ *www.popsforchampagne.com*.

Three Dots and a Dash

BARS | Once you've found the alley entrance (hint: look for the red-roped line of people waiting outside), descend the glowing skull-lined stairs to reach this hip spot that's an homage to the tiki craze of the '40s, '50s and '60s. "Three Dots and a Dash" is an old-school, rum-based tiki cocktail that gets its name from the morse code for the letter "V" as in victory, as used in WWII. There are Pan-Pacific nibbles, like the shareable pu pu platter, to accompany the strong tropical cocktails adorned with flowers and served in tiki mugs. ⊠ 435 N. Clark St., River North ☎ 312/610–4220 ⊕ www. threedotschicago.com.

DANCE CLUBS
Sound-Bar

DANCE CLUBS | Sound-Bar is a two-level labyrinth of nine bars, each with a unique design and color scheme (some even serve matching colored cocktails). Feel like dancing? Join the pulse of Chicago's best-dressed on the huge dance floor. ⊠ 226 W. Ontario St., River North ☎ 312/787–4480 ⊕ sound-bar.com.

Spybar

DANCE CLUBS | This late-night underground dance club has been in the River North area for more than 25 years. Featured are internationally renowned and up-and-coming local musicians and DJs. ⊠ 646 N. Franklin St., River North ☎ 312/337–2191 ⊕ www.spybarchicago. com.

The Underground

DANCE CLUBS | This subterranean dance club has dropped the quasi-military underground bunker theme it once sported, but it still attracts celebs, international DJs, and the clientele that follows both. ⊠ 56 W. Illinois St., River North ☎ 312/644–7600 ⊕ www.theunder- groundchicago.com.

LIVE MUSIC
Andy's Jazz Club

LIVE MUSIC | A favorite after-work watering hole with a substantial bar menu, Andy's Jazz Club has live music ranging from swing jazz to bebop. ⊠ 11 E. Hubbard St.,

River North ☎ 312/642–6805 ⊕ www. andysjazzclub.com.

Baton Show Lounge

CABARET | At Baton Show Lounge, boys will be girls. The lip-synching revues with female impersonators have catered to curious out-of-towners and bachelorette parties since 1969. Some of the regular performers, such as Chilli Pepper, have become Chicago cult figures. The more the audience tips, the better the show gets, so bring your bills. ⊠ 4713 N. Broadway, River North ☎ 312/644–5269 ⊕ www.thebatonshowlounge.com.

Blue Chicago

LIVE MUSIC | In an upscale part of downtown, Blue Chicago has none of the trademark grit or edginess of the older South Side blues clubs. What is does offer is a good sound system, a packed calendar that regularly features female vocalists, and a cosmopolitan audience that's a tad more diverse than some of the baseball-capped crowds at Lincoln Park blues clubs. ⊠ 536 N. Clark St., River North ☎ 312/661–0100 ⊕ www. bluechicago.com.

★ House of Blues

LIVE MUSIC | Though its name implies otherwise, House of Blues actually attracts big-name performers of all genres, including jazz, roots, gospel, alternative rock, hip-hop, world, and R&B. The interior is an elaborate cross between blues bar and ornate opera house. Its restaurant has a satisfying Sunday gospel brunch. Part of the Marina City complex, its entrance is on State Street. ⊠ Marina City, 329 N. Dearborn St., River North ☎ 312/923–2000 ⊕ www.houseofblues. com/chicago.

🛍 Shopping

Between the Gold Coast and Chicago River, the shopping vibe is less frenetic than Mag Mile and the retail is more focused on art galleries, antiques shops, and home furnishings stores. Some of these are housed in historic buildings.

ANTIQUES

Abraham Lincoln Book Shop

ANTIQUES & COLLECTIBLES | The shop owner here buys, sells, and appraises books, paintings, documents, and other paraphernalia associated with American military and political history. It's been around since 1938. ⊠ *824 W. Superior St., River North* ☎ *312/944–3085* ⊕ *www. alincolnbookshop.com* ⊘ *Closed Sun. and Mon., by appointment only.*

J Roberts Antiques

ANTIQUES & COLLECTIBLES | This antique dealer specializes in European furniture and accessories from the 18th century to the art deco period. By appointment only. ⊠ *149 W. Kinzie St., 3rd fl., River North* ☎ *773/369–8207* ⊕ *www.jayrobertsantiques.com.*

P.O.S.H.

ANTIQUES & COLLECTIBLES | It's hard to resist the charming, piled-up displays of vintage hotel and restaurant china here. There's also an impressive selection of silver gravy boats, creamers, hotel silver, and flatware that bear the marks of ocean liners and private clubs. P.O.S.H., in business since 1997 and in this location since 2003, is also known for its French flea market signs. ⊠ *613 N. State St., River North* ☎ *312/280–1602* ⊕ *poshchicago.com.*

ART GALLERIES

Alan Koppel Gallery

ART GALLERIES | An eclectic mix by modern masters and contemporary artists is balanced by French and Italian Modernist furniture from the 1920s to 1950s. ⊠ *806 N. Dearborn Ave., River North* ☎ *312/640–0730* ⊕ *www.alankoppel. com.*

Carl Hammer Gallery

ART GALLERIES | Lee Godie, Henry Darger, Bill Traylor, and Joseph Yoakum are among the outsider and self-taught artists whose work is shown at this

gallery. ⊠ *740 N. Wells St., River North* ☎ *312/266–8512* ⊕ *www.carlhammergallery.com.*

Echt Gallery

ART GALLERIES | Collectors of fine studio art glass are drawn here by a number of luminaries. ⊠ *210 W. Superior St., River North* ☎ *312/440–0288* ⊕ *www.echtgallery.com.*

Joel Oppenheimer, Inc.

ART GALLERIES | Established in 1969, this iconic gallery has an amazing collection of Audubon prints and specializes in antique natural-history pieces. ⊠ *10 E. Ohio St., River North* ☎ *312/642–5300* ⊕ *audubonart.com.*

Stephen Daiter Gallery

ART GALLERIES | This space showcases stunning 20th-century European and American photography, particularly avant-garde photojournalism. ⊠ *230 W. Superior St., 4th fl., River North* ☎ *312/787–3350* ⊕ *www.stephendaitergallery.com.*

CLOTHING

Blake

MIXED CLOTHING | At this haute minimalist enclave, you'll find designers like Dries van Noten and Balenciaga, as well as shoes and accessories of a similar subtle elegance. ⊠ *212 W. Chicago Ave., River North* ☎ *312/202–0047.*

HOME DECOR

The Chopping Block

HOUSEWARES | New and seasoned chefs appreciate the expertly chosen selection of cookware, bakeware, tools, ingredients, and food-friendly wines here. Intimate cooking classes are hugely popular and taught by a fun, knowledgeable staff (participants get 10% off store merchandise). ✉ *222 Merchandise Mart Plaza, River North* ☎ *312/644–6360* ⊕ *www. thechoppingblock.com.*

Lightology

HOUSEWARES | Dedicated to modern lighting, this 3-story, 20,000-square-foot showroom is an essential stop for designers and architects, not to mention passersby drawn to the window displays. Lightology is the brainchild of Greg Kay, who started out as a roller-disco lighting designer in the 1970s. ✉ *215 W. Chicago Ave., River North* ☎ *312/944–1000* ⊕ *www.lightology.com.*

Luminaire

HOUSEWARES | The international contemporary furniture in this 21,000-square-foot showroom includes pieces by Philippe Starck and Antonio Citterio. Sleek kitchen designs and tabletop pieces are from Zaha Hadid and other edgy designers from around the globe. ✉ *301 W. Superior St., River North* ☎ *312/664–9582* ⊕ *luminaire.com.*

Manifesto

HOUSEWARES | For more than 35 years, this showroom has presented the finest in elegant modern furniture from designers such as Poltrona Frau, Ceccotti, Wittmann, and COR, as well as custom in-house designs by the Manifesto Design Group. ✉ *230 West Superior St., River North* ☎ *312/664–0733* ⊕ *www. manifestofurniture.com.*

Orange Skin

HOUSEWARES | The go-to resource for modern furniture, lighting, and accessories in Chicago carries pieces by Minotti, Philippe Starck, and Piero Lissoni in a bi-level industrial space. ✉ *419 W. Superior Street, River North* ☎ *312/335–1033* ⊕ *www.orangeskin.com.*

 # Activities

SPAS

Chuan Spa

SPAS | Surrender yourself to lush amenities and treatments rooted in traditional Chinese medicine at this tranquil spot. Start by drinking in views from the calm lobby, where staffers rarely speak above a whisper; then let a personal attendant guide you through a changing room (complete with salt-stone sauna and herbal steam shower) to your own personal haven. You can linger after your session, reclining in a heated lounge chair as you gaze out onto the Chicago River. ✉ *Langham Hotel, 330 N. Wabash Ave., River North* ☎ *312/923–9988* ⊕ *www. chuanspa.com.*

PILSEN, LITTLE ITALY, AND CHINATOWN

Updated by
Jessica Mlinaric

◉ Sights	🍴 Restaurants	🛏 Hotels	🛍 Shopping	▼ Nightlife
★★★☆☆	★★★★☆	★☆☆☆☆	★★☆☆☆	★☆☆☆☆

NEIGHBORHOOD SPOTLIGHT

MAKING THE MOST OF YOUR TIME

These are exciting neighborhoods, with plenty going on. Pilsen buzzes on weekends and during the Fiesta del Sol festival (at the end of July). On the second Friday of each month, neighborhood galleries stay open late for an art crawl.

At night Little Italy's restaurants and bars bustle, and on Sunday the Maxwell Street Market, in University Village really hums. Make time to browse the shops and sample the goods along Wentworth Avenue or Chinatown Square. And don't forget to tour the nearby 19th-century Prairie Avenue homes, where many of the people who shaped Chicago lived.

GETTING HERE

If you're driving to Pilsen, take I–290 west to the Damen Avenue exit, and go south on Damen to 19th Street. There's parking at the National Museum of Mexican Art plus metered street parking. For Little Italy and University Village, take the Kennedy Expressway's Taylor Street exit and head west. Chinatown is west of Michigan Avenue via Cermak Road. There's a parking lot at Chinatown Gate, on Wentworth Avenue. Turn east off Michigan Avenue on East 21st Street to reach Prairie Avenue.

If you choose to use public transportation, the El's Pink Line stops at the 18th Street station in the Pilsen area. Check out the station's colorful murals. Take the Blue Line to UIC/Halsted for University Village and the No. 9 Ashland bus to Little Italy. For Chinatown, take the El's Red Line south to Cermak.

BRIDGEPORT ART CENTER

Over in nearby Bridgeport, the Bridgeport Art Center (*https://bridgeportart.com*) is a massive 6-story facility that's home to artists' studios, galleries, and shops. The third Friday of every month is Open Studios night, when you can see the resident artists's work, though you can visit the galleries at other times. The building used to be a Spiegel Catalog warehouse and today a small Chicago Maritime Museum on the bottom floor explains the importance of water to the city's history.

TOP REASONS TO GO

■ **Gallery-hop:** On second Fridays in Pilsen the art galleries stay open late.

■ **Shop:** Bargain with the locals at the legendary Maxwell Street Market on Sunday.

■ **Appreciate history:** See where Chicago greats like Marshall Field and George Pullman lived in the Prairie Avenue Historic District.

SAFETY

The railway tracks and vacant lots between Pilsen and Little Italy make it unsafe to walk between the two neighborhoods. Drive if possible, or take the Blue Line to either UIC–Halsted or Racine to explore University Village and Little Italy; then take the Pink Line to 18th Street for Pilsen. Chinatown and Prairie Avenue are a bit removed from the heart of the city and bordered by slowly gentrifying neighborhoods, so just be cautious and aware.

BRONZEVILLE

The Bronzeville neighborhood, southeast of Chinatown and Pilsen, was a hub of African American business and culture in the early 20th century and is experiencing a renaissance. Check out the public art, galleries, restaurants, historic homes, and more.

The jumble of ethnic neighborhoods stretching west of the Loop and from the south branch of the Chicago River to the Eisenhower Expressway (I–290) is a vibrant and diverse area. It's dominated by Pilsen's Mexican community, Little Italy, and the University of Illinois's Medical District and Circle Campus.

Pilsen

Formerly full of Bohemian and Czech immigrants, who named the area after Pilsen, the fourth largest city in Czechia, this neighborhood is now largely Mexican, with lots of Latino culture influences. The area is known for its colorful street murals, many of which showcase Mexican history, culture, and religion. There are also lots of art galleries, great restaurants, and a number of happening music venues. To get your bearings, the district is bounded on the east by 800 West Halsted Street, on the west by 2400 West Western Avenue, on the north by 16th Street, and on the south by the Chicago River.

Sights

Chicago Art Department

ARTS CENTER | You can get an education at the Chicago Art Department, where the emphasis is on workshops and classes for emerging artists. The program, housed inside the historic Fountainhead building on Halsted, also hosts an array of exhibitions. ⊠ *1926 S. Halsted St., Suite 100* ☎ *312/725–4223* ⊕ *www. chicagoartdepartment.org.*

Chicago Arts District

STREET | Since the late 1960s, Halsted Street near 18th Street has lured a large number of artists, who live and work in the mixed-use community known as the Chicago Arts District. The street-level galleries and studios have put Pilsen on the map as an art destination, and innovative spaces abound. The best time to visit is on the second Friday of each month, from 6 to 10 pm, when about 30 artists open their doors to the public. Expect visual art displays, interpretive dance, installations, music, and performance art. Most studios also have regular weekend hours or are open by appointment. ⊠ *South Halsted St., between, Pilsen* ☎ *312/738–8000.*

18th Street

STREET | Pilsen's main commercial strip is full of tempting restaurants, bakeries, and Mexican grocery stores. At 1510 West 18th is Cantón Regio, formerly Nuevo León, a family restaurant that has been an anchor in the neighborhood since the Gutiérrez family originally set up shop across the street in 1962. ⊠ *Chicago* ⊕ *www.eighteenthstreet.org.*

Lagunitas Brewing Company

BREWERY | Ever since California-based Lagunitas Brewing Company set up shop

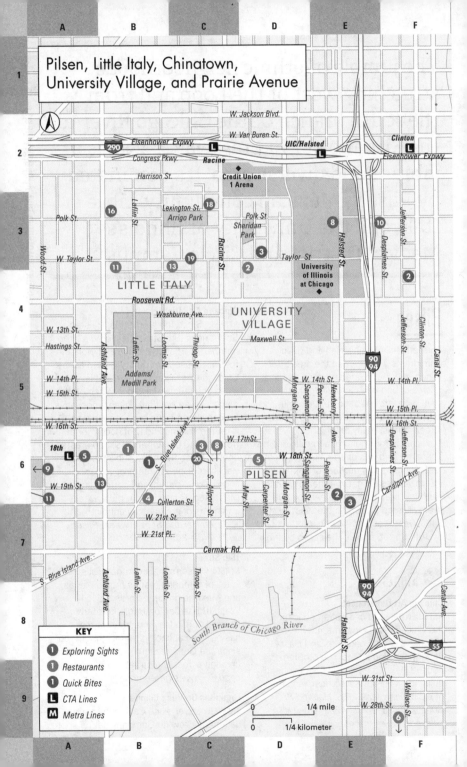

Pilsen, Little Italy, Chinatown, University Village, and Prairie Avenue

A **B** **C** **D** **E** **F**

W. Jackson Blvd.

W. Van Buren St.

Eisenhower Expwy.

Clinton **L**

290 Congress Pkwy.

UIC/Halsted **L**

Racine **L**

Eisenhower Expwy.

Harrison St.

Credit Union
1 Arena

Polk St.

Jefferson St.

16

18

Lexington St.
Arrigo Park

Polk St
Sheridan
Park

8

10

2

Laflin St.

Racine St.

Halsted St.

W. Taylor St.

3

Taylor St.

Jefferson St.

2

11

13 **19**

2

University
of Illinois
at Chicago

LITTLE ITALY

Roosevelt Rd.

Washburne Ave.

**UNIVERSITY
VILLAGE**

Wood St.

W. 13th St.

Maxwell St.

Hastings St.

Jefferson St.

Canal St.

Ashland Ave.

Laflin St.

Loomis St.

Throop St.

Addams/
Medill Park

W. 14th Pl.

W. 14th St.

W. 15th St.

W. 14th Pl.

Morgan St.

Sangamon St.

Peoria St.

Newberry Ave.

W. 15th Pl.

W. 16th St.

Jefferson St.

Desplaines St.

18th **L** **5**

1

1

S. Blue Island Ave.

S. Allport St.

3 **8**

20

W. 17th St.

5

W. 18th St.

9

PILSEN

2

3

13

W. 19th St.

11

4

Cullerton St.

W. 21st St.

May St.

Carpenter St.

Morgan St.

Sangamon St.

Peoria St.

Canalport Ave.

W. 21st Pl.

Cermak Rd.

S. Blue Island Ave.

Ashland Ave.

Laflin St.

Loomis St.

Throop St.

Halsted St.

Canal Ave.

South Branch of Chicago River

**90
94**

55

KEY

1 *Exploring Sights*

1 *Restaurants*

1 *Quick Bites*

L *CTA Lines*

M *Metra Lines*

W. 31st St.

Wallace St.

6

W. 28th St.

0   1/4 mile

0   1/4 kilometer

A **B** **C** **D** **E** **F**

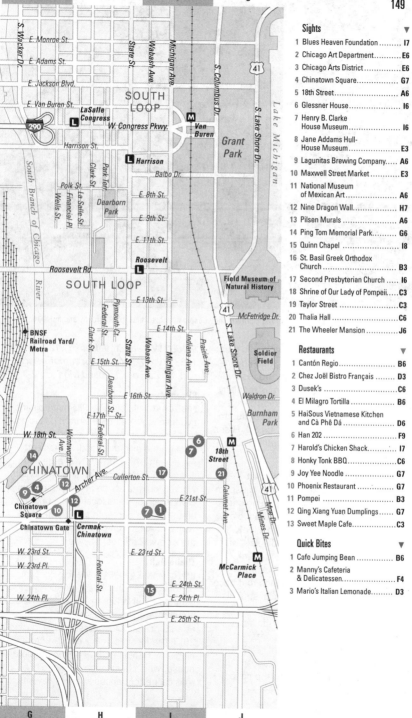

Exhibits at the National Museum of Mexican Art showcase painting, textiles, photography and much more.

in industrial West Pilsen, it's been a must-see for beer lovers. The 300,000-square-foot facility offers free tours, no reservations necessary. Its tap room is regularly buzzing with live music—as you'd expect, there's great brew and good pub grub to go with it, too. ⊠ 2607 W. 17th St., Pilsen ☎ 773/522–2097 ⊕ www.lagunitas.com ⊠ Free.

★ National Museum of Mexican Art

ART MUSEUM | The largest Latino museum in the country (and the first Latino one accredited by the American Alliance of Museums) is definitely worth a look. Its galleries house impressive displays of contemporary, traditional, and Mesoamerican art from both sides of the border, as well as vivid exhibits that trace immigration woes and political struggles. The 11,000-piece permanent collection includes pre-Cuauhtemoc artifacts, textiles, folk art, paintings, prints, and drawings. Every fall the giant "Day of the Dead" exhibit stuns Chicagoans with its altars from artists across the nation.

⊠ 1852 W. 19th St., Pilsen ☎ 312/738–1503 ⊕ www.nationalmuseumofmexicanart.org ⊠ Free ⊙ Closed Mon.

Pilsen Murals

PUBLIC ART | Murals give Pilsen its distinctive flair. You'll see their vibrant colors and bold images at many turns during a walk through the neighborhood. At Ashland Avenue and 19th Street, two large ones illustrate Latino family life and Latinos at work. More murals created by community youth groups and local artists brighten up the blocks centered at 16th and Ashland; Aztec sun-god inserts decorate the sidewalk stones. ⊠ Pilsen.

Thalia Hall

PERFORMANCE VENUE | A few blocks east of 18th Street's hustle and bustle, this neighborhood landmark was built in 1892 but shuttered for decades, and reopened as a stunning multipurpose space in 2013. The focal point is a concert hall, elegantly fashioned after a Prague opera house, which hosts a broad range of musical performances and artsy events.

Bronzeville

The historic Bronzeville neighborhood—between Douglas Boulevard (Cottage Grove Avenue) and Grand Boulevard (Martin Luther King Jr. Drive)—was an early-20th-century African American business and cultural hub. Today there's much to see in honor of the neighborhood's many influential inhabitants, as well as nearby notable sights like the Illinois Institute of Technology (IIT) campus with its Mies van der Rohe creations and the White Sox home field in Bridgeport.

Follow History's Trail

After World War I, Blacks began to move to Bronzeville to escape race restrictions prevalent in other parts of the city. Many famous African Americans are associated with the area, including Andrew "Rube" Foster, founder of the Negro National Baseball League; civil rights activist Ida B. Wells; Bessie Coleman, the first African American woman pilot; and jazz great Louis Armstrong. The symbolic entrance to the area is a tall statue at East Eastgate Place and Martin Luther King Jr. Drive that depicts a new arrival from the South bearing a suitcase held together with string. A commemorative trail along Martin Luther King Jr. Drive between 25th and 35th streets has more than 90 sidewalk plaques honoring members of the community, including Gwendolyn Brooks, whose first book of poetry was called *A Street in Bronzeville.*

A sculpture called *The Light of Truth*, inspired by the writing of Ida B. Wells, was installed in Bronzeville in 2021. The monument, designed by sculptor and Chicago native Richard Hunt, has three bronze pillars supporting a metallic torch.

Architecture 101

"Less is more," claimed Mies van der Rohe, but for fans of the master's work, more is more at IIT. The campus has an array of the glass-and-steel structures for which he is most famous. Crown Hall, the jewel of the collection, is a National Historic Landmark, but don't overlook the Robert F. Carr Memorial Chapel of St. Savior.

The McCormick Tribune Campus Center, designed by Dutch architect Rem Koolhaas, is fun to explore and pays homage to the Mies legacy. Its apparently opaque windows are actually see-through, as long as you stand head-on. Look at the glass walls near the entrance through a digital camera and you'll see depictions of IIT icons like Mies.

The campus is about 1 mile west of Lake Shore Drive on 31st Street. Both the El's Green and Red Line 35th Street stops are two blocks west of campus. *S. State St. between 31st and 35th Sts., 312/567–3000.*

Go-Go, White Sox!

The Chicago White Sox don't generate the same level of hometown hype as their North Side rivals, the Cubs but taking in a game at Guaranteed Rate Field (formerly U.S. Cellular Field, but forever Comiskey Park in the hearts of die-hard Sox fans) is a great way to spend a summer afternoon. Tickets are typically more reasonable than at Wrigley. The ballpark is located immediately west of the Red Line's 35th Street stop and two blocks west of the Green Line's IIT/Bronzeville stop.*333 W. 35th St.,312/674–1000,www.mlb.com/whitesox.*

Colorful murals highlighting community heritage are a big part of the Pilsen neighborhood.

Dusek's Tavern, an upscale neighborhood tavern, Punch House, a hip and moodily lit lounge for the cocktail crowd, and Tack Room, a cocktail bar featuring live music in the former carriage house, are also on the premises. ✉ *1807 S. Allport St., Pilsen* ☎ *312/526–3851* 🌐 *www.thaliahall-chicago.com.*

🍴 Restaurants

Pilsen has all kinds of diverse dining options, a lot of it budget-friendly. There's lots of Mexican food as well as Vietnamese and other Asian eats.

Cantón Regio

$ | **MEXICAN** | Cantón Regio rose from the ashes of Nuevo Leon, a Pilsen landmark for over 50 years before it was destroyed by a fire in 2015. The Gutierrez family rebounded with this lively Mexican steak house, across the street from the original restaurant, where an open kitchen turns out steak and chicken grilled over mesquite coals and an egg-focused breakfast menu. **Known for:** all the grilled meat; rustic, Mexican-ranch-inspired interior; fresh flour tortillas. [$] *Average main: $17* ✉ *1510 W 18th St., Pilsen* ☎ *312/733–3045* 🌐 *https://sites.google.com/view/canton-regio* 💳 *No credit cards.*

Dusek's

$$ | **ECLECTIC** | The Pilsen neighborhood plays host to some of Chicago's most diverse dining spots, including this neighborhood tavern, where sustainably sourced dishes are the perfect counterpart to*natural wine and artisan cocktails.* Make an evening of it by heading upstairs to catch a show at music venue Thalia Hall or downstairs to the basement cocktail bar, Punch House, for a retro nightcap. **Known for:** Honest Wine Wednesdays, where natural wine is paired with a seasonal dish; griddled double cheeseburger; wood-oven-roasted dishes. [$] *Average main: $22* ✉ *1227 W. 18th St., Pilsen* ☎ *312/526–3851* 🌐 *www.dusekschicago.com* 🕓 *Closed Mon.-Tues.*

HaiSous Vietnamese Kitchen and Cà Phê Dá

$$ | VIETNAMESE | Standout food and beverage options give the lively HaiSous a one-two punch of deliciousness—choose from the array of vegetable-forward, meat, or seafood specialties paired with any of the cocktails and you'll believe it. At the adjacent coffee shop, Cà Phê Dá, the focus is on more casual food, like Vietnamese-inspired chicken wings, waffles, fries, and coffee drinks. **Known for:** inventive cocktail list; $65 grand tasting menu; fried chicken wings. ⓢ *Average main: $18* ✉ *1800 S. Carpenter St., Pilsen* ☎ *312/702–1303* ⊕ *www.haisous.com* ⏱ *Closed Mon.–Wed.*

Honky Tonk BBQ

$ | BARBECUE | The twang of country meets the tang of barbecue sauce at this lively spot that's decked out in vintage Americana (including a pink fridge). The ambience sets the scene for a down-home meal of award-winning barbecued meats, either on a platter or stuffed into sandwiches, along with classic sides. **Known for:** live honky-tonk music on weekends; pulled pork; bacon candy. ⓢ *Average main: $14* ✉ *1213 W. 18th St., Pilsen* ☎ *312/226–7427* ⊕ *www. honkytonkbbqchicago.com* ⏱ *Closed Sun.-Mon.*

☕ Coffee and Quick Bites

Cafe Jumping Bean

$ | CAFÉ | You'll find Mexican hot chocolate, focaccia pizzas, and fresh sandwiches at this cozy neighborhood coffee shop. **Known for:** colorful interior; laid-back vibe; focaccia sandwiches. ⓢ *Average main: $10* ✉ *1439 W. 18th St., Pilsen* ☎ *312/455–0019* ⊕ *cafejumpingbean.wordpress.com.*

★ Manny's Cafeteria & Delicatessen

$ | JEWISH DELI | The corned-beef sandwich here is the one that other local delis aim to beat. Manny's has always been popular with Chicago politicians—as the saying goes, so if these walls could talk, they'd spill a lot of secrets. **Known for:** the corned-beef sandwich; local fave; large portions. ⓢ *Average main: $10* ✉ *1141 S. Jefferson St., West Loop* ☎ *312/939–2855* ⊕ *www.mannysdeli.com.*

🛍 Shopping

BOOKS, MUSIC, AND GIFTS

Pilsen Community Books

BOOKS | The bookshelves here are stacked high with new and used reads in all genres. The employee-owned and-operated shop also supports local literacy programs. ✉ *1102 W. 18th St., Pilsen* ☎ *312/478–9434* ⊕ *pilsencommunitybooks.com.*

CLOTHING

Knee Deep Vintage

MIXED CLOTHING | This well-stocked vintage shop is pure flashback fun. In addition to some fashion-forward pieces, Knee Deep specializes in apparel and accessories from the '20s to the '50s, with some vintage home furnishings and ephemera thrown in there for good measure. ✉ *1219 W. 18th St., Pilsen* ☎ *312/850–2510* ⊕ *kneedeepvintage. com.*

Little Italy

To the north of Pilsen is Little Italy, which, despite the encroachment by the University of Illinois at Chicago (UIC), still contains plenty of Italian restaurants, bakeries, groceries, and sandwich shops. Taylor Street is the main drag.

Sights

St. Basil Greek Orthodox Church

CHURCH | Located near Polk Street, this gorgeous Greek Revival building, erected in 1910, has an equally lavish interior. It was originally the Anshe Sholom

Synagogue. ✉ *733 S. Ashland Ave., Little Italy* ☎ *312/243–3738* ⊕ *www.stbasilchicago.org* ✉ *Free.*

Shrine of Our Lady of Pompeii

CHURCH | Completed in 1923 and built to accommodate the area's growing number of Italian immigrants, this church is the oldest continuously operating Italian American church in Chicago. Its Romanesque Revival style was popular with the famous church architects Worthman and Steinbach, and its interior is filled with statues and striking stained-glass windows. The church sometimes serves as a venue for concerts and theatrical productions. ✉ *1224 W. Lexington St., Little Italy* ☎ *312/421–3757* ⊕ *www. ourladyofpompeii.org* ✉ *Free.*

Taylor Street

STREET | In the mid-19th century, when Italians started to migrate to Chicago, about one-third of them settled in and around Taylor Street, a 12-block stretch between Ashland and the University of Illinois at Chicago. It is best known for its Italian restaurants, though Thai food, tacos, and other ethnic options are here, too. ✉ *Little Italy.*

🍴 Restaurants

Chez Joël Bistro Français

$$ | FRENCH | Unlike the rest of Taylor Street, which is predominantly Italian in allegiance, Chez Joël waves the flag for France, and it's a favorite with the locals thanks to its authentic bistro feel. The sunny, cozy bistro serves well-prepared classics along with a reasonably priced wine list favoring French and Californian selections. **Known for:** escargots; patio seating; steak frites. $ *Average main: $27* ✉ *1119 W. Taylor St., Little Italy* ☎ *312/226–6479* ⊕ *www.chezjoelbistro. com* ☾ *Closed Sun. No lunch.*

Pompei

$ | PIZZA | FAMILY | Cheerful and reasonably priced, this fast-casual Little Italy café specializes in thick, square slices of pizza, most under $5, along with salads, sandwiches, and house-made pastas. Between the nearby University of Illinois Chicago campus and workers from the Rush University Medical District, it gets busy, but the cafeteria-style service makes it a quick, satisfying meal. **Known for:** tiramisu; super-casual atmosphere; stuffed pizza. $ *Average main: $10* ✉ *1531 W. Taylor St., Little Italy* ☎ *312/421–5179* ⊕ *www.pompeiusa. com.*

Sweet Maple Cafe

$ | AMERICAN | FAMILY | This breakfast-all-day spot is easy to find on Taylor Street: just look for the line out the door, as customers ranging from students to police officers and politicians wait for a table in anticipation of warm, buttery biscuits and a side of generous hospitality. The menu has something for everyone, from breakfast classics to well-executed salads and soups come lunchtime. **Known for:** homey vibe; create-your-own home fries; delicious French toast. $ *Average main: $10* ✉ *1339 W. Taylor St., Little Italy* ☎ *312/243–8908* ⊕ *www.sweetmaplecafe.com* ☾ *No dinner.*

☕ Coffee and Quick Bites

Mario's Italian Lemonade

$ | ICE CREAM | This seasonal stand is a big hit in Chicago's hot summers, with shaved ice served with chunks of fruit in flavors from lemon to cantaloupe. Mario's was started in 1954 by Mario DiPaolo and his son, also named Mario but known as "Skip," who still runs it, with his own family. **Known for:** adorable, Instagrammable storefront; seasonal favorite; piña colada flavor. $ *Average main: $5* ✉ *1068 W. Taylor St., Little Italy* ⊕ *http://marios-lemonade.com/* ☾ *Closed Oct.–Apr.*

The Ping Tom Memorial Park is a sprawling park along the Chicago River.

Chinatown

West of the Prairie Avenue district, this Chinese microcosm sits in the shadows of modern skyscrapers. The neighborhood is anchored by the Chinatown Gate, which spans West Cermak Road and South Wentworth Avenue. Referring to the tenacity of Chicago's first Chinese settlers, the gate's four gold characters proclaim, "The world belongs to the commonwealth." Also prominent are the enormous green-and-red pagoda towers of the Pui Tak Center, a church-based community center in the former On Leong Tong Building. Many visitors only come here to dine or to hunt for bargains in the gift and furniture shops on Wentworth Avenue, but Chinatown is more than that. Take some time to wander the streets and check out the local grocery stores, where English is rarely heard, live fish and crabs fill vats, and canned and dried items bulge from shelves.

Sights

Chinatown Square
PLAZA/SQUARE | Located on Princeton and Archer, this large square is punctuated by animal sculptures, each representing one of the 12 symbols of the Chinese zodiac. Below the sculptures is a plaque explaining the personalities of those born during each year. ⊠ *2133 S. China Pl., Chinatown.*

Nine Dragon Wall
NOTABLE BUILDING | Modeled after the one in Beijing's Beihai Park, this wall is graced by nine large and 500 smaller dragons, all signifying good fortune. It is right next to the El's Red Line Cermak-Chinatown stop. ⊠ *158 W. Cermak Rd., Chinatown.*

Ping Tom Memorial Park
CITY PARK | Four pillars carved with dragon designs adorn the entrance of this beautifully landscaped park, which is named for Chinatown's most renowned civic leader. Wedged within the shadows of railroad tracks and highways, its 12 serene riverside acres include a

children's playground, winding walking trails, a fieldhouse, and a boathouse (kayak rentals are available at the last of these in summer). A large yellow-and-red pagoda provides good views of the looming Chicago skyline to the north; March through December, you can also board a water taxi here for a scenic—and cost-effective—ride to the Loop. ✉ *1700 S. Wentworth Ave., Chinatown* 🌐 *www.chicagoparkdistrict.com/parks/ping-tom-memorial-park* 🎫 *Free.*

🍴 Restaurants

Han 202

$$$ | CHINESE | Tasting menus tend to come with sky-high prices, but that's not the case at this welcoming BYOB spot in nearby Bridgeport, where $35 gets you four courses served in a sleek, comfortable dining room. The menu is eclectic, and skews toward Chinese dishes and flavors, though there are other global influences as well among the creative offerings. **Known for:** French-leaning desserts; good value; lobster and beet salad. [$] *Average main: $35* ✉ *605 W. 31st St., Chinatown* ☎ *312/949–1314* 🌐 *www.han202.com* 🕒 *Closed Mon. No lunch.*

Harold's Chicken Shack

$ | FAST FOOD | FAMILY | Back to basics soul food is what you'll get at Harold's, which has been serving made-to-order fried chicken since the 1950s and has locations all over the city. The chicken dinner is a half or a quarter chicken (white meat, dark meat, or "regular," which is a mix), fries, 2 pieces of white bread, and a cup of coleslaw. **Known for:** everyone has a favorite location but this one is very popular; a local institution; the signature "mild sauce," believed to be a blend of barbecue sauce, ketchup, and hot sauce. [$] *Average main: $6* ✉ *2132 S. Michigan Ave., Chinatown* 🌐 *www.haroldschickenscorp.com.*

Joy Yee Noodle

$ | ASIAN | The menu at this fast-casual spot is massive and spans a variety of Asian cuisines. The mouthwatering portions are large, but the prices aren't. **Known for:** casual vibe; so many choices; fast service. [$] *Average main: $12* ✉ *Chinatown Square Mall, 2139 S. China Pl., Chinatown* ☎ *312/328–0001* 🌐 *www.joyyeechicago.com.*

Phoenix Restaurant

$ | CHINESE | The weekend bustle of this dim sum house can feel overwhelming, but Phoenix softens you up with second-floor picture-window views that frame the Loop skyline and an excellent food menu. Dim sum is dispensed from rolling carts all day long on weekends, but don't overlook the regular menu, which features an array of live seafood cooked how you like it. **Known for:** dim sum carts; char siu bao (barbecue pork buns); super-busy weekends. [$] *Average main: $15* ✉ *2131 S. Archer Ave., Chinatown* ☎ *312/328–0848* 🌐 *www.chinatownphoenix.com.*

Qing Xiang Yuan Dumplings

$ | CHINESE | Handmade dumplings are the specialty at this sleek, modern restaurant. Order them fried or steamed, packed with fillings like lamb and coriander, lobster, pork and cabbage, and many more. **Known for:** many dumpling flavors; a few nondumpling options; friendly service. [$] *Average main: $16* ✉ *2002 S. Wentworth Ave., Chinatown* ☎ *312/799–1118* 🌐 *https://qxydumplings.com/.*

The 1886 Glessner House looks like a fortress but has lavish interiors and furnishings.

University Village

To the northeast of Little Italy, University Village is the University of Illinois at Chicago's booming residential area. It's centered on Halsted Street south to 14th Street.

Sights

★ Jane Addams Hull-House Museum

HISTORY MUSEUM | Hull House was the birthplace of social work. Social welfare pioneers and peace advocates Jane Addams and Ellen Gates Starr started the American settlement house movement in this redbrick Victorian in 1889. They wrought near-miracles in the surrounding community, which was then a slum for new immigrants. Pictures and letters add context to the two museum buildings, which re-create the homey setting the residents experienced. The museum, located on the UIC campus, also hosts a range of events typically geared toward progressive social movements. ⊠ *800 S. Halsted St., University Village* ☎ *312/413–5353* ⊕ *www.hullhousemuseum.org* ✉ *Suggested donation $5* ⊙ *Closed Sat.-Mon.*

Maxwell Street Market

MARKET | Until 1967 the famed Maxwell Street Market, begun in the 1880s by Jewish immigrants, was the place to go for bargain and bargaining. Then UIC took most of the property to build university housing and the market limped along and finally closed in the 1990s. A public uproar, however, led to its relocation at South Desplaines Street, between West Polk Street and West Roosevelt Road, about ½ mile from the original site. These days the market (open the first and third Sunday of the month) welcomes more than 500 vendors sell clothing, power tools, and household items; blues musicians often play; and some of the best Mexican food in town is available. ⊠ *800 S. Desplaines St., University Village* ☎ *312/745–4676* ⊕ *www.chicago.gov/city/en/depts/dca/supp_info/maxwell_street_market.html* ✉ *Free.*

Prairie Avenue

In the 1870s the **Prairie Avenue Historic District** served as Chicago's first "*Millionaire's Row.*" After the Chicago Fire of 1871, prominent Chicagoans, including George Pullman, Marshall Field, and the Armour family, had homes in the area two blocks east of Michigan Avenue, between 18th and 22nd streets. It's close to Chinatown, where Wentworth and Archer avenues are chockablock with Asian restaurants and shops.

 Sights

Blues Heaven Foundation

HISTORY MUSEUM | For a walk into history, stop by the Blues Heaven Foundation, which occupies the former home of the legendary Chess Records. Breathe the same rarefied air as blues (and rock-and-roll) legends Muddy Waters, Howlin' Wolf, Chuck Berry, and the Rolling Stones, all of whom recorded here. Check out the Chess brothers' private offices, the recording studio, and the back stairway used only by signed musicians. Be sure to see the eerie "Life Cast Portraits" wall showcasing the plaster heads of the Chess recording artists. Tours are on hold during Covid so check back for updates. ⊠ *2120 S. Michigan Ave., Prairie Avenue* ☎ *312/808–1286* ⊕ *www.bluesheaven. com* ⊒ *$15.*

★ Glessner House

HISTORIC HOME | This fortresslike residence is the only surviving building in Chicago by architect H.H. Richardson, who also designed Boston's Trinity Church. Completed in 1886, the L-shape mansion's stone construction and short towers are characteristic of the Richardsonian Romanesque Revival style. It's also one of the few great mansions left on Prairie Avenue, once home to such heavy hitters as retailer Marshall Field and meatpacking magnate Philip Armour. The area has lately seen the arrival of new, high-end construction, but nothing beats a tour of Glessner House, a remarkable relic of the days when merchant princes really lived like royalty. Enjoy the lavish interiors and the many artifacts, from silver pieces and art glass to antique ceramics and Isaac Scott carvings and furnishings. *Guided tours* run Wednesday, Friday, and Saturday year-round. ⊠ *1800 S. Prairie Ave., Prairie Avenue* ☎ *312/326–1480* ⊕ *www.glessnerhouse.org* ⊒ *$20* ⊙ *Closed Sun.-Tues. and Thurs.*

Henry B. Clarke House Museum

HISTORIC HOME | This Greek Revival structure dates from 1836, making it Chicago's oldest surviving building. It's a clapboard house in a masonry city, built for Henry and Caroline Palmer Clarke to remind them of the East Coast they left behind. The Doric columns and pilasters were an attempt to civilize Chicago's frontier image, while the everyday objects and furnishings inside evoke a typical 1850s–60s middle-class home. The house has been moved three times from its original location on Michigan Avenue between 16th and 17th streets: the last time, in 1977, it had to be hoisted above the nearby elevated train tracks. Free tours are given Wednesday and Saturday at 1 pm. ⊠ *1827 S. Indiana Ave., Prairie Avenue* ☎ *312/744–3316* ⊕ *www. clarkehousemuseum.org* ⊒ *Free.*

Quinn Chapel

CHURCH | One of Chicago's African American cornerstones, this church was founded in 1847 and served as an Underground Railroad stop. The present building, designed by Henry Starbuck, opened in 1891, and the rough-finished brick exterior is in keeping with the time. The interior has a tin ceiling and simple stained-glass windows. Many notable people have addressed the congregation, including President William B. McKinley, Booker T. Washington, and Dr. Martin Luther King Jr. ⊠ *2401 S. Wabash Ave., South Loop* ☎ *312/791–1846* ⊕ *www. quinnchicago.org* ⊒ *Free.*

Second Presbyterian Church

CHURCH | Constructed in 1874, this handsome Gothic Revival church was designed by James Renwick, also the architect of the Smithsonian's Castle and New York City's St. Patrick's Cathedral. The National Historic Landmark features one of the largest collections of Tiffany stained-glass windows anywhere. ✉ *1936 S. Michigan Ave., Prairie Avenue* ☎ *312/225–4951* ⊕ *www.2ndpresbyterian.org* 🖼 *Free.*

The Wheeler Mansion

HISTORIC HOME | At the intersection of Calumet Avenue and Cullerton Street is another of the area's great mansions, which was nearly replaced by a parking lot before it was saved and painstakingly restored in the late 1990s. Today it's a boutique hotel with the same name. ✉ *2020 S. Calumet Ave., Prairie Avenue* ☎ *312/945–2020* ⊕ *www.wheelermansion.com.*

Chapter 6

LINCOLN PARK AND WICKER PARK

Updated by
Cate Huguelet

Sights	Restaurants	Hotels	Shopping	Nightlife
★★★★☆	★★★★☆	★★★☆☆	★★★☆☆	★★★★☆

NEIGHBORHOOD SNAPSHOT

GETTING TO LINCOLN PARK

Ride the CTA Red Line or Brown Line train to either Armitage or Fullerton Avenue. Buses 22, 36, and 151 take you through the area, too. If you're driving, take Lake Shore Drive to Fullerton Avenue and go west to Sheffield Avenue.

GETTING TO LOGAN SQUARE

Take the Kennedy Expressway to California Avenue (Exit 46A). By El, take the Blue Line toward O'Hare to Logan Square. From the Loop, take Bus 20 to Homan and Bus 82 north to Logan Square.

TOP REASONS TO GO

Enjoy the lakefront: Walk—or run or bike—on the path heading south from North Avenue Beach, and take in the breathtaking views of the city along Lake Michigan.

Get caught up in the drama: Consider a performance from all angles at internationally acclaimed ensemble group Steppenwolf's intimate theater in the round.

Shop: Browse the boutiques along Lincoln Park's Armitage Avenue or shop for funky finds on Division Street, Milwaukee Avenue, and Chicago Avenue.

Visit the animals: Say hello to the apes and other animals at the Lincoln Park Zoo. The added bonus is that it's free.

PARKLAND

A decommissioned elevated rail line running east-west from Bucktown to Humboldt Park was transformed into the 606 (named for the first three digits of Chicago's ZIP Codes), a 2.7-mile recreational trail, dotted with lush greenery and public art. It's become so popular since opening in 2015, there's been talk of extending it east, across the Chicago River and into Lincoln Park.

GETTING TO WICKER PARK/ BUCKTOWN

To drive to Wicker Park/ Bucktown, take the Kennedy Expressway to North Avenue (Exit 48B), then head west to the triangular intersection of North, Milwaukee, and Damen avenues. In the evenings, competition for metered parking can be stiff, but there's also restaurant valet service. By El, take the Blue Line to Damen Avenue. For Ukrainian Village, take the Kennedy Expressway to Augusta Boulevard (Exit 49B), bear west to Ashland Avenue, and head south to Chicago Avenue. Bus 66 also connects this area to downtown.

MAKING THE MOST OF YOUR TIME

Lincoln Park can be done with or without kids. Highlights for the little ones include the Lincoln Park Zoo, the Peggy Notebaert Nature Museum, and the beach; adults will enjoy the area's shops, eateries, and entertainment: the Steppenwolf Theatre and Old Town's Second City are quintessential experiences. The hip Wicker Park/Bucktown and Ukrainian Village neighborhoods are good for funky shopping and people-watching; Logan Square has become an exciting dining and drinking destination.

In 1864 the vast park here—which extends from North Avenue to Ardmore Avenue—became the city's first public playground. Its zoo is legendary. The area adjacent to it, bordered by Armitage Avenue, Diversey Parkway, the lake, and the Chicago River, took the same name. To the west, in Wicker Park/Bucktown and Ukrainian Village, up-to-the-minute fashions mix with old-world memories and gorgeous Victorian-era architecture. Logan Square, just west of Bucktown, is notable for its historic buildings and hip restaurants.

Lincoln Park

Today Lincoln Park epitomizes all the things that people love—and love to hate—about yuppified urban areas: stratospheric housing prices, teeny boutiques with big-attitude salespeople, and plenty of fancy-schmancy coffee shops, wine bars, and cafés. It's also got some of the prettiest residential streets in the city, that gorgeous park, a great nature museum, a thriving arts scene, and the renowned Steppenwolf Theatre.

Old Town, bordered by Division Street, Armitage Avenue, Clark Street, and Halsted Street, began in the 1850s as a modest German working-class neighborhood. Now its diverse population resides in some of the oldest (and most expensive) real estate in Chicago. Its best-known tenants are the Second City and Zanies comedy clubs.

Sights

Alfred Caldwell Lily Pool

NATURE SIGHT | The work of landscape architect Alfred Caldwell, this serene oasis—comprising a gracefully curving pond and Prairie-style pavilion amid native vegetation—hides in plain sight beside Lincoln Park Zoo's parking lot, poised to allay weary zoo warriors with a zen break. ✉ *125 W. Fullerton Pkwy., Lincoln Park* ⊕ *www.chicagoparkdistrict. com/parks-facilities/lincoln-park-alfred-caldwell-lily-pool* 🎫 *Free* ⊙ *Closed Dec.–Mar.*

★ Chicago History Museum

HISTORY MUSEUM | FAMILY | Seeking to bring Chicago's often complicated history to life, this museum has several strong permanent exhibits, including "Chicago: Crossroads of America," which celebrates homegrown cultural contributions from urban blues to the skyscraper and demystifies tragedies like the Haymarket Affair, in which a bomb thrown during a labor rally in 1884 led to eight anarchists being convicted of conspiracy. In "Sensing Chicago," kids can feel what the city was once like—they can catch a fly ball at Comiskey Park (now U.S. Cellular Field), dress up like a Chicago-style hot dog, and take a spin on a penny-farthing bicycle. "City on Fire: Chicago 1871" immerses visitors in the destruction and aftermath of the notorious inferno that displaced one-third of the city's residents in just two days. ⊠ *1601 N. Clark St., Lincoln Park* ☎ *312/642–4600* ⊕ *www. chicagohistory.org* 🖼 *$19* ⊙ *Closed Mon.*

Green City Market

MARKET | FAMILY | On Wednesday and Saturday morning from May through October, the market takes over a large swath of grass at the south end of Lincoln Park. Farm stands showcase locally grown fruits and vegetables, as well as meats, cheeses, and pastas. Visitors can also dine at food booths and watch cooking demonstrations by local celebrity chefs. ⊠ *1750 N. Clark St., near N. Lincoln Ave., Lincoln Park* ☎ *773/880–1266* ⊕ *www. chicagogreencitymarket.org* 🖼 *Free.*

Lincoln Park Conservatory

GARDEN | The tranquillity and abundant greenery inside this 1892 conservatory offer a refreshing respite in the heart of a bustling neighborhood. Stroll through permanent displays in the Palm House, Fern Room, and Orchid House, or catch special events like the fragrant Spring Flower Show. ⊠ *2391 N. Stockton Dr., Lincoln Park* ☎ *312/742–7736* ⊕ *lincoln-parkconservancy.org* 🖼 *Free* ⊙ *Closed Mon. and Tues.*

Did You Know?

Begun in 1868 with a pair of swans donated by New York's Central Park, the Lincoln Park Zoo grew through donations of animals from wealthy Chicago residents and the purchase of a collection from the Barnum & Bailey Circus.

★ Lincoln Park Zoo

ZOO | FAMILY | At this urban enclave near Lake Michigan, you can watch snow monkeys unwind in the hot springs of the Regenstein Macaque Forest or ogle gorillas and chimpanzees in the sprawling Regenstein Center for African Apes, which has three separate habitats complete with bamboo stands, termite mounds, and 5,000 feet of swinging vines. Brave big cats (separated by a window, of course) outside the Pepper Family Wildlife Center, a 2021 redesign of the zoo's lion habitat conceived with input from an app that collected data on the star residents' behavior. Animals both slithery (pythons) and strange (sloths) reside in the glass-domed Regenstein Small Mammal and Reptile House, while the big guys (hippos, giraffes, and black rhinos) are in the Regenstein African Journey.

Bird lovers should make a beeline to the McCormick Bird House, which contains extremely rare species—including the Bali mynah, Guam rail, and Guam Micronesian kingfisher, some of which are extinct in the wild. Families with little ones in tow will also want to see Farm-in-the-Zoo (with its barnyard animals and learning centers), and the Lionel Train Adventure ride. Be sure to leave time for a ride (or two) on the AT&T Endangered Species Carousel, featuring a menagerie of 48 rare and endangered animals. ⊠ *2400 N. Cannon Dr, Lincoln Park* ☎ *312/742–2000* ⊕ *www.lpzoo.org*

A lioness broods atop a rock at the Lincoln Park Zoo.

✈ *Free (additional fee for rides); parking from $20.*

Louis Sullivan row houses

HISTORIC HOME | The love of geometric ornamentation that Sullivan eventually brought to such projects as the Carson, Pirie, Scott & Co. building (now the Sullivan Center) is already visible in these row houses, built in 1885. The terracotta cornices and decorative window tops are especially beautiful. ✉ *1826–1834 N. Lincoln Park W, Lincoln Park* ✈ *Free.*

North Avenue Beach

BEACH | FAMILY | The beautiful people strut their stuff at this lakefront strand. The beachhouse, which has concession stands, a restaurant, and bike rentals, resembles a steamship, complete with upper decks for surveying the skyline. There are over 50 volleyball courts (rented by the hour), an outdoor fitness center, kayak and Jet Ski rentals, and lots of sand. **Amenities:** food and drink; lifeguards (late May–early Sept.); parking (fee); toilets; water sports. **Best for:** partiers; sunrise; swimming; walking. ✉ *1601 N. Lake Shore Dr., Lincoln Park* ⊕ *www.chicagoparkdistrict.com/parks/north-avenue-beach* ✈ *Free.*

Old Town

NEIGHBORHOOD | Old Town was known in the mid-1800s as the Cabbage Patch (for its German immigrant inhabitants' proclivity for planting, well, you guessed it) and took turns in the 20th century as a stronghold for LGBTQ rights and an incubator for artists and comedians. Today the neighborhood feels more polished and less bohemian, but hints of the old world can still be found in the narrow cobbled alleys, the tolling bells of historic St. Michael's church, and the barroom banter at mainstay Old Town Ale House. Head to Wells Street, the main drag, for independent shops and good bars and clubs (including the famed Second City). ✉ *Between Armitage Ave. and Division St., Clark and Halsted Sts., Lincoln Park* ☎ *312/951–6106* ⊕ *www.oldtownchicago.org* ✈ *Free.*

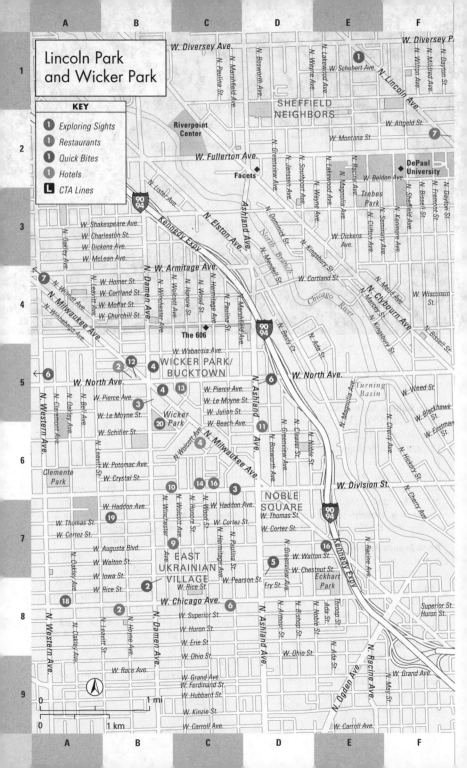

Sights ▼

1 Alfred Caldwell
   Lily Pool I2
2 Chicago History
   Museum I5
3 Division Street C6
4 Flat Iron
   Arts Building B5
5 Green City Market I4
6 Humboldt Park A5
7 Intuit: The Center for
   Intuitive and
   Outsider Art A4
8 Lincoln Park
   Conservatory..............I2
9 Lincoln Park Zoo..........I3
10 Louis Sullivan
   row houses I4
11 North Avenue Beach.....I4
12 Northwest Tower
   Building B5
13 Old Town.................H5
14 Oz Park...................G3
15 Peggy Notebaert
   Nature Museum I2
16 Polish Museum
   of America................E7
17 St. Valentine's Day
   Massacre Site H3
18 Ukrainian Institute
   of Modern Art A8
19 Ukrainian Village
   Landmark District....... B7
20 Wicker Park............. B6

Restaurants ▼

1 Alinea G4
2 All Together Now B8
3 Big Star B5
4 Boka...................... G4
5 Cafe Ba-Ba-Reeba! F3
6 Funkenhausen C8
7 Galit F2
8 Kamehachi I5
9 Kasama B7
10 Milk & Honey Café...... B6
11 Mott Street D6
12 North Pond H1
13 Piece C5
14 Smoke Daddy C6
15 Sushi Suite 202............I4
16 Tortello C6
17 Twin Anchors
   Restaurant & Tavern ... H4

Quick Bites ▼

1 Batter & Berries E1
2 Black Dog Gelato B8
3 Evette's...................H3
4 Goddess
   and Grocer B5
5 Junebug Cafe D7
6 Phodega D5
7 R.J. Grunt's H3

Hotels ▼

1 Hotel Lincoln I4
2 The Robey Chicago..... B5
3 Villa D'Citta
   Boutique Mansion....... F3
4 Wicker Park Inn..........C6

Oz Park

CITY PARK | **FAMILY** | Fans of *The Wizard of Oz* love getting up close with Dorothy, Toto, and all the other beloved characters assembled here in sculpture form. Author L. Frank Baum lived in Chicago at the turn of the 20th century. The park, located between Webster and Dickens avenues and Burling and Larrabee streets, also has a flowery Emerald Garden and play lot for pint-size visitors. ✉ *2021 N. Burling St., Lincoln Park* ☎ *312/742–7898* 🌐 *www.chicagoparkdistrict.com/parks/oz-park* 🎟 *Free.*

Peggy Notebaert Nature Museum

SCIENCE MUSEUM | **FAMILY** | Walk among hundreds of species of tropical butterflies and learn about the impact of rivers and lakes on daily life at this modern, light-washed museum. Like Chicago's other science museums, this one is perfect for kids, but even jaded adults may be excited when bright yellow butterflies land on their shoulders. The idea is to connect with nature inside without forgetting graceful Lincoln Park outside. Interesting temporary exhibits round out the offerings. ✉ *2430 N. Cannon Dr., Lincoln Park* ☎ *773/755–5100* 🌐 *www.naturemuseum.org* 🎟 *$9.*

St. Valentine's Day Massacre site

HISTORIC SIGHT | On Clark Street near Dickens, there's a rather inconspicuous parking lot next to a senior apartment building where the SMC Cartage Company once stood. There's no marker, but it's the site of the infamous St. Valentine's Day Massacre, when seven men were killed on the orders of Al Capone on February 14, 1929. The massacre targeted Capone's main rival in the illegal liquor trade, Bugs Moran. Though Moran wasn't in the warehouse that day, he was finished as a bootlegger. The event shocked the city and came to epitomize the violence of the Prohibition era. ✉ *2122 N. Clark St., Lincoln Park* 🎟 *Free.*

🍴 Restaurants

★ Alinea

$$$$ | **MODERN AMERICAN** | Believe the hype and secure tickets—yes, tickets—well in advance, since Chicago's most exciting restaurant demands an adventurous spirit and a serious commitment of time and money. If you have three hours and $295 to $435 to spare, the 10- to 18-course tasting menu that showcases Grant Achatz's stunning, cutting-edge food is a fantastic journey through intriguing aromas, visuals, flavors, and textures. **Known for:** interactive presentations; impeccable service; wine pairings. [$] *Average main: $355* ✉ *1723 N. Halsted St., Lincoln Park* ☎ *312/867–0110* 🌐 *www.alinearestaurant.com* 🕒 *Closed Mon. and Tues. No lunch.*

★ Boka

$$$$ | **MODERN AMERICAN** | If you're looking for a Steppenwolf pretheater dinner on North Halsted Street, this upscale spot gets the foodie stamp of approval. The seasonally driven menu is constantly changing, showcasing elegant fare like slow-cooked Arctic char or an elevated presentation of roasted chicken, and the slick bar and outdoor patio both serve food, so this is a big draw even for those not watching curtain time. **Known for:** excellent desserts; intimate atmosphere; notable cocktail list. [$] *Average main: $38* ✉ *1729 N. Halsted St., Lincoln Park* ☎ *312/337–6070* 🌐 *www.bokachicago.com* 🕒 *No lunch.*

Cafe Ba-Ba-Reeba!

$ | **SPANISH** | The name is so cute, you might not think the food is a selling point—but you'd be wrong: expat Spaniards swear this is one of the best Spanish restaurants in town, and the colorful Mediterranean-style interiors encourage the Spanish feel. There's a large assortment of cold and warm tapas, as well as four varieties of paella. **Known for:** Spanish wines; outdoor patio; six types of sangria. [$] *Average main:*

$15 ✉ *2024 N. Halsted St., Lincoln Park* ☎ *773/935–5000* 🌐 *www.cafebabareeba.com* ⏲ *No lunch Mon.–Thurs.*

Galit

$$$$ | **MIDDLE EASTERN** | Chef Zachary Engel has established himself as a critical favorite for his approach to Middle Eastern cuisine, which merges fine dining technique with big flavors and a disarming sense of humor that's telegraphed through cheeky menu descriptions (e.g., tehina hummus with "way too much olive oil"). **Known for:** brisket; four-course prix-fixe menu; flavorful vegetarian options. [$] *Average main: $65* ✉ *2429 N. Lincoln Ave., Lincoln Park* 🌐 *www.galitrestaurant.com* ⏲ *Closed Sun. and Mon. No lunch.*

Kamehachi

$$ | **JAPANESE** | It seems like there's a sushi spot on practically every corner in Chicago, but when Kamehachi opened in Old Town in 1967 it was the first, though the restaurant has since moved to a loftier space complete with sushi bar, upstairs lounge, and flowering garden (in season). Excellent quality fish, updated decor, and eager-to-please hospitality keep fans returning, and the combination sushi meals are a relative bargain, running from $19 to $38. **Known for:** noodle dishes; sake list; top-quality fish. [$] *Average main: $21* ✉ *1531 N. Wells St., Lincoln Park* ☎ *312/664–3663* 🌐 *www.kamehachi.com.*

★ North Pond

$$$$ | **AMERICAN** | A former Arts and Crafts–style warming house for ice-skaters at Lincoln Park's North Pond, this romantic gem in the woods fittingly champions an uncluttered culinary style amid scenic views. Organic ingredients, wild-caught fish, and artisanal farm products appear on the seasonally changing menus. **Known for:** cozy fireplace; Sunday brunch; organic and biodynamic wines. [$] *Average main: $38* ✉ *2610 N. Cannon Dr., Lincoln Park* ☎ *773/477–5845* 🌐 *www.northpondrestaurant.com*

Did You Know?

Another infamous Lincoln Park locale is the Biograph Theater, now home to the Victory Gardens Theater (*2433 N. Lincoln Ave., 773/871–3000, victorygardens.org*). Notorious bank robber John Dillinger was shot and killed here by the FBI in 1934.

⏲ *Closed Mon.–Wed. Closed for seasonal hiatus in Jan. No lunch Thurs.–Sat.*

Sushi Suite 202

$$$$ | **JAPANESE** | Hidden behind an unassuming door at Hotel Lincoln awaits one of Chicago's most intimate dining experiences, Sushi Suite 202. With just six seats and a micro lounge, the sleek space may be small, but the experience is over the top: over 75 minutes, you'll watch chef Jordan Dominguez craft a 17-course omakase-style menu of fresh and flavorful nigiri and other bites. **Known for:** sophisticated digs; Hokkaido uni; sake dispenser. [$] *Average main: $155* ✉ *1816 N. Clark St., Lincoln Park* ☎ *312/254–4700 Hotel Lincoln front desk* 🌐 *www.sushibybou.com/sushi-suite-202* ⏲ *Closed Mon. and Tues. No lunch.*

Twin Anchors Restaurant & Tavern

$$ | **AMERICAN** | For a taste of classic Chicago, stop into Twin Anchors, which has been dishing out baby back ribs since 1932—the nautically themed brick tavern was a favorite of Frank Sinatra, who still croons regularly over the speakers. You're partly visiting for the scene, as local and touring celebs often visit, but lovers of barrooms with personality don't mind the typically long waits during prime time. **Known for:** casual atmosphere; pulled pork sandwich; classic cocktails. [$] *Average main: $21* ✉ *1655 N. Sedgwick St., Lincoln Park* ☎ *312/266–1616* 🌐 *www.twinanchorsribs.com* ⏲ *No lunch weekdays.*

Did You Know?

The Lincoln Park Conservancy has developed an exciting plan for this 130-year-old pond and the 36 acres surrounding it: the lake will be deepened to improve water quality and restore aquatic habitat; existing play areas will be redeveloped; and brand-new green spaces will be created with an eye toward reducing stress on the pond's shoreline.

Coffee and Quick Bites

Batter & Berries

$ | **AMERICAN** | Bright yellow walls and a soundtrack of classic house music make for a convivial atmosphere at this daytime spot, a favorite with students from nearby DePaul University for its menu of carb-y breakfast dishes hearty enough to fuel diners till dinner. **Known for:** casual ambience; French toast flights; fried chicken-stuffed waffles. [$] *Average main: $15* ✉ *2748 N. Lincoln Ave., Lincoln Park* ☎ *773/248–7710* 🌐 *https://batterandberries.com* 🕒 *No dinner.*

Evette's

$ | **LEBANESE** | This all-day counter service spot crosses Lebanese and Mexican flavors with some kooky notions (halloumi tacos, baklava blended into a milk shake), to fun and tasty results. It's situated in cheerful digs a stone's throw from Lincoln Park Zoo–a good place to walk off overindulgence guilt. **Known for:** shawarma fries; chicken arabe tacos; hip atmosphere. [$] *Average main: $13* ✉ *350 W. Armitage Ave., Lincoln Park* ☎ *773/799–8478* 🌐 *www.evetteschicago.com* 🕒 *Closed Tues.*

R.J. Grunt's

$ | **BURGER** | **FAMILY** | Just outside Lincoln Park Zoo, R.J. Grunts has been serving killer milk shakes and burgers since 1971. **Known for:** kid-friendly environment; American diner classics; the first "Lettuce Entertain You" restaurant. [$] *Average main: $17* ✉ *2056 N. Lincoln Park W, Lincoln Park* ☎ *773/929–5363* 🌐 *www.rjgruntschicago.com.*

Hotels

Hotel Lincoln

$$ | **HOTEL** | **FAMILY** | Directly across from Lincoln Park, this historic property has a cool, kitschy vibe but still feels authentic, thanks to details like the original Hotel Lincoln sign in the lobby. **Pros:** authentic vintage Chicago feel; pet-friendly; great residential neighborhood. **Cons:** no spa; bathrooms are small and dated; a/c units are noisy. [$] *Rooms from: $279* ✉ *1816 N. Clark St., Lincoln Park* ☎ *312/254–4700 front desk, 888/591–1234 reservations* 🌐 *www.hotellincolnchicago.com* 🛏 *184 rooms* 🍴 *No Meals.*

Villa D'Citta Boutique Mansion

$$ | **B&B/INN** | This Tuscan-theme bed-and-breakfast—complete with a (shared) fully stocked gourmet kitchen—allows guests all the comforts of a top-notch hotel in a residential neighborhood where such rooms can be hard to find. **Pros:** steps away from dozens of boutiques; meticulous innkeeper keeps the rooms well cared for; bustling neighborhood. **Cons:** some rooms have detached bathrooms; on-site parking costs extra; some guests have complained of noise. [$] *Rooms from: $299* ✉ *2230 N. Halsted St., Lincoln Park* ☎ *312/771–0696, 800/228–6070* 🌐 *www.villadcitta.com* 🛏 *7 rooms* 🍴 *Free Breakfast.*

Nightlife

BARS

Delilah's

BARS | A rare dive bar amid Lincoln Park's tonier establishments, Delilah's is dark and a bit grungy. But the bar has a friendly, unpretentious vibe and a standout whiskey selection (more than 800 types are on offer). DJs spin punk, ska, and rockabilly. ✉ *2771 N. Lincoln Ave., Lincoln Park* ☎ *773/472–2771* 🌐 *www.delilahschicago.com.*

The J. Parker

COCKTAIL LOUNGES | On the 13th-floor rooftop of the Lincoln Hotel, this sprawling bar offers both excellent cocktails and the finest vantage point in the neighborhood. An impressive retractable roof means you could end up jockeying for a seat come rain or shine (or even snow). Be advised that the secret's well out among locals and access is first come, first served; a wait is probable during the warmer months. ✉ *1816 N. Clark St., Lincoln Park* ☎ *312/254–4747* ⊕ *www. jparkerchicago.com.*

Mousetrap

BREWPUBS | Local beer geeks flock to this minimalist taproom, stationed along a rather unassuming stretch of repurposed industrial buildings, to sample the latest pours from Off Color Brewing. Traditional European styles with a twist (Berliner weiss brewed with chardonnay grapes, for instance) are the order of the day here. ✉ *1460 N. Kingsbury St., Lincoln Park* ☎ *312/929–2916* ⊕ *www.offcolor-brewing.com.*

★ **Old Town Ale House**

BARS | Just a stone's throw from Second City, Old Town Ale House has attracted a diverse cast of characters since it opened in 1958, including comedy legends John Belushi and Bill Murray. With eclectic artwork, a mural of bar denizens painted in the '70s, and an on-site lending library, it's a dingy neighborhood bar unlike any other in the city—perhaps the country. Esteemed film critic Roger Ebert called it "the best bar in the world." ✉ *219 W. North Ave., Near North Side* ☎ *312/944–7020* ⊕ *www.theoldtownalehouse.com.*

COMEDY AND IMPROV CLUBS

★ **Second City**

COMEDY CLUBS | The epicenter of comedy since 1959, The Second City has launched the careers of countless comedy legends. Alumni include Bill Murray, Catherine O'Hara, Stephen Colbert, Tina Fey, and Keegan-Michael Key. The revues on the company's historic Mainstage and more intimate e.t.c. space are fully realized sketch comedy shows, but the prescripted material is developed through improvisation in front of audiences. There's always plenty of time in each show devoted to demonstrating the comedy chops of the quick-witted performers. Most nights, a free improv set after the late show features cast members and invited guests (sometimes famous, sometimes not). UP Comedy Club

presents award-winning touring shows, comedy festivals, and special guest performances. In Donny's Skybox upstairs, you're likely to see one of Chicago's many fledgling improv comedy troupes debuting fresh material. ✉ *230 W. North Ave., Near North Side* ☎ *312/337–3992* ⊕ *www.secondcity.com.*

Zanies Comedy Night Club

COMEDY CLUBS | Zanies books outstanding national talent and is Chicago's best stand-up comedy spot. Dave Chappelle, Ali Wong, and Jeff Garlin have all performed at this intimate venue. ✉ *1548 N. Wells St., Near North Side* ☎ *312/337–4027* ⊕ *chicago.zanies.com.*

MUSIC VENUES

BLUES

Kingston Mines

LIVE MUSIC | In 1968, Kingston Mines went down in Chicago history as the first blues club to open on the North Side. Though it's since moved to bigger digs, it still offers the same traditional sounds and late-night hours as the original club. Swarms of blues lovers and partying singles take in the good blues and tasty barbecue. ✉ *2548 N. Halsted St., Lincoln Park* ☎ *773/477–4646* ⊕ *www.kingston-mines.com* ⊙ *Closed Sun.–Wed.*

ROCK

Lincoln Hall

LIVE MUSIC | The owners of Lincoln Hall transformed a former movie theater into an intimate concert space with great sight lines, an excellent sound system, and a wraparound balcony with seating. The booking is always on point, so it's worth taking a chance on a lesser-known band. A separate bar up front pours pre-show pints from local breweries. ✉ *2424 N. Lincoln Ave., Lincoln Park* ☎ *773/525–2501* ⊕ *www.lh-st.com.*

 Performing Arts

FILM

Facets
FILM | FAMILY | Film buffs shouldn't leave Lincoln Park without visiting this long-running nonprofit movie theater, which presents an eclectic selection of films from around the world. Each year, Facets also hosts the Academy Award–qualifying Chicago International Children's Film Festival: the massive (think upward of 250 screenings) event showcases the best in culturally diverse, value-affirming new cinema for kids and offers young viewers opportunities to chat with film-makers. ⊠ *1517 W. Fullerton Ave., Lincoln Park* ☎ *773/281–9075* ⊕ *www.facets.org* ◔ *Closed Mon.–Thurs.*

THEATER

★ Steppenwolf
THEATER | Steppenwolf's alumni roster speaks for itself: John Malkovich, Gary Sinise, Joan Allen, and Laurie Metcalf all honed their chops with this troupe. The company's trademark cutting-edge acting style and consistently successful productions have won national acclaim. An ultramodern 2021 expansion added a 400-seat theater in the round, an educa-tion center, and two bars to the compa-ny's already-impressive assets. ⊠ *1650 N. Halsted St., Lincoln Park* ☎ *312/335–1650* ⊕ *www.steppenwolf.org.*

Victory Gardens Theater
THEATER | Known for diverse storytelling and Chicago premieres, this company stages all of its plays in the impressive 299-seat, proscenium-thrust Biograph Theater (the site of John Dillinger's infa-mous demise). ⊠ *2433 N. Lincoln Ave., Lincoln Park* ☎ *773/871–3000* ⊕ *www. victorygardens.org.*

🛍 Shopping

Upscale Lincoln Park features a mix of distinctive boutiques and national chains. It's been an established shopping destination for more than 25 years and still retains its character and homey feel (chalk it up to those tree-lined streets and brownstone residences). On Armitage Avenue is a key street, where you'll find everything from stylish clothing and shoes to bath products and pet accessories. Around the corner on Halsted Street, independent shops like the Chicago-born Monica + Andy kids and baby boutique are dotted in among big-name clothing stores. Hit North and Clybourn avenues for hip housewares from interior designer favorite Jayson Home and others.

BEAUTY

Aroma Workshop
PERFUME | Customize lotions, massage oils, and bath salts with more than 150 essential and eau de parfum-grade fragrance oils during a 40–60 minute, perfumer-led Signature Scent Creation session in this beauty boutique. Every customer-created formula is stored in an online database, so reordering your new trademark aroma is a breeze. ⊠ *2110 N. Halsted St., Lincoln Park* ☎ *773/871–1985* ⊕ *www.aromaworkshop.com.*

BOOKS, STATIONERY, AND MUSIC

Judy Maxwell Home
GENERAL STORE | Off-kilter fun is the unify-ing principle behind the eclectic goods at Judy Maxwell Home, a modern general store owned by Chicago-bred actress Joan Cusack. Pop in to buy exploding golf balls, an ant farm, or earrings shaped like tiny pizza slices for that friend with the wacky sense of humor. ⊠ *1349 N. Wells St., Lincoln Park* ☎ *312/787–9999* ⊕ *www.judymaxwellhome.com.*

CHILDREN'S CLOTHING

Monica + Andy
CHILDREN'S CLOTHING | FAMILY | A beautiful boutique that is also where moms and moms-to-be find a social scene, thanks to story and music times. The clothing for newborns, babies, and toddlers is

Continued on page 179

CHICAGO SINGS THE BLUES

Cool, electric, urban blues are the soundtrack of the Windy City. The blues traveled up the Mississippi River with the Delta sharecroppers during the Great Migration, settled down on Maxwell Street and South Side clubs, and gave birth to such big-name talent as Muddy Waters, Howlin' Wolf, Willie Dixon, and, later, Koko Taylor. Today, you can still hear the blues in a few South Side clubs where it all began, or check out the current scene on the North Side. *Check the listings in the chapters for specifics.*

Clockwise from top left: Chicago Jazz & Blues at the Chicago History Museum; Chicago Blues Festival; Chicago Blues Festival; Carlos Johnson performing at Rosa's Lounge

THE BIRTH OF THE CHICAGO BLUES

CHESS RECORDS

Founded by Philip and Leonard Chess, Polish immigrant brothers, in 1947. For the first two years, the label was called Aristocrat. Its famous address, 2120 S. Michigan Avenue, was the nucleus of the blues scene. Up-and-comers performed on the sidewalk out front in hopes of being discovered. Even today, locals and visitors peek through the windows of the restored studio (now the Blues Heaven Foundation) looking for glimpses of past glory.

The label's first hit record was Muddy Waters' *I Can't Be Satisfied.*

The brothers were criticized for having a paternalistic relationship with their artists. They reportedly bought Muddy Waters a car off the lot when he wasn't able to finance it himself.

The company was immortalized in the excellent 2008 film *Cadillac Records*, which starred Adrian Brody.

Did you know? When the Rolling Stones recorded the track "2120 South Michigan Avenue" (off the *12 x 5* album) at the Chess Records studio in June 1964, the young Brits were reportedly so nervous about singing in front of Willie Dixon (Buddy Guy and Muddy Waters were also hanging around the studio that day) that they literally became tongue-tied. As a result, the song is purely instrumental.

WILLIE DIXON (July 1, 1915–Jan. 29, 1992) Chess Records' leading A & R (artist and repertoire) man, bass player, and composer. Founded the Blues Heaven Foundation, Chess Records' restored office and studio. *See Blues Heaven Foundation review next page.*

Famous compositions: "Hoochie Coochie Man" (recorded by Muddy Waters), "My Babe" (recorded by Little Walter), and "Wang Dang Doodle" (recorded by Koko Taylor)

MUDDY WATERS: KING OF ELECTRIC BLUES (4/1915–4/1983)

When Muddy Waters gave his guitar an electric jolt, he didn't just revolutionize the blues. His electric guitar became a magic wand: Its jive talk (and cry) turned country-blues into city-blues, and it gave birth to rock and roll. Waters's signature sound has been firmly imprinted on nearly all subsequent musical genres.

Best known for: Riveting vocals, a swooping pompadour, and, of course, plugging in the guitar

Biggest break: Leonard Chess, one of the Chess brothers of Chess Records, let Waters record two of his own songs. The record sold out in two days, and stores issued a dictum of "one per customer."

Biggest song: "Hoochie Coochie Man"

Lyrics: *Y'know I'm here / Everybody knows I'm here / And I'm the hoochie-coochie man*

Awards: 3 Grammies, Lifetime Achievement induction into the Rock and Roll Hall of Fame

Local honor: A strip of 43rd Street in Chicago is renamed Muddy Waters Drive.

HOWLIN' WOLF (June 10, 1910–Jan. 10, 1976)

In 1951, at the age of 41, Wolf recorded with Sun Studios in Memphis, TN. Shortly thereafter, Sun sold Wolf's only two songs, "Moanin' At Midnight" and "How Many More Years," to Chess Records, kicking off his prolific recording career with Chess.

Most popular songs: "Backdoor Man" and "Little Red Rooster"

Instruments: Electric guitar and harmonica

Dedication to his craft: Wolf was still taking guitar lessons even a year before his death, even though he was long recognized as one of the two greatest blues musicians in the world.

DON'T-MISS ACTS

Classic slide-guitar and hard-driving blues beats mixed with jazz and even rock 'n' roll influences makes **Melvin Taylor & The Slack Band** a must-see. Call Rosa's Lounge for details. **Billy Branch and the Sons of Blues** frequently bring their forward-thinking sounds (steeped in blues tradition) to Rosa's Lounge and Kingston Mines, though they have been known to make rousing onstage appearances at the Chicago Blues Festival.

top-quality, with organic fabrics in adorable original prints you'll want to post on Instagram. ⊠ *2052 N. Halsted St., Lincoln Park* ☎ *312/600–8530* ⊕ *www.monicaandandy.com.*

CLOTHING
Art Effect

WOMEN'S CLOTHING | This modern-day general store stocks trendy clothes and accessories at a wide range of price points. Pretty prairie dresses, stylish denim, and handmade necklaces share space with quirky-cool gifts and home furnishings, ranging from candles and bath products to mortar-and-pestle sets and cookbooks. ⊠ *934 W. Armitage Ave., Lincoln Park* ☎ *773/929–3600* ⊕ *www.shoparteffect.com.*

FOOD AND TREATS
★ The Spice House

FOOD | The Spice House draws rave reviews from local home cooks and glossy national food mags alike for its head-spinning range of top quality spices sourced from around the globe. At the brand's Old Town outpost, an aromatic storefront with a modern apothecary vibe, you can shop for edible reminders of your Chicago sojourn in the form of spice blends created to capture the essence of the city's neighborhoods. ⊠ *1512 N. Wells St., Lincoln Park* ☎ *312/274–0378* ⊕ *www.thespicehouse.com.*

HOME DECOR
★ Jayson Home

HOUSEWARES | Loaded with new and vintage European and American furnishings, this decor store is elegance defined, with an offbeat touch thrown in for good measure. Look for tribal throws, geometric vases, handsome art and gardening books and the decorative odds and ends you never knew you needed. (Antique player piano roll anyone?) ⊠ *1885 N. Clybourn Ave., Lincoln Park* ☎ *800/472–1885* ⊕ *www.jaysonhome.com.*

JEWELRY AND ACCESSORIES
The Tie Bar

MEN'S CLOTHING | If you're in need of a new necktie, the Tie Bar's flagship store is the place for you. It stocks everything from funky bow ties to more traditional styles, with pocket squares to match—all bargain-priced, considering the quality. ⊠ *918 W. Armitage Ave., Lincoln Park* ☎ *312/241–1299* ⊕ *www.thetiebar.com.*

LINGERIE
Underthings

LINGERIE | For over 40 years this small but well-stocked boutique has furnished locals with pretty but functional bras, panties, and pajamas as well as sexy lingerie. Nowadays, owner Maria Ashby reports outfitting the offspring of her original customers—a testament to her personable service. ⊠ *804 W. Webster Ave., Lincoln Park* ☎ *773/472–9291.*

SHOES, HANDBAGS, AND LEATHER GOODS
Fleet Feet Sports

SPORTING GOODS | Serious runners sprint over here for expert running shoe fittings, which entail 3-D foot mapping and a thorough gait analysis. Athletic wear and sports gear round out the offerings at its four Chicago stores. ⊠ *1706 N. Wells St., Lincoln Park* ☎ *312/587–3338* ⊕ *www.fleetfeetchicago.com.*

★ Lori's Designer Shoes

SHOES | Owner Lori Andre's obsession with shoes takes her on regular trips to Europe to hunt for styles you won't likely see at department stores. The result is an inventory that many consider to be the best in Chicago. Shoes by designers like Jeffrey Campbell, Vagabond, and Marc Fisher are sold in a self-serve atmosphere. Terrific handbags, jewelry, bridal shoes, and other accessories are also available. ⊠ *824 W. Armitage Ave., Lincoln Park* ☎ *773/281–5655* ⊕ *www.lorisshoes.com.*

TOYS

Rotofugi

TOYS | A toy store for grown-up kids, Rotofugi specializes in artist-created, limited-edition playthings. You'll find dozens of lines from the United States, Hong Kong, China, and Japan, like Pop Mart blind boxes and fanciful figures by artists like Kasing Lung and Shoko Nakazawa. The store also hosts revolving gallery exhibitions. ⊠ *2780 N. Lincoln Ave., Lincoln Park* ☎ *773/868–3308* ⊕ *rotofugi. com.*

Wicker Park

Wicker Park, the area south of North Avenue to Division Street, is inhabited by creative types, young families, university students, and older but hip professionals. Art galleries, coffeehouses, nightclubs, and funky shops line its streets—it's a far cry from the Mag Mile. Along Hoyne and Pierce avenues, near the triangular park that gives the neighborhood its name, you'll find some of the biggest and best examples of Chicago's Victorian-era architecture. So many brewery owners built homes in this area that it was once dubbed Beer Baron Row. Farther south is Ukrainian Village, so named for the influx of immigrants who began settling there in the late 19th century. The area's Slavic identity remains very real today; notices written exclusively in Cyrillic script pepper the windows of local businesses, and on Chicago Avenue you're never more than a *varenyky*'s throw from a Ukrainian deli. Make no mistake, though: gentrification has arrived here, and old school spots co-exist (for now) with tasting menu restaurants and vintage stores patronized by young residents well-heeled enough to afford the burgeoning rents.

 Sights

Division Street

BUSINESS DISTRICT | Serving as the border that separates Wicker Park from Ukrainian Village to its south, Division Street has become a shopping and dining destination in its own right. Bars, boutiques, and trendy restaurants line the once-gritty thoroughfare, which lent its name to journalist Studs Terkel's 1967 book about urban life. To start your exploration, head west on the stretch of Division between Ashland and Leavitt avenues. ⊠ *Division St. between Ashland Ave. and Leavitt St., Ukrainian Village* ☒ *Free.*

Flat Iron Arts Building

NOTABLE BUILDING | This distinctive three-story, terracotta structure sits opposite the Northwest Tower. Its creaky upper floors have long served as a sort of informal arts colony, providing studio and gallery space for a number of visual artists, whose work can be viewed at monthly First Friday open studio events (or on impromptu strolls through the hallways). ⊠ *1579 N. Milwaukee Ave., Wicker Park* ⊕ *www.flatironartists.com* ☒ *Free.*

Humboldt Park

CITY PARK | **FAMILY** | Another Chicago under-the-radar gem, this park was designed by William Le Baron Jenney in the mid-1800s and his work was expanded upon several years later by Jens Jensen. The 1907 Prairie School boathouse is the park's centerpiece, home to free cultural events and swan pedal boat rentals. The park has a formal garden, tennis courts, baseball fields, bike paths, and the city's only inland beach. In 2019 Humboldt Park temporarily became the subject of local obsession when an immature alligator—likely someone's illegal pet—was spotted in its lagoon; rest assured Chance the Snapper (as he was lovingly dubbed) was quickly captured and relocated to a Florida gator sanctuary. ⊠ *1400 N. Sacramento Ave.,*

Logan Square ☎ *312/742–7549* ⊕ *www.chicagoparkdistrict.com/parks-facilities/humboldt-alexander-von-park* 🖃 *Free.*

Intuit: The Center for Intuitive and Outsider Art

ART MUSEUM | Intuit showcases work from creators outside the artistic mainstream, many of whom used whatever supplies they had at their disposal to realize their vision. Collectively it's a testament to the force of the creative impulse, no matter one's background. Temporary exhibitions change throughout the year, but the heart of the center is its Henry Darger collection, a vast selection of oversize works and ephemera—think volumes of writing, balls of twine, pencil stubs, hordes of comic books—discovered in the cramped one-room apartment where the then-anonymous Chicagoan lived at the time of his death. A re-creation of Darger's living quarters was disassembled for conservation assessment in late 2021, but some of the artist's work will remain on view while the room's needs are examined. ⊠ *756 N. Milwaukee Ave., West Town* ☎ *312/624–9487* ⊕ *art.org* 🖃 *$5* ⊗ *Closed Mon.–Wed.*

Northwest Tower Building (*Coyote Building*)

HOTEL | Erected in 1929, this triangular, 12-story art deco office building is the anchor of the North-Milwaukee–Damen intersection and is used as a reference point from miles around. According to the *Chicago Tribune*, some artists dubbed it the Coyote Building in the 1980s, because they thought that the base attaching the flagpole to the rest of the tower "resembled a coyote howling at the moon." The tower has a café on the ground floor, a hotel (The Robey Chicago), a lounge, and a club. ⊠ *1600 N. Milwaukee Ave., Wicker Park* ☎ *872/315–3050* ⊕ *www.therobey.com* 🖃 *Free.*

Polish Museum of America

HISTORY MUSEUM | The Chicago Metro area has the largest Polish population of any city outside Warsaw, and this museum celebrates that fact. Take a trip to the old country by strolling through exhibits of folk costumes, memorabilia from Pope John Paul II, American Revolutionary War heroes Tadeusz Kosciuszko and Casimir Pulaski, and pianist and composer Ignacy Paderewski. There's also Hussar armor and an 8-foot-long sleigh in the shape of a dolphin. It's a good place to catch up on your reading, too—the library has almost 100,000 volumes in Polish and English. ⊠ *984 N. Milwaukee Ave., Wicker Park* ☎ *773/384–3352* ⊕ *www.polishmuseumofamerica.org* 🖃 *$10* ⊗ *Closed Sun., Mon., Wed., and Fri.*

Ukrainian Institute of Modern Art

ART MUSEUM | Modern and contemporary art fans with an interest in the artistic achievements of the Ukrainian diaspora head to this small museum at the far western edge of the Ukrainian Village. One of its two galleries is dedicated to changing exhibitions; the other features the museum's permanent collection of mixed media, sculpture, and painting from the 1950s to the present. Some of the most interesting works are kinetic steel-wire sculptures by Konstantin Milonadis, the constructed reliefs of Ron Kostyniuk, and painted wood structures by Mychajlo Urban. ⊠ *2320 W. Chicago Ave., Ukrainian Village* ☎ *773/227–5522* ⊕ *www.uima-chicago.org* 🖃 *$5* ⊗ *Closed Mon. and Tues.*

Ukrainian Village Landmark District

HISTORIC DISTRICT | For a glimpse of how the working class lived at the turn of the 20th century, head south of Wicker Park to the Ukrainian Village. In its center, on Haddon Avenue and on Thomas and Cortez streets between Damen Avenue and Leavitt Street, you'll find a well-preserved group of workers' cottages and apartments. At the corner of Leavitt and Haddon Streets, gilded cupolas mark Holy Trinity Orthodox Cathedral (tours offered occasionally; schedule at holytrinitycathedral.net), an early-20th-century church designed by renowned Chicago

The Wicker Park neighborhood is named after this small park with a fountain at its center.

architect Louis Sullivan. ✉ *Between Division St. and Chicago Ave., Western and Damen Aves.., Ukrainian Village* 🎟 *Free.*

Wicker Park

CITY PARK | This triangular little patch of green, donated to the city in 1870 by politician Charles Wicker, is a neighborhood favorite and home to softball fields, a children's water playground, a winter ice rink, a dog park, and outdoor movies. It's a great spot for chilling out and people-watching in warm weather. ✉ *Between N. Damen and N. Wicker Park Aves. and W. Schiller St., Wicker Park* ☎ *312/742–7553* 🌐 *www.wickerpark-bucktown.com* 🎟 *Free.*

🍴 Restaurants

All Together Now

$$ | **WINE BAR** | The mood is easy-breezy but the food and beverage offerings are seriously good at this snug Ukrainian Village all-day café/bottle shop/grocery. Nibble on artisan charcuterie, low-intervention wine at hand, or feast on seasonally changing mains. **Known for:** vegetarian-friendly; oenophile staffers; light-filled digs. $ *Average main: $22* ✉ *2019 W. Chicago Ave., Wicker Park* 🌐 *https://alltogethernow.fun* 🕒 *Closed Mon.*

★ Big Star

$ | **MEXICAN** | The second the sun peeks out each spring, locals make a beeline for the 250-seat patio at Big Star because the tacos and margaritas are some of the best in the city. Most of this honky-tonk taqueria's star power comes from executive chef/partner Paul Kahan and chef de cuisine Chris Miller, who serve a small menu of tasty Mexican classics—if it's a taco emergency, skip the wait for a table and head to the take-out window or try the larger Wrigleyville location. **Known for:** tacos, tacos, tacos; whiskey list; queso fundido. $ *Average main: $8* ✉ *1531 N. Damen Ave., Wicker Park* ☎ *773/235–4039* 🌐 *www.bigstarchicago.com.*

Funkenhausen

$$ | **GERMAN** | German-meets-Southern-American might not be a culinary mashup you see every day, but it's being executed to tasty ends here—think Oktoberfest-worthy pretzels served with pimento cheese and bratwurst with briny chow-chow to stand in for sauerkraut. The large, convivial dining room is playfully appointed with just enough Germanic tchotchkes (a cuckoo clock here, a stein there) to be on point without veering into full-on kitsch. **Known for:** vegetarian "schnitzel"; daily happy hour specials; Sunday brunch. $ *Average main: $27* ✉ *1709 W. Chicago Ave., Wicker Park* ☎ *312/929–4727* 🌐 *www.funkenhausen.com* 🕒 *Closed Mon. No lunch Tue.–Sat.*

Kasama

$ | **FILIPINO** | Homey Filipino dishes executed with upscale flair are the order of the day at this Ukrainian Village charmer. Don't overlook the pastry case, stocked by co-owner and baking vet Genie Kwon; treats like purple potato Basque cake and ham and raclette danish are absolutely worth the calories. **Known for:** welcoming patio; Filipino breakfast with longanisa sausage; mushroom adobo. $ *Average main: $14* ✉ *1001 N. Winchester Ave., Wicker Park* 🌐 *kasamachicago.com* 🕒 *Closed Mon. and Tues. No dinner.*

Milk & Honey Café

$ | **CAFÉ** | **FAMILY** | Division Street has long been a prowl of night owls but with the growing number of spas and boutiques in the area, not to mention the many work-from-home locals, this neighborhood needed a good breakfast and lunch spot. Milk & Honey exceeds expectations with hearty, healthful breakfasts and creative sandwiches at lunch—grab a seat on the sidewalk café in warm weather or in near the fireplace in cooler temperatures. **Known for:** casual, airy atmosphere; avocado and gouda sandwich; weekend huevos rancheros. $ *Average main: $10* ✉ *1920 W. Division St., Wicker Park* ☎ *773/395–9434* 🌐 *www.milkandhoney-cafe.com* 🕒 *No dinner.*

Mott Street

$$ | **ASIAN** | Everything is big and bold at this perennial neighborhood favorite, from the Asian flavors that infuse chef Edward Kim's dishes to the colorful graffiti-esque art that adorns the exterior to the high-energy tunes that bop all night. The legendary house burger is only served until 7 pm, but its fans are so legion that ownership finally caved and launched Mini Mott, a casual burger and shake spot, in nearby Logan Square. **Known for:** Szechuan Negroni; great enclosed patio; oyster mushrooms in miso butter. $ *Average main: $22* ✉ *1401 N. Ashland Ave., Wicker Park* ☎ *773/687–9977* 🌐 *www.mottstreetchicago.com* 🕒 *Closed Mon. No lunch.*

Piece

$ | **PIZZA** | **FAMILY** | The antithesis of Chicago-style deep-dish pizza, Piece's thin-crust pies mimic those made famous in New Haven, Connecticut—they're somewhat free-form in shape and come in plain (tomato sauce, Parmesan, and garlic), white (olive oil, garlic, and mozzarella), or traditional red, with lots of topping options. Salads balance out the menu, while the award-winning house-brewed beers pair perfectly with the food. **Known for:** European-style ales; Hot Doug's atomic sausage pizza; clam pizza. $ *Average main: $17* ✉ *1927 W. North Ave., Wicker Park* ☎ *773/772–4422* 🌐 *www.piecechicago.com.*

Smoke Daddy

$ | **BARBECUE** | **FAMILY** | A ribs-and-blues emporium in the funky Wicker Park neighborhood, Smoke Daddy is a full night out, serving tangy barbecued ribs to accompany the frequent, no-cover R&B and jazz bands. Fans pack the bar and the booths for the wide range of barbecue options and drinks, so if you're looking for more space, head to the Wrigleyville location. **Known for:** top-notch Bloody Mary; pulled pork; fun music. $ *Average main: $17* ✉ *1804 W. Division St., Wicker*

Park ☎ 773/772–6656 🌐 www.thesmoke-daddy.com.

Tortello

$$ | **ITALIAN** | A selection of fresh handmade pasta produced with top-quality Italian flour anchors the menu at this counter service spot, where checkered linoleum flooring and a Vespa suspended from the ceiling give the snug, always-packed dining room a cheery retro vibe. Popular group classes let pasta novices try their hand at forming gnocchi and lumache. **Known for:** grocery section stocked with Italian wines and olive oils; tortelli di burrata; take-home pasta kits. [$] *Average main: $21 ✉ 1746 W. Division St., Wicker Park ☎ 773/360–1293 🌐 www.tortellopasta.com ⏲ No lunch Mon. and Tues.*

Coffee and Quick Bites

Black Dog Gelato

$ | **ICE CREAM** | **FAMILY** | Things can get weird on the flavor front at this cheerful Ukrainian Village scoop shop—goat cheese, moscato, and even basil have been known to make appearances. Suspend disbelief and give it a go; flavors rotate throughout the year, but you'd be hard pressed to find a dud in the mix. **Known for:** pleasant patio; gelato spun fresh daily; honey butter almond gelato. [$] *Average main: $6 ✉ 859 N. Damen Ave., Wicker Park ☎ 773/235–3116 🌐 blackdoggelato.com ⏲ Closed Nov.–May (check website to confirm).*

Goddess and Grocer

$ | **CAFÉ** | **FAMILY** | Tasty sandwiches, salads, and pastries that please vegans and carnivores alike are served at daytime spot Goddess and Grocer. A selection of prepared foods comes in handy for stocking picnics at nearby Wicker Park. **Known for:** rock and roll influence; rainbow cake; rooftop patio. [$] *Average main: $10 ✉ 1649 N. Damen Ave., Bucktown ☎ 773/342–3200 🌐 www.goddessand-grocer.com.*

Junebug Cafe

$ | **CAJUN** | **FAMILY** | The good times roll all day long at this New Orleans-inspired café, where locals pop in for fried-to-order beignets served piping hot and absolutely piled with powdered sugar. **Known for:** lavender lemonade; meat pies; café au lait. [$] *Average main: $6 ✉ 851 N. Ashland Ave., Wicker Park ☎ 312/624–9423 🌐 www.junebugchicago.com ⏲ Closed Mon. No dinner.*

Phodega

$ | **VIETNAMESE** | An urban bodega merges with a Vietnamese noodle shop at this quirky corner store that's won accolades for its fragrant chicken, beef, and vegan pho, based on a family recipe. In the grocery section, hard-to-find imported Thai chips and Japanese chocolates mingle with household essentials. **Known for:** come-as-you-are vibe; Hainan-style chicken; Vietnamese iced coffee. [$] *Average main: $11 ✉ 1547 N. Ashland Ave., Wicker Park ☎ 773/687–8187 🌐 www.phodega.com ⏲ Closed Mon.*

Hotels

The Robey Chicago

$$ | **HOTEL** | Located in the heart of Wicker Park, this boutique luxury revival hotel has curated art deco features, a mazelike layout, and two very distinct categories of rooms: Tower Rooms, which are snug but strong on mid-century style, and industrial, family-friendly Annex Lofts. **Pros:** design-lovers' dream; seasonal rooftop; scene-y brunch spot. **Cons:** rooms may be too small for some; no spa; a bit of a trek to downtown. [$] *Rooms from: $306 ✉ 2018 W. North Ave., Wicker Park ☎ 872/315-3050 🌐 www.therobey.com 🛏 89 rooms 🍴 No Meals.*

Wicker Park Inn

$$ | **B&B/INN** | One of the condo-like rooms in this small B&B is a great choice for anyone who wants to venture outside downtown Chicago and sample two of its most popular neighborhoods—Wicker

Park and Bucktown. **Pros:** dozens of restaurants and bars just blocks away; rooms are spacious, very well maintained, and homey; top-notch service. **Cons:** enclosed on-site parking is extra; communal space is minimal; some complain of noise problems from the El or other guests. [$] *Rooms from: $249* ✉ *1331 N. Wicker Park Ave., Wicker Park* ☎ *773/486–2743* 🌐 *www.wickerparkinn.com* 🛏 *9 rooms* 🍴 *Free Breakfast.*

Nightlife

BARS

Davenport's Piano Bar & Cabaret

PIANO BARS | Davenport's, a sophisticated cabaret booking both local and touring acts, brings a grown-up presence to the Wicker Park club scene. The piano lounge is set up for casual listening, while the cabaret room is reserved for ticketed performances with a two-drink minimum. ✉ *1383 N. Milwaukee Ave., Wicker Park* ☎ *773/278–1830* 🌐 *www.davenportspianobar.com.*

Emporium Arcade Bar

THEMED ENTERTAINMENT | Two of America's favorite pastimes—drinking and playing classic arcade games—come together here. More is more is the governing M.O.: there are over three dozen arcade games to choose from, along with skeeball, pinball machines, and 24 beer taps. There's also a Logan Square location at 2363 North Milwaukee Avenue. ✉ *1366 N. Milwaukee Ave., Wicker Park* ☎ *773/697–7922* 🌐 *emporiumchicago.com.*

The Map Room

BARS | The Map Room might help you find your way around Chicago, if not the world. Guidebooks decorate the walls of this self-described "travelers' tavern," and the craft beers represent much of the globe. This is a favorite gathering spot for soccer fans, so expect it to be roaring during World Cup season. ✉ *1949 N. Hoyne Ave., Bucktown* ☎ *773/252–9351* 🌐 *www.maproom.com.*

★ **The Matchbox**

BARS | In West Town near Wicker Park, the Matchbox isn't much bigger than a you-know-what, but the hodgepodge of regulars don't seem to mind. In fact, many claim it's the dark, cramped quarters (we're talking 3 feet wide at its narrowest) that keep them coming back. A heated front patio comes in handy when you need to reclaim a little personal space. You're practically required to try the signature drink, a margarita. ✉ *770 N. Milwaukee Ave., Wicker Park* ☎ *312/666–9292* 🌐 *www.matchboxbar.com.*

★ **The Queen Mary**

BARS | Lovers of vintage bar rooms will be in heaven at this veritable 1950s-era time capsule on Division Street: After shuttering in 1975, it was left undisturbed until 2015, when a local hospitality group dusted off the warm wooden interior and reopened the doors. Today there's an emphasis on nautical quaffs like grog and navy strength gin. The Sunday and Monday oyster and martini happy hour is a favorite with locals. ✉ *2125 W. Division St., Wicker Park* ☎ *773/697–3522* 🌐 *www.queenmarytavern.com.*

Rainbo Club

BARS | Chicago hipsters and indie rockers have made Rainbo Club their unofficial meeting place. Apart from the working photo booth wedged into a corner, the stripped-down hangout is pretty barren, but drinks are dirt cheap and the crowd is loyal. ✉ *1150 N. Damen Ave., Wicker Park* ☎ *773/489–5999.*

Sportsman's Club

BARS | This Ukrainian Village bar's roots as a nightspot for local Polish immigrants can still be felt in its warm wood accents and retro back bar. Classic cocktails are the drink of choice; they pair perfectly with the warmth of the back patio's brick fireplace. ✉ *948 N. Western Ave., Wicker*

Park ☎ 872/206–8054 ⊕ drinkingandgath-
ering.com/.

The Violet Hour

COCKTAIL LOUNGES | The Violet Hour
channels a Prohibition-era speakeasy—an
unmarked door in the mural-covered
facade leads to a mysterious, curtained
hallway. Inside, twinkling crystal chande-
liers cast a glow on cornflower-blue walls,
and extremely high-backed blue leather
chairs encourage intimate conversa-
tions. Add to that pricey, but flawlessly
executed cocktails and a sign discour-
aging cell-phone use, and it's our idea of
nightlife heaven. ⊠ 1520 N. Damen Ave.,
Wicker Park ☎ 773/252–1500 ⊕ www.
theviolethour.com.

MUSIC CLUBS
COUNTRY
★ The Hideout

LIVE MUSIC | The Hideout, which is literally
hidden away in a North Side industrial
zone, has managed to make country
music hip in Chicago. Players on the
city's alternative country scene have
adopted the friendly hole-in-the-wall,
and bands ranging from the obscure to
the semifamous take the stage. Late
night DJ sets, standup, trivia, and even
a music-theme talk show round out
the entertainment offerings. ⊠ 1354 W.
Wabansia Ave., Wicker Park ☎ 773/227–
4433 ⊕ www.hideoutchicago.com.

ECLECTIC
★ The Empty Bottle

LIVE MUSIC | This place, in the Ukrainian
Village near Wicker Park, may have toys
and knickknacks around the bar (including
a case of macabre baby-doll heads), but
when it comes to booking rock, punk,
and jazz bands from the indie scene, it's
a serious place with no pretensions. Grab
some grub next door at Pizza Friendly
Pizza before the show—the thick Sicil-
ian-style squares, created in collaboration
with fine dining vet Noah Sandoval, are
among the best pizza bets in the whole
city. ⊠ 1035 N. Western Ave., Wicker Park

☎ 773/276–3600 ⊕ www.emptybottle.
com ⊘ Closed Mon. and Tues.

ROCK
Subterranean

LIVE MUSIC | Check the letter board over
the front door of this Wicker Park storefront for a list of the rising indie rock and
hip-hop acts playing there soon, often
on their first Chicago gigs. Chances are
good they'll be playing a larger venue the
next time through. Locals also come for
the popular Thursday reggae nights and
regular hip-hop open mike events. ⊠ 2011
W. North Ave., Wicker Park ☎ 773/278–
6600 ⊕ www.subt.net.

Shopping

Former artists' enclaves in Wicker Park
were long ago taken over by style-con-
scious boutiques, cocktail bars, and
restaurants (with the Slavic-accented
hair salons and blue collar taverns of
Ukrainian Village increasingly following
suit). Today the ever-more-gentrified areas
are buzzing with activity, mostly around
the intersection of North, Damen, and
Milwaukee avenues and along Division
Street and Chicago Avenue. Walk around
and you'll find everything from Asrai Garden, a floral boutique with a Goth twist,
to Reckless Records, one of Chicago's
original vinyl parlors. Unable to resist a
captive market, large retailers such as
Urban Outfitters, John Fleuvog, and Adi-
das have also moved into the area.

ART GALLERIES
Catherine Edelman Gallery

ART GALLERIES | Relocated from River
North in May 2019, this now-4,400
square-foot space showcases contemporary photography that explores the work
of emerging, mixed-media, photo-based
artists such as Carlos Diaz, Sandro Miller,
and Jack Spencer. CEG has also expanded its program to include panel discussions, artists readings and a dedicated
video room. ⊠ 1637 W. Chicago Avenue,
West Town ☎ 312/266–2350 ⊕ www.

edelmangallery.com ☞ *Open Tues.-Sat. by appointment only.*

The Golden Triangle

ANTIQUES & COLLECTIBLES | In a block-long, 10,000-square-foot space, Asian furnishings and artifacts are arranged in vignettes depicting various eras and regions, from a British Colonial reception hall to a Chinese scholar's courtyard. The vast collection includes a line of custom-designed modern furnishings made from reclaimed wood. ✉ *2035 W. Grand Avenue, West Town* ☎ *312/755–1266* ⊕ *www.goldentriangle.biz* ۞ *Closed Sun.*

BEAUTY

Plant Salon

FLORIST | The impressive range of lush houseplants that do double duty as merchandise and decorative feature here impart an Instagrammable, #life-goals vibe. But even if you have black thumbs, there's still reason to visit: In addition to plants, the shop specializes in reasonably priced, botanical-forward beauty products and candles from artisan makers. ✉ *957 N. Ashland Ave., Wicker Park* ☎ *708/600–6225* ⊕ *plantsalon.com* ۞ *Closed Mon.-Tues.*

RR#1 Chicago

STATIONERY | A wood-paneled 1930s pharmacy is the setting for this charming gift shop, which stocks eclectic wares for everyone on your list, plus a tempting selection of bath and beauty products. ✉ *814 N. Ashland Ave., West Town* ☎ *312/421–9079* ⊕ *www.rr1chicago.com.*

BOOKS, MUSIC, AND GIFTS

Dusty Groove

MUSIC | The retail outlet of a massive online business, Dusty Groove stocks an enormous collection of new and used jazz, soul, hip-hop, Latin, rock, and other genres in both LP and CD formats. It also buys used records and CDs. ✉ *1120 N. Ashland Ave., Wicker Park* ☎ *773/342–5800* ⊕ *www.dustygroove.com.*

★ Myopic Books

BOOKS | One of Chicago's largest used-book dealers carries more than 80,000 titles and buys books from the public on Friday evening and Saturday afternoon. ■ TIP➜ **This community mainstay also hosts regular music and poetry events.** ✉ *1564 N. Milwaukee Ave., Wicker Park* ☎ *773/862–4882* ⊕ *www.myopicbookstore.com.*

Paperish Mess

STATIONERY | All sorts of paper goods are on offer here, from sassy letterpress cards and stickers to journals and hip art prints. Many of the offerings have a Chicago theme, making this a good spot to pick up souvenirs of the Windy City. ✉ *1945 W. Chicago Ave., Wicker Park* ⊕ *www.paperishmess.com.*

Quimby's Bookstore

BOOKS | This indie bookstore offers one of the city's most diverse selections of reading material. You'll find everything from fancy coffee-table art books and flashy comics to hand-drawn zines created by obscure local artists here. ✉ *1854 W. North Ave., Wicker Park* ☎ *773/342–0910* ⊕ *www.quimbys.com* ۞ *Closed Tues.-Wed.*

The Secret Agent Supply Co.

TOYS | FAMILY | Outfit your aspiring sleuth with the necessary spy paraphernalia and secret agent supplies—such as mirror glasses, fake mustaches, and voice amplifiers—as well as stationery, books, and puzzles at this shop run by writer Dave Eggers's nonprofit group 826CHI. Proceeds help fund the group's after-school tutoring and writing programs for kids. ✉ *1276 N. Milwaukee Ave., Wicker Park* ☎ *773/772–8108* ⊕ *www.secretagentsupply.com.*

CLOTHING

Alcala's Western Wear

OTHER SPECIALTY STORE | Alcala stocks more than 8,000 pairs of cowboy boots—many in exotic skins—for men, women, and children. The amazing array of Stetson hats and rodeo gear makes this a must-see for cowboys, caballeros, and country-and-western dancers. ✉ *1733 W. Chicago Ave., Ukrainian Village* ☎ *312/226–0152* ⊕ *www.alcalas.com.*

Eskell
HOUSEWARES | Although this women's boutique can be a bit on the pricey side, Eskell's selection of new and vintage jewelry, fragrances, wall art, and assorted home goods is ever-evolving and truly one-of-a-kind. ✉ *2029 N. Western Ave., Bucktown* ☎ *773/486–0830* ⊕ *www. eskell.com.*

Kokorokoko
SECOND-HAND | This unusual vintage shop specializes in loud, bold clothing, shoes, and accessories from the '80s and '90s. ✉ *1323 N. Milwaukee Ave., Wicker Park* ☎ *773/252–6996* ⊕ *www.kokorokokovintage.com.*

Lost Girls Vintage
WOMEN'S CLOTHING | Once a mobile shop operating out of a 1976 Dodge RV, Lost Girls is now a brick and mortar store in Ukrainian Village (with an additional location in Logan Square). True to its theme of fun and adventure, you never know what you'll stumble upon. But you're sure to leave with a gem, be it a '50s cocktail dress or '70s beaded handbag. ✉ *1947 W. Chicago Ave., Ukrainian Village* ⊕ *www.lostgirlsvintage.com.*

Mulberry & Me
WOMEN'S CLOTHING | Snag work-appropriate blouses, cute dresses, tie dye athleisure wear, and accessories in this boutique with a New York feel. ✉ *2019 W. Division St., Wicker Park* ☎ *773/952–7551* ⊕ *mulberryandme.com* ☾ *Closed Mon.*

Penelope's
MIXED CLOTHING | Step inside this spacious Ukrainian Village shop for flirty dresses from Compania Fantastica, SMF, and Just Female, as well as funky accessories such as Casa 184 earrings. Menswear by the likes of Native Youth and Rollas plus a selection of housewares and gift items round out the collection. ✉ *1913 W. Division St., Wicker Park* ☎ *773/395–2351* ⊕ *shoppenelopes.com* ☾ *Closed Tues.*

Una Mae's
MIXED CLOTHING | This Wicker Park favorite is bursting at the seams with affordable styles for guys and girls. The accessories here, often even more fun than the clothing, may include vintage bow ties, Mexican blankets, backpacks, and incredibly colorful jewelry. ✉ *1528 N. Milwaukee Ave., Wicker Park* ☎ *773/276–7002* ⊕ *www.unamaeschicago.com* ☾ *Closed Tues.*

HOME DECOR
Asrai Garden
FLORIST | Although you'd be hard-pressed to find fresher blooms or more carefully constructed bouquets, this quirky boutique is more than a flower shop. It also contains a thoughtful, visually stunning collection of leather pouches, jewelry, soaps, scented candles, ornate tableware, scrimshaw, stationery, and other gifts. ✉ *1935 W. North Ave., Wicker Park* ☎ *773/782–0680* ⊕ *www.asraigarden. com* ☾ *Closed Mon.-Tues.*

Sprout Home
HOUSEWARES | Sprout's original location deals in all things green: think terrariums, planters, and bud vases for your indoor life, plus unusual plants and gardening products for your outdoor one. A newer annex directly across the street is geared more toward beautifying your tabletop with boho handmade ceramics, linen textiles, and handsome culinary journals. ✉ *744 and 745 N. Damen Ave., Ukrainian Village, Wicker Park* ☎ *312/226–5950* ⊕ *www.sprouthome.com.*

JEWELRY AND ACCESSORIES
Dovetail
SECOND-HAND | Vintage and handmade pieces that run the gamut from kitschy to avant garde make this store feel nostalgic and timeless at once. Owner Julie Ghatan scours estate sales and flea markets to salvage those perfect items worth an (often modest) investment. The

jewelry is the main draw, but clothing, accessories, and barware are equally noteworthy. ✉ *1452 W. Chicago Ave., West Town* 🌐 *dovetailchicago.com.*

Bucktown

North of Wicker Park, Bucktown got its name from the goats kept by the area's original Polish and German immigrants. These days it's mostly a home base for a fairly wealthy population of young professionals and families, but evidence of its ethnic roots remains. For shopping—window or otherwise—with wares you won't likely find elsewhere, head to Damen Avenue between North and Fullerton. Fun restaurants and bars (many of them tucked along residential streets) keep things busy at night, too.

👁 Sights

★ The 606

CITY PARK | **FAMILY** | Similar to New York City's High Line, this abandoned elevated rail line—open since 2015—is now a fun place to walk and take in art all at once. Edgy, splashy and bright murals are depicted along the 2.7-mile route, which you can access by hopping on the CTA's Blue Line and getting off at the Western or Damen stops. The route runs through the Wicker Park, Humboldt Park, Bucktown and Logan Square neighborhoods. Take along some water and sunscreen; on summer days the more exposed stretches of the trail get rather sunbaked. ✉ *Bloomingdale Ave. between Ashland and Ridgeway Aves., Bucktown* 🌐 *www.the606.org* 🎟 *Free.*

🍴 Restaurants

The Bristol

$$$ | **MODERN AMERICAN** | While Bucktown isn't wanting for dining options, the Bristol sets itself apart by focusing intently on the food—crowds turn out to the convivial dining room night after night for the pastas, sustainably raised meats, and seasonal produce. The wine program simultaneously celebrates revered producers as well as young gun winemakers challenging traditional styles. **Known for:** seamless table service; 8-course tasting menu; milk bread. [$] *Average main: $32* ✉ *2152 N. Damen Ave., Bucktown* ☎ *773/862–5555* 🌐 *www.thebristolchicago.com* 🕒 *Closed Mon. and Tues. No lunch.*

Etta

$$ | **AMERICAN** | A wood-fired hearth comprises the primary cooking equipment here, and many of chef Danny Grant's dishes, from pizza to pork collar, take their turn getting kissed by the flames. Brunch adds another layer of deliciousness with flaky, gooey treats from locally revered pastry chef Aya Fukai. **Known for:** happy hour specials; modern farmhouse vibe; fresh pastas. [$] *Average main: $21* ✉ *1840 W. North Ave., Bucktown* ☎ *312/757–4444* 🌐 *ettarestaurant.com.*

Le Bouchon

$$$ | **BISTRO** | The Lyonnais comfort food at this charming, cozy bistro in Bucktown is in a league of its own thanks to pitch-perfect classics along with some light twists on favorite dishes. Evenings can get busy so reservations are recommended; note that Mondays mean half-price bottles of wine, while the royale burger is only served at lunch. **Known for:** whole roasted duck for two; cozy Old World atmosphere; onion tart. [$] *Average main: $28* ✉ *1958 N. Damen Ave., Bucktown* ☎ *773/862–6600* 🌐 *www.lebouchonofchicago.com* 🕒 *Closed Sun.*

☕ Coffee and Quick Bites

Ipsento 606

$ | **CAFÉ** | Power up after a brisk walk on the adjacent 606 trail with nitro drafts and lattes brewed with the shop's own range of beans. There are sandwiches and mini donuts to snack on during the

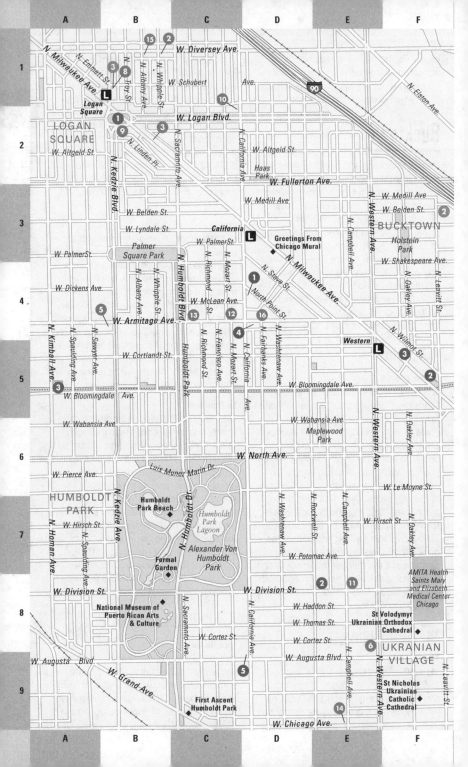

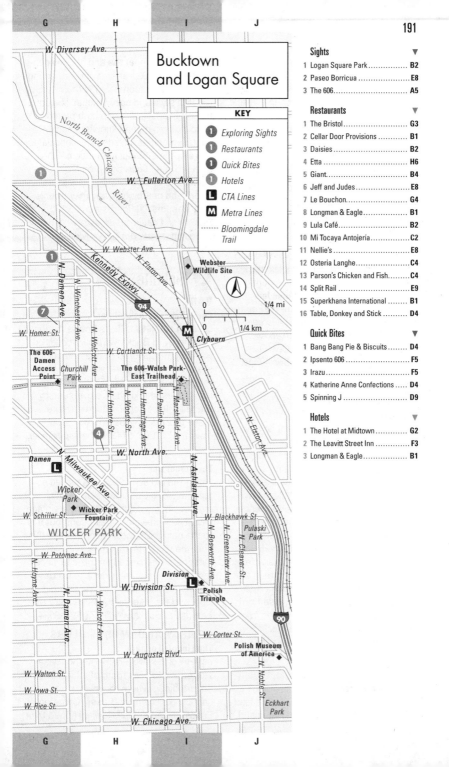

Bucktown and Logan Square

KEY

1 Exploring Sights
1 Restaurants
1 Quick Bites
1 Hotels
L CTA Lines
M Metra Lines
...... Bloomingdale Trail

Sights ▼

1 Logan Square Park B2
2 Paseo Borricua E8
3 The 606 .... A5

Restaurants ▼

1 The Bristol G3
2 Cellar Door Provisions B1
3 Daisies B2
4 Etta H6
5 Giant B4
6 Jeff and Judes E8
7 Le Bouchon G4
8 Longman & Eagle B1
9 Lula Café B2
10 Mi Tocaya Antojeria C2
11 Nellie's E8
12 Osteria Langhe C4
13 Parson's Chicken and Fish C4
14 Split Rail E9
15 Superkhana International B1
16 Table, Donkey and Stick D4

Quick Bites ▼

1 Bang Bang Pie & Biscuits D4
2 Ipsento 606 .... F5
3 Irazu F5
4 Katherine Anne Confections D4
5 Spinning J D9

Hotels ▼

1 The Hotel at Midtown G2
2 The Leavitt Street Inn F3
3 Longman & Eagle B1

day, and a curated selection of local beers to lubricate customers come happy hour. **Known for:** work on the go-friendly setup; signature coconut cayenne latte; light-filled storefront. Ⓢ *Average main: $9* ✉ *1813 N. Milwaukee Ave., Bucktown* ☎ *872/206–8697* ⊕ *ipsento.com/606* ⊘ *No dinner.*

Irazu

$ | **COSTA RICAN** | **FAMILY** | This BYOB Costa Rican spot has been going strong since 1990, thanks to its range of empanadas, mixed grill platters, and sandwiches that offer good value but don't skimp on flavor. The casual, brightly colored dining room and patio call to mind a laid-back beach shack–a welcome vision during Chicago's rough winters. **Known for:** fried pork chifrijo; oatmeal shake; Pepito sandwich with skirt steak. Ⓢ *Average main: $12* ✉ *1865 N. Milwaukee Ave., Bucktown* ☎ *773/252–5687* ⊕ *www. irazuchicago.com* ⊘ *Closed Sun.–Tues.*

 ## Hotels

The Hotel at Midtown

$$ | **HOTEL** | Far from just a generic amenity, the fitness facilities are the raison d'être at this independently owned Bucktown property; after all, it got its start as a tennis club that's hosted the likes of Billie Jean King and Venus Williams (who kindly pitched in and designed a lounge when the club was overhauled and the hotel added in 2017). **Pros:** modern, stylish bathrooms; food and amenities from local makers; child care available. **Cons:** no El stop nearby; all common areas shared with fitness club members; some guests report hearing noise from fitness facility in rooms. Ⓢ *Rooms from: $250* ✉ *2444 N. Elston Ave., Bucktown* ☎ *773/687–7600* ⊕ *www.midtown-hotelchicago.com* ⦿ *No Meals* ⇌ *55 rooms.*

The Leavitt Street Inn

$ | **B&B/INN** | The friendly proprietors (and longtime Bucktown denizens) launched this guesthouse, at the end of a residential street, in 2021 after lovingly restoring its three guest rooms with a mix of crisp modern style and cozy touches like butter-soft linens and Aesop bath products. **Pros:** welcoming and knowledgeable hosts; amenities include local chocolates and a bottle of wine; authentic neighborhood vibe. **Cons:** common areas are limited; no El stop nearby; downstairs tavern and nearby highway may trouble light sleepers. Ⓢ *Rooms from: $190* ✉ *2345 N. Leavitt St., Bucktown* ⊕ *www. theleavittstreet.com* ⦿ *No Meals* ⇌ *3 rooms.*

 ## Nightlife

BARS

Chef's Special Cocktail Bar

COCKTAIL LOUNGES | Chef's Special brings fun energy to Bucktown's bar scene with brightly flavored cocktails in colorful shabby-chic digs. Don't snooze on the menu of kitschy classic Chinese American dishes; the kitchen is overseen by the team from Logan Square favorite Giant. ✉ *2165 N. Western Ave., Bucktown* ☎ *773/666–5143* ⊕ *chefsspecialbar. com.*

The Corner Bar

BARS | The old school taverns tucked at random along Bucktown's residential streets—many distinguished by a vintage Old Style sign—are a major contributor to the neighborhood's character, and this one (the latest iteration of a series of bars that have existed on this site since the 1950s) is a prime example. Come for the ice cold beer, the easy going dive vibe, and the jukebox tunes. ✉ *2224 N. Leavitt St., Bucktown* ☎ *773/697–9934.*

COMEDY AND IMPROV CLUBS

The Lincoln Lodge

COMEDY CLUBS | This comedy showcase started in the back room of a Lincoln Square diner, where for years young comics like Hannibal Buress, Cameron Esposito, and Kumail Nanjiani honed their

stand-up. The Lodge now has its own venue in Bucktown, where you can find the next generation of comedians working the room most nights of the week. ⊠ *2040 N. Milwaukee Ave., Bucktown* ⊕ *www.thelincolnlodge.com.*

Shopping

CHILDREN'S CLOTHING
The Red Balloon

CHILDREN'S CLOTHING | FAMILY | A good selection of books, toys, and games plus darling toddler duds and Chicago-centric onesies are on offer at this long-running favorite for children's gifts. ⊠ *1940 N. Damen Ave., Bucktown* ☎ *773/489–9800* ⊕ *www.theredballoon.com.*

CLOTHING
p.45

WOMEN'S CLOTHING | This store is a must-hit for its fashion-forward collection by a cadre of hip women's designers like Katharine Kidd, Rachel Comey, and Ulla Johnson. Customers from all over the city and well beyond come for adventurous to elegant styles at prices that don't get out of hand. ⊠ *1643 N. Damen Ave., Bucktown* ☎ *773/862–4523* ⊕ *www.p45.com* ⊗ *Closed Mon.*

Robin Richman

WOMEN'S CLOTHING | Robin Richman showcases interesting sculptural housewares and oversize vintage necklaces alongside pieces from lesser-known European labels and local clothes designers. The eclectic displays never disappoint. ⊠ *2108 N. Damen Ave., Bucktown* ☎ *773/278–6150* ⊕ *www.robinrichman.com* ⊗ *Closed Mon.-Thurs.*

The T-Shirt Deli

SOUVENIRS | FAMILY | Order up a customized T-shirt with iron-on letters or throwback '70s decals. Your creation will be served to you on the spot, wrapped in paper like a sandwich, and packed with a bag of chips for good measure. ⊠ *1739 N. Damen Ave., Bucktown* ☎ *773/276–6266* ⊕ *www.tshirtdeli.com* ⊗ *Closed Sun.*

JEWELRY AND ACCESSORIES
Virtu

JEWELRY & WATCHES | The perfect place to find a gift for the person that has everything, Virtu's focus is fine jewerly but the stationery and kitchenware selection is also on point. They also carry ceramic, paper and metal pieces for the home. ⊠ *2035 N. Damen Ave., Bucktown* ☎ *773/235–3790* ⊕ *virtuforyou.com.*

SHOES, HANDBAGS, AND LEATHER GOODS
City Soles

SHOES | This on-trend shop is a mecca for shoe lovers. There's a vast selection of edgy men's and women's footwear from Cabloco, Mia Sheridan, Camper, and more. ⊠ *1630 N. Milwaukee Ave., Wicker Park* ⊕ *www.citysoles.com.*

Logan Square

Logan Square sits just west of Wicker Park/Bucktown. Over the years, it has been a melting pot for immigrants—first European (primarily Scandinavian, English, Polish, and Jewish), then later Latino. Spacious tree-lined boulevards are the dominant aspect of the area, and many historic buildings still line the streets. But Logan Square's "cool quotient" has risen significantly in recent decades, leading some to compare it to Brooklyn, and these days its dining scene rivals its East Coast analog for creativity. Directly to the south, Humboldt Park mixes Puerto Rican traditions, green space, and increasingly, trendy shops and restaurants that cater to those who have been priced out of nearby hoods.

Sights

Logan Square Park

CITY PARK | The park that gives Logan Square its name can look a little worse for the wear—the colossal eagle-top column at its center has seen its fair share of graffiti tagging—but that doesn't stop locals from setting up shop for the afternoon with a book and a portable hammock. An old-world Norwegian church and restaurants with busy sidewalk patios fringe the square (really more of an oval, to be exact), imparting a cosmopolitan vibe. Wide, rambling Kedzie and Logan Boulevards—two of the neighborhood's loveliest assets—radiate outward from the park; pick out your dream mansion on a postprandial stroll. ✉ *3200 W. Logan Blvd., Logan Square* 🎫 *Free.*

Paseo Borricua

STREET | Massive steel Puerto Rican flags proudly straddle the road along this six-block stretch of Division Street in Humboldt Park, marking out the nucleus of Chicago's large Puerto Rican community. This is the place to be for mofongo and cafe con leche in easygoing sidewalk cafes. Keep your eyes peeled for murals by street artists and a walk of fame celebrating Puerto Rican luminaries. ✉ *Division St. between Western and California Aves., Humboldt Park* 🌐 *prcc-chgo.org/* 🎫 *Free.*

🍴 Restaurants

Cellar Door Provisions

$$$$ | **AMERICAN** | Seasonality is the watchword at this modern spot, where the menu changes constantly but the dishes are always executed with the utmost care. Filled with blonde wood and lovely light, the dining room makes a fine place to unwind with wine and snacks in the afternoon, or tuck into heartier plates at dinnertime. **Known for:** sourdough bread; natural wines; seasonal fruit desserts. [$] *Average main: $40* ✉ *3025 W. Diversey Ave., Logan Square* ☎ *773/697–8337* 🌐 *www.cellardoorprovisions.com* ⏲ *Closed Sun.–Tues. No lunch.*

Daisies

$$ | **AMERICAN** | Neighborhood foodies flock to this minimalist dining room for handmade pastas dressed in the season's best produce and kooky but quaffable cocktails like a margarita infused with fermented mushrooms. At lunchtime there's an excellent roster of rustic sandwiches. **Known for:** smoked trout agnolotti; French onion dip; daytime grab and go market. [$] *Average main: $19* ✉ *2523 N. Milwaukee Ave., Logan Square* ☎ *773/661–1671* 🌐 *www.daisieschicago.com* ⏲ *Closed Mon. and Tues.*

★ Giant

$ | **AMERICAN** | Huge flavors come roaring out of the tiny kitchen at Giant, where chef Jason Vincent takes crowd-pleasers like pasta, vegetarian dishes, and American classics and cranks the umami up to an 11. Beverage director Josh Perlman seeks to pair diners with interesting wines from small producers without an unwanted chaser of snootiness. **Known for:** cajeta (goat milk) ice cream; happening, fun vibe; rigatoni with albacore tuna. [$] *Average main: $17* ✉ *3209 W. Armitage Ave., Logan Square* ☎ *773/252–0997* 🌐 *www.giantrestaurant.com* 💳 *No credit cards* ⏲ *Closed Mon. No lunch.*

Jeff and Judes

$ | **JEWISH DELI** | A self-professed Jew-ish deli, this bright corner spot in Humboldt Park serves sandwiches and other classics of the genres made extra special courtesy of house-smoked meats and breads produced by owner Ursula Siker, a baker by training. There's a spacious patio in back. **Known for:** pastrami on rye; savory hamanstaschen; matzo fried chicken sandwich. [$] *Average main: $16* ✉ *1024 N. Western Ave., Humboldt Park* ☎ *773/661–1227* 🌐 *www.jeffandjudes.com* ⏲ *Closed Tues.–Wed. No dinner.*

Longman & Eagle

$$ | **MODERN AMERICAN** | Chef Maxwell Robbins' menu adheres to a farm-to-table aesthetic, so expect the offerings at this hip gastropub to change often, with options ranging from bar snacks to substantial entrées, all with clever twists. Chase your meal with one of more than 100 whiskeys on offer (one of the thoughtfully curated flight options is a good way to sample a few), or swing around to the back bar for a nightcap; late night, it serves a small menu of elevated drinking food (wild boar sloppy joes, vegan "sour cream" and onion dip) that's exactly perfect after a evening on the town. **Known for:** well-chosen beer selection; hip atmosphere; raw beef tartine. [$] *Average main: $22* ✉ *2657 N. Kedzie Ave., Logan Square* ☎ *773/276–7110* 🌐 *www.longmanandeagle.com.*

★ Lula Café

$$ | MODERN AMERICAN | Locals worship Lula Café, a neighborhood favorite that has been serving modern, seasonal dishes (and a cult-favorite brunch menu) in a spacious location with counter seating and an intimate dining room since 1999. The food is stellar, with menus that change frequently and champion farm sources. **Known for:** neighborhood vibe; pasta yiayia (bucatini in a brown butter sauce); breakfast burrito. [$] *Average main: $18* ✉ *2537 N. Kedzie Blvd., Logan Square* ☎ *773/489–9554* 🌐 *www.lulacafe.com* 🕒 *Closed Tues.-Wed.*

Mi Tocaya Antojeria

$$ | MEXICAN | Chef Diana Dávila offers a deeply personal, richly flavored take on Mexican cuisine at this colorful restaurant, which serves everything from snacks and tacos to heartier plates. Grab a patio seat in warm weather for people-watching along Logan Boulevard, or hang out at the bar for smoky mezcal cocktails or Mexican beers served alongside food that's wildly creative but endlessly satisfying. **Known for:** peanut butter lengua; lively atmosphere; nitro horchata. [$] *Average main: $24* ✉ *2800 W. Logan Blvd., Logan Square* ☎ *872/315–3947* 🌐 *www.mitocaya.com* 🕒 *Closed Sun.–Mon. No lunch.*

Nellie's

$ | PUERTO RICAN | FAMILY | A long-running fixture on Division Street in Humboldt Park—also known as the Paseo Boricua—family-owned Nellie's is especially popular on weekends, when locals come out in droves for the generously sized breakfast and brunch dishes. It's a good place to sample a *jibarito*, the Puerto Rican contribution to Chicago's sandwich pantheon: it's an assemblage of grilled meat and toppings surrounded by flattened, fried plantains. **Known for:** sidewalk patio; coconut oatmeal; café con leche. [$] *Average main: $12* ✉ *2458 W. Division St., Humboldt Park* ☎ *773/252–5520* 🌐 *www.nelliesrestaurant.com* 🕒 *No dinner Mon.-Wed.*

Osteria Langhe

$$$ | PIEDMONTESE | Chefs Cameron Grant and Cooper O'Brien serve some of Chicago's most soul-satisfying Italian food at this cozy and convivial Logan Square Piedmontese restaurant. The pastas are flawless and come stuffed and topped with seasonal accompaniments, while the hearty meat and seafood main courses pair perfectly with the Northern Italian wine list—save room for the classic Italian desserts or order a bittersweet digestif to end the meal. **Known for:** seasonally changing panna cotta; plin (stuffed pasta); daily risotto special. [$] *Average main: $29* ✉ *2824 W. Armitage Ave., Logan Square* ☎ *773/661–1582* 🌐 *www.osterialanghe.com* 🕒 *Closed Mon.-Tues. No lunch.*

Parson's Chicken and Fish

$ | AMERICAN | The crowd at this casual spot serving fried chicken and fish is decidedly hipster, but even if that's not your scene, the food and cocktails are worth making your way to to the location on the southern end of Logan Square. During the summer, the beer garden is packed with folks playing table tennis, chowing down on shareable snacks and sandwiches, and sipping boozy slushies and cheap beer. **Known for:** games!; negroni slushy; hush puppies. [$] *Average* *main: $12 ✉ 2952 W. Armitage Ave., Logan Square ☎ 773/384–3333 🌐 www.parsonschickenandfish.com.*

Split Rail

$ | **SOUTHERN** | Split-Rail's Zoe Schor is a champion for equality: she's eliminated tipping to ensure staff earn a fair wage, foregrounds wines produced by people of color and women, and donates part of the restaurant's profits to community organizations in recognition of the debt her menu owes to African American foodways. If that sounds a bit heavy, the dining room's anything but: it's a warm neighborhood gathering spot that serves fried chicken and biscuits you won't soon forget. **Known for:** crab gravy with Carolina rice; spicy Caesar salad; happy hour specials. [$] *Average main: $16 ✉ 2500 W. Chicago Ave., Humboldt Park ☎ 773/697–4413 🌐 www.splitrailchicago.com 🕓 Closed Tues. No lunch weekdays.*

Superkhana International

$ | **INDIAN** | Indian flavors drive the menu at this merry all-day spot on the northern fringes of Logan Square, but this isn't your grandma's tikka masala (even though that *might* be her calico upholstery in the quirky industrial-meets-cottagecore dining room). Instead, Zeeshan Shah and Yoshi Yamada take a witty approach to familiar dishes, sealing butter chicken into calzones and dressing french toast in halvah and gulab jamun syrup. **Known for:** bun omelet; lots of vegetarian options; cardamom ice-cream sandwich. [$] *Average main: $14 ✉ 3059 W. Diversey Ave., Logan Square ☎ 773/661–9028 🌐 www.superkhanachicago.com 🕓 Closed Mon. and Tues. No lunch Wed.-Fri. No dinner Sun.*

Table, Donkey and Stick

$$ | **EUROPEAN** | This cozy spot is influenced by the Alpine cuisine of France, Germany, Italy, and Austria, and takes an old-world approach to local ingredients; baking, butchering, curing, pickling, and smoking everything in house. The same region informs the beverage program, translating to an interesting selection of wine, amari, and liqueurs. **Known for:** charcuterie selection; eau-de-vie and schnapps; warm ambience. [$] *Average main: $21 ✉ 2728 W. Armitage Ave., Logan Square ☎ 773/486–8525 🌐 www.tabledonkeystick.com 🕓 Closed Mon. No lunch.*

☕ Coffee and Quick Bites

Bang Bang Pie & Biscuits

$ | **BAKERY** | **FAMILY** | If you thought sausage gravy was as creative as biscuit toppings get, you obviously haven't been to Bang Bang. The buttery, fluffy specimens here serve as a base for an assortment of tasty accompaniments, like herbed ricotta with roasted seasonal veggies. **Known for:** chicken pot pie; key lime pie; sausage and cheese biscuit. [$] *Average main: $9 ✉ 2051 N. California Ave., Logan Square ☎ 773/276–8888 🌐 www.bangbangpie.com 🕓 Closed Sun.–Tues. No dinner.*

Katherine Anne Confections

$ | **DESSERTS** | **FAMILY** | Hand-rolled truffles are the signature item here; some flavor combinations are staples while others change with the seasons, but all are highly inventive. (Goat cheese walnut or peanut butter coconut curry anyone?) For many, the real star of the show is the absurdly thick hot chocolate topped with house-made marshmallows. **Known for:** vegan hot chocolate options; at-home truffle making kits; salted caramels. [$] *Average main: $6 ✉ 2745 W. Armitage Ave., Logan Square ☎ 773/245–1630 🌐 www.katherine-anne.com 🕓 No dinner.*

Spinning J

$ | **AMERICAN** | **FAMILY** | A 1920s-era marble bar salvaged from a Milwaukee drugstore anchors this darling dining room in Humboldt Park, where the young and young at heart flock for old-fashioned sodas and malts. No mere one-note, the shop also serves an all-day breakfast menu, warm and cold sandwiches, and tempting pastries. **Known for:** chocolate egg cream; freshly baked scones; savory strata. [$] *Average main: $11* ✉ *1000 N. California Ave., Humboldt Park* ☎ *872/829–2793* 🌐 *www.spinningj.com* 🕓 *Closed Mon.-Tues. No dinner.*

Hotels

Longman & Eagle

$ | **B&B/INN** | The restaurant known for whiskey and nose-to-tail cuisine has opened a six-room inn by the same name, and each of these homey quarters is full of original art and handcrafted furnishings. **Pros:** no two rooms are the same; award-winning restaurant downstairs; great local feel. **Cons:** not kid-friendly; no concierge or public amenities; need to take a 15-minute El ride downtown. [$] *Rooms from: $185* ✉ *2657 N. Kedzie Ave., Logan Square* ☎ *773/276–7110* 🌐 *www.longmanandeagle.com* 🛏 *6 rooms* 🍴 *No Meals.*

Nightlife

BARS

Billy Sunday

COCKTAIL LOUNGES | This Logan Square cocktail go-to with an impressive catalog of vintage spirits focuses on elevating classic drink recipes by using unexpected ingredients. The Charlie Trotter's alums who opened Billy Sunday cheekily named the bar for the Prohibition-era temperance evangelist. ✉ *3143 W. Logan Blvd., Logan Square* ☎ *773/661–2485* 🌐 *www.billy-sunday.com.*

Bungalow by Middlebrow

BREWPUBS | Bungalow by Middlebrow wears a lot of hats—brewery, sourdough bread bakery, pizzaiolo, all-day neighborhood third place—and looks darned good in all of them. There's a relaxed, come-one-come-all feeling to the dining room and patio here; indie folk types play mellow sets while friends sip wild ales and families linger over pizza. The owners also run an apprenticeship program that helps train at-risk youth for employment in the hospitality industry. ✉ *2840 W. Armitage Ave., Logan Square* 🌐 *www.middlebrowbeer.com* 🕓 *Closed Mon.-Tues.*

Estereo

BARS | Mexican spirits like mezcal, sotol, and raicilla are the focus at petite Estereo, which has an unusual triangular shape due to its position on an angled corner lot. When the garage-style windows that surround the room are rolled up and the vintage Latin tunes are pumping, you'd be forgiven for thinking you'd been transported to a city much nearer to the equator. ✉ *2450 N. Milwaukee Ave., Logan Square* ☎ *773/360–8363* 🌐 *www.estereochicago.com.*

Lost Lake

COCKTAIL LOUNGES | No one took tropical cocktails seriously until James Beard Award finalist Paul McGee came along; his concoctions have a cerebral edge—we're talking unaccustomed ingredients like byrrh, Sfumato, and even kelp—but they're served up in kitschy mugs that keep things from getting too serious. Palm print wallpaper and lots of rattan flesh out the island escape vibe. ✉ *3154 W. Diversey Ave., Logan Square* 🌐 *www.lostlakechicago.com* 🕓 *Closed Sun.-Tues.*

Revolution Brewing

BREWPUBS | Chicago has evolved one of the country's best craft brewing scenes, but back when the pickings were slim, Revolution was here, satisfying drinkers thirsty for something more interesting than watery macrobrews. The Milwaukee Avenue location is a good place to work your way through a flight of the house beers—the offerings skew toward classic German styles and hop-forward IPAs—while lining your stomach with unfussy pub grub like burgers and fried cheese curds. (There's also a taproom on nearby Kedzie Avenue with a less polished vibe and a limited menu of nibbly things.) ✉ *2323 N. Milwaukee Ave.,*

Logan Square ☎ 773/588–2267 ⊕ www.revbrew.com.

Scofflaw

COCKTAIL LOUNGES | That the once-shabby stretch on which the Scofflaw sits grows hipper by the month is no coincidence; the cozy, brick-walled cocktail bar, which boasts a huge collection of gin, put the intersection of Kedzie and Armitage Avenues on the map. It's an open secret that the kitchen serves a stellar cheeseburger. ⊠ 3201 W. Armitage Ave., Logan Square ⊕ www.scofflawchicago.com.

Slippery Slope

DANCE CLUBS | With its giant dance floor, craft cocktails, and dim, red-hue lighting, Slippery Slope has brought a cool, clubby vibe to Logan Square. (It gets bonus points for the Skeeball machines located next to the door.) This place gets especially crowded on the weekends, when the dancing gets serious. ⊠ 2357 N. Milwaukee Ave., Logan Square ☎ 773/799–8504 ⊕ www.slipperyslope-chicago.com.

Webster's Wine Bar

WINE BARS | This cozy, candlelit bar is a romantic place for a date. It stocks more than 500 bottles of wine (at least 20 are available by the glass) plus ports, sherries, single-malt Scotches, a few microbrews, and a menu of small tasting entrées at reasonable prices. If you're looking for carryout provisions, there's a wine shop with tempting picnic fixings, too. ⊠ 2601 N. Milwaukee Ave., Logan Square ☎ 773/292–9463 ⊕ www.websterwinebar.com.

MUSIC VENUES
BLUES
★ Rosa's Lounge

LIVE MUSIC | On a given night at Rosa's Lounge, near Bucktown, you'll find Tony, the owner, working the crowd. What makes the club special is that he moved here from Italy out of a pure love for the blues. Stop by and partake in Rosa's winning mixture of big-name and local talent,

stiff drinks, and friendly service—the same since it opened in 1984. ⊠ 3420 W. Armitage Ave., Logan Square ☎ 773/342–0452 ⊕ www.rosaslounge.com.

ECLECTIC
FitzGerald's Nightclub

LIVE MUSIC | Although it's a 30-minute schlep west of downtown Chicago, FitzGerald's draws crowds from all over the city and suburbs with its mix of folk, jazz, blues, zydeco, and rock. This early 1900s roadhouse has both great sound and sight lines. There's a menu of fantastic barbecue fare by fine dining vet John Manion, so do come hungry, and if you just can't bear trekking back to the city, consider booking into the so-called Sleepover Castle, a three-bedroom boho rental apartment above the bar. ⊠ 6615 W. Roosevelt Rd., Berwyn ☎ 708/788–2118 ⊕ www.fitzgeraldsnightclub.com.

Performing Arts

FILM
Logan Theatre

FILM | It used to be that folks only came here because of the low ticket prices. But, after an ambitious remodel, the historic 1915 theater is now a neighborhood gem. Expect a well-curated mix of current blockbusters, indie films, and cult classics as well as a full bar off the lobby. ⊠ 2646 N. Milwaukee Ave., Logan Square ☎ 773/342–5555 ⊕ www.thelogantheatre.com.

Shopping

CLOTHING
Birdseye Rule

WOMEN'S CLOTHING | Run by two sisters and their mom, Birdseye is an homage to the Midwest, especially summers in northern Michigan—think reupholstered vintage chairs, twill duffle bags, and that perfect pair of jeans. ⊠ 2319 N. Milwaukee Ave., Logan Square ☎ 773/904–8038 ⊕ www.birdseyerule.com ☉ Closed Mon.

Felt

WOMEN'S CLOTHING | Up-and-coming and established women's clothing designers are artfully showcased in a space that's airy, bright, and uncluttered. The owners are pros at mixing fabrics and patterns, and putting unexpected pieces together with wonderful results. Refreshingly, staff put a premium on personable service, making you feel genuinely welcome whether you've come to drop a paycheck or just to browse. ✉ *2317 N. Milwaukee Ave., Logan Square* ☎ *773/772–5000* ⊕ *feltchicago.com.*

Squasht

WOMEN'S CLOTHING | Friendly owner Lesley Timpe stocks her Humboldt Park boutique with fun accessories and vibrantly printed dresses and cropped tees in easy-wearing fabrics that manage to tick the boxes for both style and comfort. Some of the stock comes from her own line, which shares the shop's name. ✉ *2556 W. Chicago Ave., Humboldt Park* ☎ *773/292–4123* ⊕ *squashtboutique. com.*

Tusk

ANTIQUES & COLLECTIBLES | A minimalist shop that carries a small selection of vintage clothing along with other one-of-a-kind wearables, objects, and accessories selected by forward-thinking owner Mary Eleanor Wallace. Wallace also invites local artists to show their work there. The shop is usually open only on weekends. ✉ *3205 W. Armitage Ave., Logan Square* ⊕ *instagram.com/tuskchicago.*

Wolfbait & B-Girls

WOMEN'S CLOTHING | More than 300 local designers have showcased their work at this longtime favorite. Owners Shirley Kienitz and Jenny Stadler carry clothing, jewelry, home goods, and art at very reasonable prices. They also have occasional workshops. ✉ *3131 W. Logan Blvd., Logan Square* ☎ *312/698–8685* ⊕ *wolfbaitchicago.com.*

HOME DECOR

Fleur

FLORIST | Kelly Marie Thompson has expanded her popular floral boutique to include home goods, linens, and fine jewelry. Unfortunately, there's no way to bottle the lush, floral scent of the shop's interior, but the selection of artisan candles and fragrances are a good substitute. ✉ *2651 N. Milwaukee Ave., Logan Square* ☎ *773/395–2770* ⊕ *www. fleurchicago.com.*

Humboldt House

HOUSEWARES | This Humboldt Park lifestyle boutique is packed with stylish treasures. The selection of tableware is a particular strength, favoring natural woods, ceramics and enamelware in a 1970s palette. There's also cool clutches, handmade earrings, letterpress cards, and feminist buttons and stickers. ✉ *1045 N. California Ave., Humboldt Park* ☎ *312/785–1442* ⊕ *humboldthouseco.com.*

TOYS

Little Peach Fuzz

TOYS | FAMILY | This thoughtfully curated shop features beautiful wooden toys, kid-appropriate art supplies, whimsical costumes, and a range of storybooks chosen so every child can see themselves represented on the page. The goods aren't cheap, but they're built to last. ✉ *1005 N. California Ave., Humboldt Park* ☎ *312/785–1442* ⊕ *www.littlepeach-fuzz.com.*

Play

TOYS | FAMILY | Owner Ann Kienzle has cornered the neighborhood toy market with wonderful books, games, and stuffed toys that spark the imagination. Favorite throwbacks include Slinkys, jacks, and Lite Brite. ✉ *3109 W. Logan Blvd., Logan Square* ☎ *773/227–6504* ⊕ *playtoysandbooks.com.*

Chapter 7

LAKEVIEW AND THE FAR NORTH SIDE

Updated by
Kris Vire

👁 **Sights**
★★☆☆☆

🍴 **Restaurants**
★★★★☆

🛏 **Hotels**
★☆☆☆☆

🛍 **Shopping**
★★★★☆

🍸 **Nightlife**
★★★★☆

NEIGHBORHOOD SPOTLIGHT

MAKING THE MOST OF YOUR TIME

A Wrigleyville and Lakeview stroll takes about 90 minutes; add another two hours to browse the Southport shops. To experience the *real* Chicago, take in a Cubs game from Wrigley Field's bleachers.

To see all of the Far North's neighborhoods, allow a day. Visit Graceland Cemetery for an hour or two. Leave three hours for Andersonville's shops and Swedish American Museum Center, then two more for shopping on Devon Avenue.

GETTING HERE BY PUBLIC TRANSPORTATION

You may need to take a combination of bus and El. Buses 22 and 36 go to Lakeview from downtown, as do the Brown Line (Southport) and the Purple and Red lines (Belmont). Take the El's Red Line north toward Howard to Lawrence for Uptown, Berwyn for Andersonville, and Loyola for Devon. The 155 bus from Devon reaches the Far North. The Brown Line El north toward Kimball to Western takes you to Lincoln Square.

PARKLAND

One of the great things about Chicago is its many parks. The recently completed **RiverRun 312** (named for the Chicago's original telephone area code), is a biking/running trail that links several park areas along the Chicago River, from California Park to Horner Park. The LaBagh Woods, also on the Chicago River is a popular spot for bird-watching, with a 5.7-mile observation trail winding through it.

TOP REASONS TO GO

- **Take yourself out to the ball game:** Sit in the bleachers with the locals at Wrigley Field, and be ready to throw the ball back onto the field if the opposing team hits a homer. When the Cubs are on the road, take a tour of the park.

- **Go to the movies:** Catch a classic or indie flick at the vintage Music Box Theatre.

- **Tour Graceland Cemetery:** Visit such famous "residents" as Marshall Field, George Pullman, and others at their final resting place.

- **Go Swedish:** Check out the Swedish enclave, Andersonville, for authentic Swedish restaurants and bakeries.

GETTING HERE BY CAR

By car, take Lake Shore Drive north to Belmont (Lakeview), but keep in mind that parking can be scarce. When the Cubs play, take public transit. Head north up Western Avenue to between Montrose and Lawrence for Lincoln Square, Lawrence Avenue for Uptown, Foster Avenue for Andersonville, and Devon Avenue for the Far North.

Stretching north in a rough row that runs parallel and close to the lake, the primarily residential neighborhoods in Lakeview and the Far North Side aren't the place for major museums or high-rises. Instead, they're best at giving you a feel for how local Chicagoans live. Whether you wander one of the many ethnic neighborhoods, contemplate the dignitaries (and scoundrels) buried in Graceland Cemetery, or celebrate a hard-won victory at Wrigley Field, this area is perfect for connecting with the sights and sounds that make Chicago the great city it is.

Lakeview

Initially a settlement and then a township independent of Chicago, Lakeview became part of the city in 1889. Today it is a massive neighborhood made up of small enclaves, each with its own distinct personality. There's Wrigley Field surrounded by the beer-swilling, Cubby-blue-'til-we-die sports-bar fanaticism of Wrigleyville; the gay bars, shops, and clubs along Halsted Street in Boystown (now known as Northalsted); and an air of urban chic along Southport Avenue, where young families stroll amid the trendy boutiques and ice-cream shops.

 Sights

★ **Northalsted**

NEIGHBORHOOD | Just east of Wrigleyville lies this section of Lakeview; it's been a major "gayborhood" since the 1970s, which also makes it one of the country's first. In recent years there's been an admirable push by activists and local merchants alike to rename Boystown to something more inclusive of the larger LGBTQ community, such as "Northalsted" (most of its gay-oriented shops, bars, and restaurants are concentrated on and around North Halsted Street), but the change has been slow to catch on. In June the street becomes a sea of people, when Chicago's gay pride parade

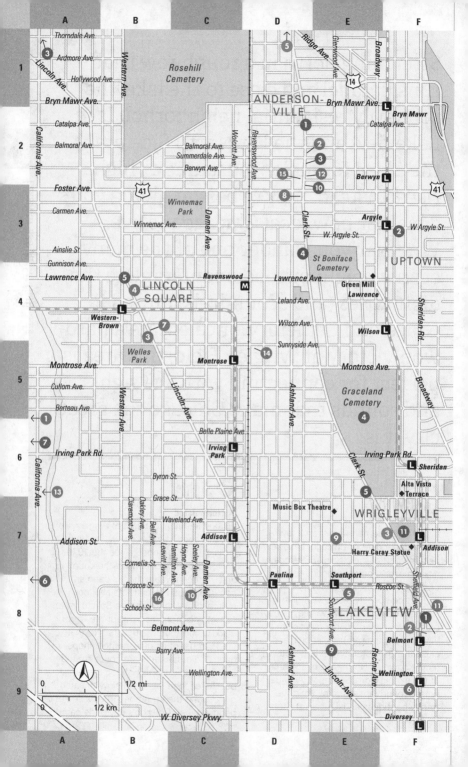

Lakeview, Far North and Far Northwest Sides

KEY

- 1 Exploring Sights
- 1 Restaurants
- 1 Quick Bites
- 1 Hotels
- L CTA Lines
- M Metra Lines

Sights ▼

1 Andersonville D2
2 Argyle Strip F3
3 Devon Avenue A1
4 Graceland Cemetery E5
5 Lincoln Square B4
6 National Italian American Sports Hall of Fame A8
7 National Veterans Art Museum A6
8 Northalsted G7
9 Southport Avenue E8
10 Swedish American Museum Center E2
11 Wrigley Field F7

Restaurants ▼

1 Arun's A5
2 Big Jones E2
3 Bistro Campagne B4
4 Café Selmarie B4
5 Coda di Volpe E8
6 DMK Burger Bar F9
7 Gather B4
8 Hopleaf D3
9 Julius Meinl Café E7
10 Kitsch'n on Roscoe C8
11 Mia Francesca F8
12 Reza's E2
13 Smoque BBQ A6
14 Spacca Napoli Pizzeria D5
15 Svea D2
16 Turquoise Restaurant and Café B8

Quick Bites ▼

1 Ann Sather F8
2 Intelligentsia G8
3 Kopi, a Traveler's Cafe E2
4 Pick Me Up Café D3
5 Uncommon Ground E6

Hotels ▼

1 Best Western Plus Hawthorne Terrace Hotel G8
2 City Suites Hotel F8
3 Hotel Zachary F7
4 The Majestic Hotel G7
5 Margarita European Inn D1
6 The Willows Hotel Chicago G9

Lake Michigan

Lake Shore Drive

Halsted St.

Montrose Beach

Montrose Point Bird Sanctuary

Montrose Harbor

41

Lincoln Park

BOYS-TOWN

N. Broadway

Belmont Ave.

Belmont

Belmont Harbor

Chicago Yacht Club

Barry Ave.

Clark St.

W Surf St.

Pay homage to the greats of Chicago's past at Graceland Cemetery.

floats down the block; Market Days, a massive LGBTQ street fest, floods the area with visitors in August. ✉ *Between Broadway, Belmont Ave., and Halsted St., Boystown.*

★ Graceland Cemetery

CEMETERY | Near Irving Park Road, this graveyard has crypts that are almost as strikingly designed as the city skyline. A number of Chicago's most prominent citizens, including Daniel Burnham and Marshall Field, are spending eternity here. Architect Louis Sullivan (also a resident) designed some of its more elaborate mausoleums. Free maps, available at the cemetery office, will help you find your way around the pastoral 119-acre property. ✉ *4001 N. Clark St., Lakeview* ☎ *773/525–1105* ⊕ *www.gracelandcemetery.org* ✉ *Free.*

Southport Avenue

BUSINESS DISTRICT | Southport and other streets that travel north to Irving Park Road are lined with independent shops,

many of which cater to well-dressed young women with money to burn. ✉ *Southport Ave., between Grace St. and Belmont Ave., Wrigleyville* ⊕ *www. southportneighbors.com.*

★ Wrigley Field

SPORTS VENUE | **FAMILY** | The nation's second-oldest major league ballpark—venerable, ivy-covered Wrigley Field—hosted its first major league game in 1914 and has been home to the Chicago Cubs since 1916. The original scoreboard is still used (score-by-innings, players' numbers, strikes, outs, hits, and errors are all posted manually), and though renovations have modernized the park, the character that makes this place so special remains intact. If you look up along Sheffield and Waveland Avenues beyond the bleachers, you can see the rooftop patios where baseball fans pay high prices to cheer for the home team; devoted "ball hawks" sit in lawn chairs on Sheffield, waiting for foul balls to fly their way. While you're here, check out the Harry Caray statue commemorating the late Cubs announcer; at the seventh-inning stretch, fans sing "Take Me Out to the Ballgame" in his honor. Tours of the park and dugouts are given from April to October. Note that big-name concerts by the likes of Elton John and Bruce Springsteen are also staged here when the team is out of town. ✉ *1060 W. Addison St., at Sheffield St., Wrigleyville* ☎ *800/843–2827* 🌐 *www.mlb.com/cubs/ballpark* 🎫 *Tours $30.*

🍴 Restaurants

Coda di Volpe

$$ | **ITALIAN** | With Vera Pizza Napoletana-certified pizza (that means these are legit Neapolitan-style pies), an airy dining room, a lively bar, and a drinks list packed with Italian wines and aperitivos, Coda di Volpe expertly channels a Southern Italian feel. Use scissors to cut through blistered, chewy-crust pies or opt for the excellent housemade pastas—but save room for the updated takes on Italian sweets on the dessert menu. **Known for:** house-cured meats; brunch; restaurant-exclusive wines. [$] *Average main: $21* ✉ *3335 N. Southport Ave., Lakeview* ☎ *773/687–8568* 🌐 *www.cdvolpe.com* 🕒 *No lunch weekdays.*

DMK Burger Bar

$ | **BURGER** | **FAMILY** | Chef and co-owner Michael Kornick knows fine dining, but he's also a longtime fan of the simple burger, and the two worlds mingle at DMK Burger Bar, where grass-fed beef patties can come topped with green chiles or chipotle ketchup, and fries are often adorned with truffle aioli. If you're not in the mood for beef, any burger can be made with turkey, bison, or a veggie patty. **Known for:** big DMK burger; creamy shakes; beer list. [$] *Average main: $14* ✉ *2954 N. Sheffield Ave., Lakeview* ☎ *773/360–8686* 🌐 *www.dmkburgerbar.com.*

Julius Meinl Café

$ | **CAFÉ** | **FAMILY** | Comfortable banquettes and a supply of international newspapers entice coffee sippers to stick around at this very European café in an unexpected location at the intersection of Addison and Southport, just a few blocks from Wrigley Field. The menu offers classic sandwiches, salads, and pastries, perfect for fueling up for a day of shopping along Southport. **Known for:** specialty coffee drinks; Austrian breakfast; weekend classical and jazz combos. [$] *Average main: $12* ✉ *3601 N. Southport Ave., Lakeview* ☎ *773/868–1857* 🌐 *www.juliusmeinlchicago.com* 🕒 *No dinner.*

Kitsch'n on Roscoe

$ | **AMERICAN** | **FAMILY** | If you love all things '70s, you'll love Kitsch'n as much as the regulars—it's a diner in retro garb, with lava lamps and vintage appliances that have been turned into table lamps, along with clever takes on old-school favorites. The menu has high kid appeal (hello green eggs and ham) but there are plenty of comfort food options for everyone, as well as some international flavors. **Known for:** family-friendly; Twinkies tiramisu; kitschy decor. [$] *Average main: $11* ✉ *2005 W. Roscoe St., Lakeview* ☎ *773/248–7372* 🌐 *www.kitschn.com* 🕒 *No dinner.*

Mia Francesca

$ | **ITALIAN** | Moderate prices and a smart, urbane style drive crowds to this Lakeview storefront for enlightened Northern Italian dishes like pasta, pizza, and antipasti made with fresh ingredients. Have a drink at the bar while you wait for one of the small, tightly spaced tables. **Known for:** bruschetta; daily food and drink specials; outdoor seating. [$] *Average main: $16* ✉ *3311 N. Clark St., Lakeview* ☎ *773/281–3310* 🌐 *www.miafrancesca.com* 🕒 *No lunch.*

Turquoise Restaurant and Café
$$ | **TURKISH** | This bustling Turkish-owned café offers a mixed menu of Continental and Turkish foods, but it's the latter that star here, with a menu of tasty pide (flatbread), salads, and an array of lamb dishes. The vested servers, white tablecloths, and wood-trimmed surroundings add elegance to the low-key Roscoe Village location. **Known for:** salt-crusted branzino; chill vibe; selection of raki. [$] *Average main: $22* ✉ *2147 W. Roscoe St., Lakeview* ☎ *773/549–3523* 🌐 *www.turquoisedining.com.*

Coffee and Quick Bites

Ann Sather
$ | **SCANDINAVIAN** | This Scandinavian minichain, open since 1945, is a Chicago institution for good reason: the aroma of fresh, gooey cinnamon rolls put this place on the map. It still draws a mob—at this location and at the handful of other spots on the city's North Side—where hungry diners line up along the block for weekend breakfasts as well as Scandinavian specialties and standard café sandwiches and salads at lunch. **Known for:** creative eggs Benedict offerings; potato pancakes with applesauce; Swedish pancakes with ligonberries. [$] *Average main: $11* ✉ *909 W. Belmont Ave., Lakeview* ☎ *773/348–2378* 🌐 *www.annsather.com* ⏲ *No dinner.*

Intelligentsia
$ | **AMERICAN** | This place was named to invoke the pre-chain days when cafés were forums for discussion, but the long, broad farmer's tables and handsome couches are usually occupied by students and other serious types who treat the café like their office. Intelligentsia does all of its own coffee roasting and sells its house blends to local restaurants. **Known for:** Black Cat espresso; expert baristas; industrial-chic decor. [$] *Average main: $6* ✉ *3123 N. Broadway, Lakeview* ☎ *773/348–8058* 🌐 *www.intelligentsiacoffee.com* ⏲ *No dinner.*

Uncommon Ground
$$ | **AMERICAN** | The original location of Uncommon Ground is roomy and inviting, with a hand-carved bar and large street-facing windows offering views of passersby. Patrons brave the wait for bowls of coffee and hot chocolate. **Known for:** coffee by the bowl; craft beer selection; Sunday open mics. [$] *Average main: $17* ✉ *3800 N. Clark St., Lakeview* ☎ *773/929–3680* 🌐 *www.uncommonground.com.*

Hotels

Best Western Plus Hawthorne Terrace Hotel
$$ | **HOTEL** | Centrally located in the Lakeview neighborhood, this Best Western offers all essential amenities at a reasonable price: the rate includes a free continental breakfast plus use of the business facilities and fitness center. **Pros:** close to Wrigley Field and popular bars and restaurants; free Wi-Fi; helpful staff. **Cons:** parking is not ideal; no on-site restaurant; no pool. [$] *Rooms from: $269* ✉ *3434 N. Broadway, Lakeview* ☎ *773/244–3434, 888/675–2378* 🌐 *www.hawthorneterrace.com* 🛏 *83 rooms* 🍴 *Free Breakfast.*

City Suites Hotel
$ | **HOTEL** | European travelers love this hotel for its residential feel; the rooms have black-and-white linens plus mid-century-inspired accents, and two-thirds of them have separate sitting areas with pull-out couches. **Pros:** flat-screen TVs in all rooms; convenient to public transit; great neighborhood. **Cons:** rooms are on the small side; an underwhelming breakfast; possible El noise. [$] *Rooms from: $239* ✉ *933 W. Belmont Ave., Lakeview* ☎ *773/404–3400, 800/248–9108* 🌐 *www.chicagocitysuites.com* 🛏 *45 rooms* 🍴 *Free Breakfast.*

Hotel Zachary
$$$ | **HOTEL** | Across from Wrigley Field, this much-anticipated arrival is a home run on all accounts, from the Cubs-centric design to the buzzing bar scene to the private balconies where you can overlook all the brouhaha below. **Pros:** upscale cocktail bar; luxury accommodations near Wrigley; lively neighborhood feel. **Cons:** at least a 20-minute ride downtown; no spa; rowdy neighborhood, especially on game nights. [$] *Rooms from: $349* ✉ *3630 N. Clark St., Wrigleyville* ☎ *773/302–2300* 🌐 *www.hotelzachary.com* 🛏 *173 rooms* 🍴 *No Meals.*

The Majestic Hotel
$$ | **HOTEL** | Everything at this charming boutique hotel says homey—from the quiet, side-street location to the roaring fireplace in the lobby and the complimentary cookies served each afternoon. **Pros:** free Wi-Fi and continental breakfast; friendly staff; some rooms have pullout couches. **Cons:** some have complained of issues with the heating; rooms can be small; you'll have to walk a block for a cab. [$] *Rooms from: $299* ✉ *528 W. Brompton Ave., Lakeview* ☎ *773/404–3499, 800/727–5108* 🌐 *www.majestic-chicago.com* 🛏 *52 rooms* 🍴 *Free Breakfast.*

The Willows Hotel Chicago
$$ | **HOTEL** | Designed in French Provincial style, the lobby of this 1920s hotel opens onto a tree-lined street in Lakeview, just three blocks from the lake and central to stores, restaurants, and movie theaters. **Pros:** just steps away from bars, restaurants, and public transit; 24-hour coffee service; free Wi-Fi. **Cons:** modestly decorated rooms; some say air-conditioning is inadequate; no on-site fitness center, but guests have access to a nearby gym. [$] *Rooms from: $279* ✉ *555 W. Surf St., Lakeview* ☎ *773/528–8400, 800/787–3108* 🌐 *www.willowshotelchicago.com* 🛏 *55 rooms* 🍴 *Free Breakfast.*

Nightlife

BARS

Gman Tavern
BARS | Up the street from Wrigley Field, Gman Tavern deftly manages to avoid being pigeonholed as a sports bar. The back room is outfitted with a small stage and top-notch sound system for live music and comedy shows; in the front room, the well-stocked jukebox and extensive beer list keep regulars and Cubs fans coming back. ✉ *3740 N. Clark St., Lakeview* ☎ *773/549–2050* 🌐 *www.gmantavern.com* 🕒 *Closed Mon.–Wed. except Cubs game and Metro show days.*

Nisei Lounge
BARS | This unassuming joint claims the mantle of Wrigleyville's oldest bar, operating continuously since 1951. Whether it's thronged with Cubs fans on game days or by its loyal regulars in mid-winter, the Nisei exudes a welcoming, divey vibe. If you want to sample Malört, an only-in-Chicago liqueur best described as an acquired taste, no bar will be happier to introduce it to you. ✉ *3439 N. Sheffield Ave., Wrigleyville* ☎ *773/525–0557* 🌐 *www.niseiloungechicago.com.*

Sheffield's
BEER GARDENS | With a shaded beer garden in summer and a roaring fireplace in winter, Sheffield's spans the seasons. The laid-back neighborhood pub has billiards and more than 100 kinds of bottled beer, including regional microbrews. You can also choose from 18 brands on tap or opt for the bartender's "bad beer of the month" (think a cheap can of PBR). ✉ *3258 N. Sheffield Ave., Lakeview* ☎ *773/281–4989* 🌐 *www.sheffieldschicago.com.*

Sluggers
BARS | Sluggers is packed after Cubs games in the nearby stadium, and the ballplayers make occasional appearances

There were no lights—or night games—at Wrigley Field until 1988.

in summer. Check out the fast- and slow-pitch batting cages on the second floor, as well as the pool tables, air-hockey tables, and electronic basketball. ✉ 3540 N. Clark St., Lakeview ☎ 773/248–0055 ⊕ www.sluggersbar.com.

COMEDY AND IMPROV CLUBS

★ The Annoyance Theatre & Bar

COMEDY CLUBS | This is home base for Annoyance Productions, an irreverent group best known for hits like *Skinprov* and *Hitch*Cocktails*. ✉ 851 W. Belmont Ave., Lakeview ☎ 773/697–9693 ⊕ www.theannoyance.com.

DANCE CLUBS

★ Berlin Nightclub

DANCE CLUBS | A multicultural, pansexual dance club near the Belmont El station, Berlin has progressive electronic dance music and fun themed nights (Madonna is celebrated on the first Sunday of every month, and Björk is honored with a quarterly party). The venue also hosts drag matinees, comedy shows, and vogue-offs. The crowd tends to be predominantly queer on weeknights,

mixed on weekends. ✉ 954 W. Belmont Ave., Lakeview ☎ 773/348–4975 ⊕ www.berlinchicago.com ⊗ Closed Tues. and Wed. ☞ A cash-only cover is charged on Fri. and Sat.

GAY AND LESBIAN

Charlie's

DANCE CLUBS | A country-and-western dance spot, Charlie's lets you two-step nightly to achy-breaky tunes (club music takes over after midnight). It's mostly a boots-and-denim crowd on weekends. ✉ 3726 N. Broadway St., Lakeview ☎ 773/871–8887 ⊕ www.charlieschicago.com.

The Closet

BARS | This compact dive bar—one of the few that caters to lesbians, though it draws gay men, too—can be especially lively after 2 am when most other bars close. Stop by Sunday afternoons when bartenders serve up what are hailed as the best Bloody Marys in town. ✉ 3325 N. Broadway St., Lakeview ☎ 773/477–8533 ⊕ www.theclosetchicago.com.

Hydrate

DANCE CLUBS | Hydrate combines a relaxed front lounge with a late-night, high-energy dance floor in the back. Weekly events include drag shows. ⊠ *3458 N. Halsted St., Lakeview* ☎ *773/975–9244* ⊕ *www.hydratechicago. com.*

North End

BARS | A sports bar with a twist, the North End is a favorite spot to watch the big game or play some pool. Later at night, it has more of a typical gay-bar atmosphere. ⊠ *3733 N. Halsted St., Lakeview* ☎ *773/477–7999* ⊕ *www.north-endchicago.com.*

Progress Bar

DANCE CLUBS | A neighborhood lounge that turns DJ-driven dance spot late at night, this newer entry on the Halsted Street strip makes a striking statement with its signature visual, a cloud-like illuminated ceiling sculpture that's visible from the street. ⊠ *3359 N. Halsted St., Boystown* ☎ *773/697–9268* ⊕ *www. progressbarchicago.com.*

Roscoe's Tavern and Cafe

BARS | A longtime favorite, Roscoe's Tavern has a lot to offer its preppy patrons, including a jam-packed front bar, a dance floor, a pool table, an outdoor garden, and lively music. The sidewalk café is open May through September. ⊠ *3356 N. Halsted St., Lakeview* ☎ *773/281–3355* ⊕ *www.roscoes.com.*

Sidetrack

BARS | Focusing on a different theme every night of the week, Sidetrack broadcasts videos on TV screens that never leave your sight. Attractive professionals pack the sprawling strike-a-pose bar and rooftop deck; order a vodka slushie (the house specialty) and join the crowd. ⊠ *3349 N. Halsted St., Lakeview* ☎ *773/477–9189* ⊕ *www.sidetrackchicago.com.*

MUSIC CLUBS

Beat Kitchen

LIVE MUSIC | North Side stalwart Beat Kitchen brings in the crowds because of its good sound system and solid rock, alternative-rock, country, and rockabilly acts. It also serves soups, salads, sandwiches, pizzas, and desserts. ⊠ *2100 W. Belmont Ave., Lakeview* ☎ *773/281–4444* ⊕ *www.beatkitchen.com.*

Metro

LIVE MUSIC | Progressive, nationally known artists and the cream of the local crop play at Metro, a former movie palace. It's an excellent place to see live bands, whether you're moshing on the main floor or above the fray in the balcony. In the basement is **Smart Bar**, a late-night dance club that starts hopping after midnight. ⊠ *3730 N. Clark St., Lakeview* ☎ *773/549–4140* ⊕ *www.metrochicago. com.*

Schubas Tavern

LIVE MUSIC | Built in 1903 by the Schlitz Brewing Company, Schubas Tavern favors local and national power pop, indie rock, and folk musicians. The laid-back, wood-paneled back room is the perfect place to hear artists who are just about to make it big. The attached restaurant, Tied House, serves creative comfort food. ⊠ *3159 N. Southport Ave., Lakeview* ☎ *773/525–2508* ⊕ *www.lh-st. com.*

⬤ Performing Arts

FILM

Music Box Theatre

FILM | If you love old theaters, old movies, and ghosts (rumor has it the theater is haunted by the spirit of its original manager), don't miss a trip to the Music Box. Certain screenings in the vintage 1929 venue get extra atmosphere thanks to a live pipe organ introduction. ⊠ *3733 N. Southport Ave., Lakeview* ☎ *773/871–6604* ⊕ *www.musicboxtheatre.com* ✉ *$11.*

THEATER

Briar Street Theatre

THEATER | Originally built as a horse stable for Marshall Field, Briar Street Theatre is the spot to catch the long-running hit *Blue Man Group*. ⊠ *3133 N. Halsted St., Lakeview* ☎ *773/348–4000* ⊕ *www. blueman.com/chicago.*

Theater Wit

THEATER | This cozy three-theater complex hosts Theater Wit's own productions (which tend toward highbrow comedies) as well as those by like-minded small companies without spaces of their own. ⊠ *1229 W. Belmont Ave., Lakeview* ☎ *773/975–8150* ⊕ *theaterwit.org.*

VENUES

Athenaeum Theatre

THEATER | The 1,000-seat Athenaeum Theatre, adjacent to St. Alphonsus Church, stages comedy, dance, children's theater performances, and more. ⊠ *2936 N. Southport Ave., Lakeview* ☎ *773/935–6875* ⊕ *www.athenaeumtheatre.com.*

Constellation/Links Hall

ARTS CENTERS | A converted warehouse on Western Avenue is home to an eclectic mix of adventurous performance, ranging from genre-fluid jazz and new music to small, scrappy dance troupes to cutting-edge solo performance art. ⊠ *3111 N. Western Ave., Lakeview* ☎ *773/281–0824* ⊕ *www.constellation-chicago.com.*

🛍 Shopping

Home to Wrigley Field, this North Side neighborhood is broken into several smaller shopping areas, each with a distinct flavor and each making for a fun afternoon out. Clark Street, between Diversey Avenue and Addison Street, is Cubs central, with shops hawking sports-centric paraphernalia. A slew of upscale boutiques draws trend seekers to Southport Avenue between Belmont Avenue and Grace Street. Antiquers and bargain hunters should head straight for the intersection of Lincoln Avenue and Diversey Parkway and meander north on Lincoln.

ANTIQUES

Antique Resources

ANTIQUES & COLLECTIBLES | Choice antiques from Europe and elsewhere are sold at fair prices here. This is an excellent source for stately desks and dignified dining sets, but the true find is a huge trove of antique crystal and gilt chandeliers from France. ⊠ *1741 W. Belmont Ave., Lakeview* ☎ *773/871–4242* ⊕ *www. antiqueresourcesinc.com* ⊙ *Closed Sun. and Mon.*

Father Time Antiques

ANTIQUES & COLLECTIBLES | Father Time bills itself as the Midwest's largest retailer of vintage timepieces. In addition to pocket watches and clocks, it carries accessories like watch holders and display cases. ⊠ *2108 W. Belmont Ave., Lakeview* ☎ *773/880–5599* ⊕ *www.fathertimeantiques.com* ⊙ *Closed Mon. and Tues.*

Urban Artifacts

ANTIQUES & COLLECTIBLES | This store's superb collection of furniture, lighting, and decorative accessories from the 1940s to the '70s emphasizes industrial designs. ⊠ *2928 N. Lincoln Ave., Suite 1, Lakeview* ☎ *773/404–1008* ⊙ *Closed Mon. and Tues.*

BOOKS, MUSIC, AND GIFTS

Gramaphone Records

MUSIC | Local DJs and club kids go to Gramaphone to find vintage and cutting-edge dance, house, and hip-hop releases. You can hear them on the spot at one of the store's listening stations. It also stocks DJ gear. ⊠ *2843 N. Clark St., Lakeview* ☎ *773/472–3683* ⊕ *www. gramaphonerecords.com* ⊙ *Closed Mon.–Wed.*

Inkling

STATIONERY | This quirky hole-in-the-wall specializes in locally made cards, art prints, jewelry, and other hipster-friendly gifts. Every first Friday, Inkling hosts a reception showcasing whichever artist's work is featured on the shop's gallery wall that month. ⊠ *2917½ N. Broadway, Lakeview* ☏ *773/248–8004* ⊕ *www. theinklingshop.com.*

★ Reckless Records

MUSIC | Reckless Records ranks as one of the city's leading alternative and secondhand record stores. Besides the indie offerings, you can flip through jazz, classical, and soul recordings, or catch a live appearance by an up-and-comer passing through town. Look for other locations in the Loop (*26 East Madison Street*) and Wicker Park (*1379 North Milwaukee Avenue*). ⊠ *929 W. Belmont Ave., Lakeview* ☏ *773/404–5080* ⊕ *www. reckless.com.*

★ Unabridged Bookstore

BOOKS | Since 1980 this independent bookshop has maintained a loyal clientele who love its vast selection and dedicated staff. Known for having one of the most extensive gay and lesbian sections in the city, it also has an impressive array of children's books. ⊠ *3251 N. Broadway St., Lakeview* ☏ *773/883–9119* ⊕ *www. unabridgedbookstore.com.*

CLOTHING

Kickin'

WOMEN'S CLOTHING | Hip, urban women snap up their maternity wear at this shop. There's an emphasis on workout and yoga gear. ⊠ *2033 W. Roscoe St., Lakeview* ☏ *773/281–6577* ⊕ *www. kickinmaternity.com.*

Krista K Boutique

WOMEN'S CLOTHING | An inventory of must-haves for women from designers like Citizens of Humanity, Theory, and Splendid reflects the style of this neighborhood. The boutique has become a go-to spot for the latest denim, too. ⊠ *3458 N. Southport Ave., Lakeview* ☏ *773/248–1967* ⊕ *www.kristak.com.*

HOME DECOR

Waxman Candles

HOUSEWARES | The candles sold here are made on the premises and come in countless shapes, colors, and scents. There's an incredible selection of candle holders and incense, too. ⊠ *3044 N. Lincoln Ave., Lakeview* ☏ *773/929–3000* ⊕ *www.waxmancandles.com.*

PET STORES

Wigglyville

PET STORES | Everything you need for your furry friend (leashes, collars, bedding, carriers, shampoo, and more), along with pet-theme artwork, is carefully arranged in this inviting pet boutique. Another branch is at 1137 West Madison Street, in the West Loop. ⊠ *3337 N. Broadway Ave., Lakeview* ☏ *773/528–3337* ⊕ *www. wigglyville.com.*

TOYS

Building Blocks

TOYS | From cars and train sets to puzzles and musical instruments, Building Blocks carries classic toys designed to appeal to kids' natural curiosity and imagination—and they'll gift wrap them for you at no charge. In Wicker Park, stop by the store at 2130 West Division Street. ⊠ *3306 N. Lincoln Ave., Lakeview* ☏ *773/525–6200* ⊕ *www.buildingblockstoys.com.*

WINE

Lush Wine and Spirits

WINE/SPIRITS | This full-service liquor store specializes in wine, microbrews, and obscure spirits from small-batch distilleries. Attend one of the frequently held wine tastings to try before you buy. There is also a branch in West Town (*1412 West Chicago Avenue*). ⊠ *2232 W. Roscoe St., Lakeview* ☏ *773/281–8888* ⊕ *www. lushwineandspirits.com.*

In Andersonville, as elsewhere in the city, wood houses were banned after the Great Chicago Fire of 1871.

Far North and Far Northwest Sides

The Far North and Far Northwest sides of Chicago are home to several of the city's most colorful neighborhoods. Just north of Lakeview, Uptown's beautiful architecture and striking old marquees are a testament to the time when it was a thriving entertainment district.

The area around Broadway and Argyle is known variously as Little Vietnam, Little Chinatown, and North Chinatown. Andersonville was named for the Swedish community that settled near Foster Avenue and Clark Street in the 1960s, and it still maintains a huge concentration of Swedes.

Double street signs attest to Devon Avenue's diversity—in some places named for Gandhi, in others for Golda Meir, although much of the Jewish population has moved to Skokie. Whatever the name, the area is best explored on foot.

South of Devon via Western Avenue is the former German enclave of Lincoln Square, now a happening dining and shopping destination. One of the best ways to discover all these neighborhoods' cultural diversity is by sampling the food.

Sights

★ Andersonville

NEIGHBORHOOD | FAMILY | Just north of Uptown there's a neighborhood that feels like a small town and still shows signs of the Swedish settlers who founded it. Andersonville has some great restaurants and bakeries, many of which pay tribute to its Scandinavian roots. In winter months, be sure to drop by **Simon's Tavern**, at 5210 North Clark, for a glass of *glögg* (mulled wine)—it's a traditional favorite. Helping anchor the area is the **Women & Children First** bookstore, at 5233

North Clark, which stocks an extensive selection of feminist tomes and children's lit. ⊠ *Between Glenwood, Foster, Ravenswood, and Bryn Mawr Aves., Andersonville* ☎ *773/728–2995* ⊕ *www. andersonville.org.*

Argyle Strip

NEIGHBORHOOD | Also known as Little Vietnam (and Little Chinatown and North Chinatown), this area is anchored by the red pagoda of the El's Argyle Street stop. Home to many Vietnamese immigrants, the Strip teems with storefront noodle shops, bakeries, and pan-Asian grocery stores that are a huge draw for locals and tourists alike. Roasted ducks hang in shop windows and fish peer out from large tanks. ⊠ *Between Foster, Lawrence, Broadway, and Lake Michigan, Uptown.*

Devon Avenue

NEIGHBORHOOD | Chicagoans flock here to satisfy cravings for Indian, Middle Eastern, and Asian fare, or, as the avenue moves west, a good Jewish challah. Indian restaurants and sari shops start popping up just west of Western Avenue. Though west of Talman Avenue was once an enclave for orthodox Jews and Russian immigrants, many of the people, along with the shops, have migrated to the northern suburbs. ⊠ *Devon Ave., between Kedzie and Ridge Aves., Far North Side.*

Lincoln Square

NEIGHBORHOOD | Long known for its Teutonic heritage, Lincoln Square is home to two annual German fests—Mayfest in late May (held around a 30-foot-tall maypole) and German-American Fest in September—both featuring plenty of beer, brats, German-style pretzels, and folks dressed in lederhosen. Thursday evenings in summer bring free concerts and a farmers' market. Popular bars and restaurants line Lincoln Avenue between Montrose and Lawrence; shopping is a draw, too. Many credit Lincoln Square's

renaissance to the relocation of the Old Town School of Folk Music, which moved to a long-vacant art deco building at 4544 North Lincoln Avenue in 1998. Each July, it sponsors the Square Roots festival. But those longing for a taste of Lincoln Square's ethnic roots shouldn't despair. You'll still find a handful of German restaurants and bars along the avenue. Also still here is the 1922 Krause Music Store building (*4611 North Lincoln Avenue*), with its ornate green terracotta facade; it was the last work commissioned by architect Louis Sullivan. ⊠ *Between Foster, Montrose, and Damen Aves. and the Chicago River, Lincoln Square* ⊕ *www. lincolnsquare.org.*

National Italian American Sports Hall of Fame

HISTORY MUSEUM | The NIASHF was founded by George Randazzo in 1978 to honor Italian American athletes. Among the first inductees was baseball legend Joe DiMaggio; others include Rocky Marciano, Yogi Berra, Mary Lou Retton, and Phil Rizzuto. Originally housed in Elmwood Park, then Arlington Heights, then Little Italy, the collection is now located in the Dunning neighborhood. If you're interested in relics like the last coat worn by Vince Lombardi as the Green Bay Packers coach or Mario Andretti's Indy 500 race car, this is your kind of place. ⊠ *3417 N. Harlem Ave., Far Northwest Side* ☎ *312/226–5566* ⊕ *www.niashf.org* ☞ *Free.*

★ National Veterans Art Museum

OTHER MUSEUM | Located in Portage Park, this museum is dedicated to collecting, preserving, and exhibiting art inspired by combat and created by veterans. Founded in 1981, its goal is to serve as a space for civilians, veterans, and current military alike to share an open dialogue on the lasting impacts of warfare. The museum features haunting works from all wars in which the United States has participated. ⊠ *4041 N. Milwaukee Ave.,*

2nd fl., Far Northwest Side ☎ *312/326-0270* 🌐 *www.nvam.org* 🎫 *Free* 🕒 *Closed Sun.–Tues. and Thurs.*

★ Swedish American Museum Center

OTHER MUSEUM | FAMILY | You don't have to be Swedish to find this tiny and welcoming museum interesting. Permanent displays include trunks immigrants brought with them to Chicago and a map showing where in the city different immigrant groups settled. On the third floor, in the only children's museum in the country dedicated to immigration, kids can climb aboard a colorful Viking ship. ✉ *5211 N. Clark St., Andersonville* ☎ *773/728-8111* 🌐 *www.swedishamericanmuseum.org* 🎫 *$6* 🕒 *Closed Mon. and Tues.*

🍴 Restaurants

★ Arun's

$$$$ | THAI | One of the finest Thai restaurants in Chicago—some say in the country—offers a culinary tour through Thailand via a nine-course tasting menu. (An à la carte menu is also available.) The elegant dining room is in an out-of-the-way location in a residential neighborhood on the Northwest Side, but it doesn't discourage a strong following among locals and visiting foodies. **Known for:** unique cocktails; artful food presentations; mango sticky rice. [$] *Average main: $100* ✉ *4156 N. Kedzie Ave., Irving Park* ☎ *773/539-1909* 🌐 *www.arunsthai.com* 🕒 *Closed Mon.-Wed. No lunch.*

Big Jones

$$ | SOUTHERN | Even if you weren't raised by a Southern grandmother, the cooking at this bright, comfortable Andersonville restaurant will make you feel right at home, but the Southern heirloom cooking has more depth than you might expect. The brunch, lunch, and dinner menus revive century-old recipes scrupulously sourced out of historical cookbooks from New Orleans to Appalachia and re-create them with high-quality, sustainable ingredients. **Known for:** bourbon list; fried chicken; brunch beignets. [$] *Average main: $19* ✉ *5347 N. Clark St., Far North Side* ☎ *773/275-5725* 🌐 *www.bigjoneschicago.com.*

Bistro Campagne

$$$ | FRENCH | For rustic French fare on the North Side, this is the place to come: the classic, seasonally changing French dishes are top-notch, while the lovely, wood-trimmed Arts and Crafts interior is the perfect complement to a relaxing meal. In warmer weather, ask for a table in the torch-lighted garden and a bottle off the French-centric wine list. **Known for:** commitment to sustainability; steak frites; Sunday brunch. [$] *Average main: $29* ✉ *4518 N. Lincoln Ave., Lincoln Square* ☎ *773/271-6100* 🌐 *www.bistrocampagne.com* 🕒 *Closed Mon. and Tues. No lunch.*

Café Selmarie

$ | CAFÉ | A long-standing favorite among locals, this bakery-turned-restaurant is a great spot for a light meal—especially during warmer months, when the outdoor patio beckons. The restaurant is open all day and serves perfectly executed sandwiches, salads, pastas, and other staples; head in on Tuesday for half-price bottles of wine and don't miss the fabulous pastries (you can also buy them to go at the front counter). **Known for:** cinnamon roll griddlecakes; signature tortes; $24 prix-fixe dinners Wednesday. [$] *Average main: $16* ✉ *4729 N. Lincoln Ave., Lincoln Square* ☎ *773/989-5595* 🌐 *www.cafeselmarie.com* 🕒 *Closed Mon.*

★ Gather

$$ | AMERICAN | FAMILY | Class meets comfort in this upscale Lincoln Square neighborhood eatery, where the service is top-notch and everything on your plate is made in-house from scratch, right down to the fresh breads and condiments. The seasonally driven dinner and brunch menus feature farm-fresh ingredients applied to inventive riffs on classic dishes, at prices that feel like a steal. **Known for:** back patio; Sunday night family-style dinners (plus à la carte); pastas. $ *Average main: $20* ✉ *4539 N. Lincoln Ave., Lincoln Square* ☎ *773/506–9300* ⊕ *www. gatherchicago.com* ⊗ *Closed Mon. and Tues. No lunch.*

★ Hopleaf

$$ | **AMERICAN** | When hops devotee Michael Roper added a dining room onto the back of his beloved tavern, swillers were thrilled with the opportunity to sop their suds with delectable specialties from the Belgian-inspired kitchen. Even with the expansion of a second full dining room and upstairs space, it's still best to arrive early to avoid waiting for a table—though exploring the massive beer list at the bar is never a bad idea. **Known for:** shaded back patio; CB&J (cashew butter sandwich); Belgian-style mussels. $ *Average main: $20* ✉ *5148 N. Clark St., Far North Side* ☎ *773/334–9851* ⊕ *www. hopleaf.com* ☞ *21+ only.*

Reza's

$ | **PERSIAN** | This bright spot with lots of windows serves outstanding Persian cuisine, like kebabs, dolmas, and charbroiled ground beef with rice. On weekdays, its $13.95 lunch buffet is the best deal in town. **Known for:** large portions; signature kebabs; terrific baba ghannouj. $ *Average main: $12* ✉ *5255 N. Clark St., Andersonville* ☎ *773/561–1898* ⊕ *www. rezasrestaurant.com.*

Smoque BBQ

$ | **BARBECUE** | **FAMILY** | The sweet smoky aroma wafting out of this casual barbecue spot always attracts a crowd, and while the line to order at the counter extends out the door on weekends, it moves quickly. Smoque covers a range of barbecue styles, from St. Louis ribs to 14-hour cooked Texas-style brisket, so if you can't make up your mind between brisket or shredded pork shoulder, order the half-and-half—a sandwich with half of

each. **Known for:** the ribs; Texas sausage; BYOB. $ *Average main: $14* ✉ *3800 N. Pulaski Rd., Irving Park* ☎ *773/545–7427* ⊕ *www.smoquebbq.com* ⊗ *Closed Mon.*

★ Spacca Napoli Pizzeria

$ | **PIZZA** | **FAMILY** | Despite Chicago's renown for deep-dish pizza, locals are swept away by the thin-crust Neapolitan pies at this bright Ravenswood gem, where finely ground Italian flour, imported buffalo mozzarella, hand-stretched dough, and a brick, wood-fired oven built by Italian craftsmen produce the bubbling, chewy crusts of these pies. Antipasti, a well-priced selection of Italian wines and beers, and desserts like tiramisu round out the menu. **Known for:** Italian beverages; sidewalk patio; gluten-free pizza. $ *Average main: $16* ✉ *1769 W. Sunnyside Ave., Ravenswood* ☎ *773/878–2420* ⊕ *www.spaccanapolipizzeria.com* ⊗ *Closed Mon.*

Svea

$ | **SCANDINAVIAN** | **FAMILY** | The North Side's Andersonville neighborhood was once a haven for Swedes; though that's changed over the decades, the humble Svea, a Swedish version of an American diner, carries the torch with hearty breakfast and lunch options. The daytime-only menu is packed with Swedish classics (the huge "Viking Breakfast" is legendary) and burgers; while the digs are no-frills, the service is unvariably friendly. **Known for:** super-friendly vibe; pancakes with lingonberries; Swedish meatballs. $ *Average main: $10* ✉ *5236 N. Clark St., Andersonville* ☎ *773/275–7738* 🖃 *No credit cards* ⊗ *Closed Mon. and Tues. No dinner.*

☕ Coffee and Quick Bites

Kopi, a Traveler's Cafe

$ | **CAFÉ** | This casual, bohemian café serves healthy vegetarian fare as well as decadent desserts, and has a full bar, too. While here, you can browse through a selection of travel books and global gifts. **Known for:** live music on Mondays; convivial crowd; vegan snacks. Ⓢ *Average main: $13* ✉ *5317 N. Clark St., Far North Side* ☎ *773/989–5674* ⊕ *www.kopicafechicago.com.*

Pick Me Up Café

$ | AMERICAN | A CTA construction project forced the Pick Me Up out of its longtime Lakeview location, but its new digs preserve its quirky, neighborhood café charm. The thrift-store treasures hanging on the walls are as eclectic as the crowd that comes at all hours of the day to drink bottomless cups of coffee or dine on sandwiches, appetizers, and desserts. **Known for:** vegetarian-friendly menu; all-day breakfast; vegan milkshakes. Ⓢ *Average main: $10* ✉ *4882 N. Clark St., Far North Side* ☎ *773/248–6613* ⊕ *www.pmucafe.com.*

Hotels

Margarita European Inn

$$ | B&B/INN | While the varied room sizes and narrow corridors may bring to mind a college dormitory, you won't find a more charming place to stay in Chicago's Near North suburbs. **Pros:** small but helpful staff; a fun, off-the-beaten-path place; close to Northwestern University. **Cons:** no parking; breakfast is merely adequate. Ⓢ *Rooms from: $250* ✉ *1566 Oak Ave., Evanston* ☎ *847/869–2273* ⊕ *www.margaritainn.com* ⤴ *46 rooms* ⦿ *Free Breakfast.*

Nightlife

Lakeview, Uptown, and Andersonville, all on the Far North Side, have one thing in common: affordability. Unbelievable as it sounds, there are places in the city where $20 stretches beyond the price of admission and a martini. Drink deals are frequently offered at many bars. If you're heading out early, take the El or a bus, but you'll probably want to cab it back to your hotel.

BARS

Cubby Bear Lounge

BARS | Diagonally across the street from Wrigley Field stands the Cubby Bear, a Chicago institution since 1953. It is the place where Cub fans come to drown their sorrows in beer or lift one to celebrate. There are plenty of TVs for game watching, plus live music and a menu featuring burgers and other bar food. ✉ *1059 W. Addison St., Wrigleyville* ☎ *773/327–1662* ⊕ *www.cubbybear.com* ⊗ *Closed Mon. and Tues. except during Cubs home games.*

Holiday Club

COCKTAIL LOUNGES | Rat Pack aficionados will appreciate the 1950s decor at this self-described "Swinger's mecca." Down a pint of beer and scan the typical (but tasty) bar menu as you listen to Frank Sinatra crooning on the well-stocked CD jukebox. The back room, in contrast, hosts karaoke, trivia and storytelling events on weeknights and '80s and '90s dance parties on the weekends. ✉ *4000 N. Sheridan Rd., Far North Side* ☎ *773/348–9600* ⊕ *www.holidayclubchicago.com.*

★ Hopleaf

BARS | An anchor in the Andersonville corridor, Hopleaf continues the tradition of the classic Chicago bar hospitable to conversation (there's not a TV in sight). The lengthy beer menu emphasizes Belgian varieties and regional microbrews, and the Belgian fare served here far surpasses typical bar food. Don't miss the ale-steamed mussels and delectable skinny fries with aioli on the side. ✉ *5148 N. Clark St., Far North Side* ☎ *773/334–9851* ⊕ *www.hopleaf.com.*

Marty's Martini Bar

COCKTAIL LOUNGES | Minuscule Marty's serves up some of the tastiest cocktails in town. Roughly the size of a one-bedroom apartment, the bar can get very crowded, so come early in the night. ✉ *1511 W. Balmoral Ave., Andersonville*

☏ 773/944–0082 ⊕ www.martysmartinibar.com.

Rogers Park Social

BARS | It's hard to imagine a bar feeling homier than Rogers Park Social. The community-oriented spot has an impressive menu of craft beers plus fresh cocktails that pack deep layers of flavor into every glass. ✉ 6920 N. Glenwood Ave. ☏ 773/791–1419 ⊕ www.rogersparksocial.com.

★ Simon's Tavern

BARS | This classic Andersonville bar honors the neighborhood's Swedish roots with its signature drink, glögg—mulled Swedish wine, served hot in a mug in winter and in frozen slushie form in summer. The Viking/Midwestern-chic decor is eclectic and dive-y, but in a very good way. This is where the locals hang out. Simon's often hosts live music from area bands as well. ✉ 5210 N. Clark St., Andersonville ☏ 773/878–0894.

GAY AND LESBIAN

★ Big Chicks

BARS | In the Uptown area of the Far North Side, Big Chicks is a striking alternative to the Halsted strip, with a funky crowd that appreciates the owner's art collection hanging on the walls. The fun-loving staff and their self-selected eclectic music are the payoffs for the hike to get here. Special attractions include weekend dancing and free Sunday-afternoon buffets. ✉ 5024 N. Sheridan Rd., Far North Side ☏ 773/728–5511 ⊕ www.bigchicks.com ☺ Closed Wed.

MUSIC VENUES

★ Green Mill Cocktail Lounge

LIVE MUSIC | A Chicago institution, the Green Mill has stood sentinel in the Uptown neighborhood since 1907. Deep leather banquettes and ornate wood paneling line the walls, and a photo of former patron Al Capone occupies a place of honor on the piano behind the bar. The jazz entertainment is both excellent and contemporary—the club launched the careers of Kurt Elling and Patricia Barber. ✉ 4802 N. Broadway Ave., Far North Side ☏ 773/878–5552 ⊕ www.greenmilljazz.com ☞ Cash only.

Martyrs'

LIVE MUSIC | Martyrs' brings mostly local rock bands (and the occasional major-label act) to North Center, a small neighborhood sandwiched between Lincoln Square and Roscoe Village. Music fans can see the stage from just about any corner of the bar, while the more rhythmically inclined gyrate in the large standing-room area. A mural opposite the stage memorializes late rock greats. ✉ 3855 N. Lincoln Ave., Far Northwest Side ☏ 773/404–9494 ⊕ www.martyrslive.com.

★ Old Town School of Folk Music

LIVE MUSIC | Chicago's oldest folk-music school has served as folk central in the city since it opened in 1957. The welcoming spot in Lincoln Square hosts outstanding performances by national and local acts in an intimate-feeling 420-seat concert hall that has excellent acoustics. A major expansion in 2012 added a new, environmentally friendly facility across the street, with a 150-seat performance hall and acoustically engineered classrooms. ✉ 4544 N. Lincoln Ave., Lincoln Square ☏ 773/728–6000 ⊕ www.oldtownschool.org.

🎭 Performing Arts

THEATER

Black Ensemble Theater

THEATER | The Black Ensemble Theater has a penchant for long-running musicals based on popular African American icons. Founder and executive producer Jackie Taylor has written and directed such hits as The Jackie Wilson Story and The Other Cinderella. ✉ 4450 N. Clark St., Far North Side ☏ 773/769–4451 ⊕ www.blackensembletheater.org.

City Lit Theater

THEATER | City Lit Theater Company produces notable staged readings and full productions of famous literary works—by the likes of Henry James, Alice Walker, and Raymond Carver—as well as original material with a literary bent. ⊠ *1020 W. Bryn Mawr Ave., Edgewater* ☎ *773/293– 3682* ⊕ *www.citylit.org.*

★ Neo-Futurists

THEATER | Neo-Futurists perform their long-running, late-night hit *The Infinite Wrench* in a ramshackle second-floor space in Andersonville. The piece is a series of 30 ever-changing plays performed in 60 minutes; the order of the plays is chosen by the audience. ⊠ *5153 N. Ashland Ave., Far North Side* ☎ *773/878–4557* ⊕ *www.neofuturists.org.*

🛍 Shopping

In the Far North, Swedish-settled Andersonville specializes in antiques and home furnishings. If you need a break while perusing the stores, many funky coffee shops and casual restaurants await.

ANTIQUES

★ Broadway Antique Market

ANTIQUES & COLLECTIBLES | More than 75 handpicked dealers make it worth the trek to the Broadway Antique Market (known as BAM by its loyal fans). Mid–20th century is the primary emphasis, but items range from Arts and Crafts and art deco to Heywood-Wakefield. All are wonderfully presented, and the building itself is a prime example of deco architecture. ⊠ *6130 N. Broadway St., Far North Side* ☎ *773/743–5444* ⊕ *www. bamchicago.com* ☽ *Closed Mon.–Wed.*

Evanstonia Antiques and Restoration

ANTIQUES & COLLECTIBLES | Dealer Ziggy Osak has a rich collection of fine 19th-century English and Continental antiques that are prized for being as functional as they are striking. ⊠ *6417*

N. Ravenswood Ave., Lincoln Square ☎ *773/907–0101* ⊕ *evanstoniaantiques. com* ☽ *Closed Sun.*

Lincoln Antique Mall

ANTIQUES & COLLECTIBLES | Dozens of dealers carrying antiques and collectibles share this large space. There's a good selection of French and mid-20th-century modern furniture, plus estate jewelry, oil paintings, and photographs, but you can find virtually anything here. ⊠ *3115 W. Irving Park Rd., Far Northwest Side* ☎ *773/604–4700.*

★ Woolly Mammoth Antiques, Oddities & Resale

ANTIQUES & COLLECTIBLES | In the market for a stuffed giraffe head? How about a bracelet made of human hair or some vintage medical supplies? Woolly Mammoth has an ever-evolving selection of strange, unusual, and sometimes disturbing items—but herein lies the magic. For those who are so inspired, the shop also hosts its own taxidermy classes. ⊠ *1513 W. Foster Ave., Far North Side* ☎ *773/989–3294* ⊕ *www.woollymammothchicago.com.*

BEAUTY

★ Merz Apothecary

OTHER HEALTH & BEAUTY | In addition to being a normal pharmacy, this old-fashioned druggist also stocks all manner of homeopathic and herbal remedies, as well as hard-to-find European toiletries, cosmetics, candles, and natural laundry products. ⊠ *4716 N. Lincoln Ave., Lincoln Square* ☎ *773/989–0900* ⊕ *merzapothecary.com* ☽ *Closed Sun.*

BOOKS, MUSIC, AND GIFTS

The Book Cellar

BOOKS | The bright, inviting Book Cellar has a well-edited selection of works ranging from local interest to popular fiction. There's also a small wine bar/coffee shop on-site, where customers can linger over their purchases. Readings and other literary events are held here frequently.

Ethnic Enclaves

Chicago's ethnic neighborhoods give you the chance to shop the globe. Just southwest of the Loop is **Pilsen**, the city's largest Latino neighborhood. A walk along 18th Street between Halsted Street and Western Avenue leads you to a colorful array of bakeries, religious-goods shops, vintage stores, and a burgeoning art-gallery district. Stretching south and east from the intersection of Cermak Road and Wentworth Avenue, **Chinatown** has shops selling Far Eastern imports, including jade and ginseng root. On the north side in **Uptown**, a heavy concentration of Vietnamese shops and imported food stores around the intersection of Broadway and Argyle Street have earned the area the title of "New Chinatown" or Little Vietnam. In the **Lincoln Square** neighborhood on a stretch of Lincoln Avenue between Leland and Lawrence avenues on the city's North Side, you'll still find German restaurants and stores that sell European-made health and beauty products amid the swell of newer upscale clothing and gift boutiques attracting the young families who now call this area home. Heading east to **Andersonville**, you'll find a slew of Swedish restaurants, bakeries, and gift shops along Clark Street between Foster and Balmoral avenues, plus specialty boutiques that sell everything from fine chocolates to eclectic home furnishings. Many non–U.S. visitors make the trek to **Devon Avenue** (between Western and Washtenaw avenues) in an Indian neighborhood on the city's Far North Side. The attraction is a chance to buy electronics that run on 220 volts. Because the United States has no value-added tax, it's often cheaper for international visitors to buy here than at home.

■ TIP→ The same stretch of Devon Avenue is also home to a hodgepodge of great Indian groceries, Bollywood video stores, and fabric shops where you can while away your time.

⊠ *4736 N. Lincoln Ave., Far Northwest Side* ☎ *773/293–2665* ⊕ *www.bookcellarinc.com.*

Enjoy

SOUVENIRS | Calling itself an "urban general store," this welcoming Lincoln Square go-to stocks a wide selection of greeting cards, cute kids' clothes, toys, and fun gift items. A second location in Andersonville (*5307 North Clark Street*) opened in 2019. ⊠ *4723 N. Lincoln Ave., Far Northwest Side* ☎ *773/334–8626* ⊕ *www.urbangeneralstore.com.*

Gallimaufry Gallery

CRAFTS | Browse the tightly packed selection of greeting cards, wood carvings, jewelry, and incense in this eclectic little shop. ⊠ *4712 N. Lincoln Ave., Lincoln Square* ☎ *773/728–3600* ⊕ *www.gallimaufry.net* ⊙ *Closed Mon.–Thurs.*

★ **Women & Children First**

BOOKS | This feminist bookstore stocks fiction and nonfiction, periodicals, journals, small-press publications, and a strong selection of LGBTQ titles. The children's section also has a great array of books, all politically correct. Authors, both local and world-famous, often give readings here. ⊠ *5233 N. Clark St., Andersonville* ☎ *773/769–9299* ⊕ *www.womenandchildrenfirst.com* ⊙ *Closed Mon.*

FOOD AND TREATS
City Olive
OTHER SPECIALTY STORE | This cute shop in Andersonville sells olive oil in every imaginable form, from bottles of the extra-virgin variety to bath and body products made with the stuff. Other gourmet foods from around the globe also fill the shelves. ✉ *5644 N. Clark St., Andersonville* ☏ *773/942–6424* ⊕ *www.cityolive.com* ⊙ *Closed Mon.*

HOME DECOR
Neighborly
SOUVENIRS | Living up to its name, Neighborly focuses on ethically sourced, independently made home goods and gifts with a local vibe. ✉ *4710 N. Lincoln Ave., Far North Side* ☏ *773/234–1424* ⊕ *www.neighborlyshop.com.*

MARKETS
Vintage Garage
MARKET | One Sunday a month in the warmer half of the year, dozens of Chicago area vintage and antiques vendors descend on an empty parking garage for one of the city's finest markets. A local DJ typically spins records while shoppers browse through clothes, furniture, housewares, music, and the like. Admission is $6. ✉ *1800 Maple Ave., Evanston* ⊕ *www.vintagegaragechicago.com.*

TOYS
Timeless Toys
TOYS | This old-timey toy shop has a Santa's-workshop feel. Lose yourself in a magical mix of classic wooden toys alongside fanciful dress-up costumes, plush puppets, cuddly stuffed animals, board games, puzzles, and books. ✉ *4749 N. Lincoln Ave., Lincoln Square* ☏ *773/334–4445* ⊕ *www.timelesstoyschicago.com.*

Activities

SPAS
Sir Spa
SPAS | This is where the guys go. It's a sleek Zen den—a minimalist mix of black leather, exposed brick, and marble. It also includes a Grooming Club Lounge with armchairs, a plasma TV, and beer-stocked fridge. With services like a back buff and detoxifying mud wrap, treatments are just as focused on cleaning and revitalizing as they are on purely relaxing. ✉ *5151 N. Clark St., Andersonville* ☏ *773/271–7000* ⊕ *www.sirspa.com* ☞ *$110 60-min massage, from $220 3-treatment packages, $210 couple packages. Services: facials, massages, manicures, pedicures, waxing, body wraps.*

Chapter 8

HYDE PARK

Updated by
Matt Beardmore

◉ Sights	🍴 Restaurants	🛏 Hotels	🛍 Shopping	🍸 Nightlife
★★★★☆	★★☆☆☆	★☆☆☆☆	★☆☆☆☆	★★☆☆☆

NEIGHBORHOOD SPOTLIGHT

GETTING HERE

By car, take Lake Shore Drive south to the 57th Street, exit, and turn left into the parking lot of the Museum of Science and Industry. You can also take the Metra train from the Millennium Station at Randolph Street and Michigan Avenue; get off at the 55th-56th-57th Street stop and walk east through the underpass two blocks, then south two blocks. From Indiana, take the South Shore Line to the 57th Street station. CTA Buses 2, 6, 10, and 28 will also get you here from downtown.

MAKING THE MOST OF YOUR TIME

Visiting the Museum of Science and Industry will probably take most of a day. Go during the week to avoid crowds. Wind down by meandering through Jackson Park, the University of Chicago campus, or the Midway Plaisance, the main walkway for the 1893 World's Columbian Exposition.

PULLMAN NATIONAL MONUMENT

It's a fair bit south of Hyde Park but the Pullman National Monument is a worth excursion. America's first planned industrial community—otherwise known as a company town—this former home of the workers employed by a railcar manufacturer is notable for its architecture as well as its role in the civil rights and labor movements. Start at the new visitors' center, opened in 2021 in the former factory administration building, to learn more about Pullman's history.

TOP REASONS TO GO

- **Get caught up in wonderment:** Spend a few hours at the Museum of Science and Industry.

- **Enjoy Jackson Park:** Revel in the tranquil mood and do some exotic-bird-watching.

- **Appreciate Frank Lloyd Wright:** Take a tour of the fantastic Robie House.

- **Enjoy the views:** Pack a picnic for Promontory Point.

KENWOOD

The Kenwood area of Hyde Park was once home to the city's elite but after many of the residents moved to the suburbs, the neighborhood became run-down—it has since rebounded to a large degree. These days it might be best known as where you'll find former President Barack Obama's house. Another notable landmark is **Saint Gabriel Church** (4500 S. Wallace St., 773/268–9595), designed in 1887 by Daniel Burnham and John Root. It's marked by a tower, arched doorways, and a large round window. The church parish was organized to serve Irish workers at the Union Stock Yards, once in operation nearby.

Hyde Park is something of a trek from downtown Chicago, but it's worth the extra effort. Rich in academic and cultural life, it is also considered to be one of the country's most successfully integrated neighborhoods—a fact reflected in everything from the people you'll meet on the street to the diverse cuisine served in local eateries.

Best known as the home of the University of Chicago, Hyde Park began to see significant growth only in the late 19th century, with the university opening in 1892 and the World's Columbian Exposition drawing an international influx a year later. The exposition spawned numerous Classical Revival buildings (including the behemoth Museum of Science and Industry) as well as the Midway Plaisance, which still runs along the southern edge of the University of Chicago's original campus. Sprawling residences were soon erected for school faculty in neighboring Kenwood, and the area began to attract well-to-do types who commissioned famous architects to build them spectacular homes.

Among the architecturally riveting buildings here are two by Frank Lloyd Wright, the Robie House and Heller House, as different as night and day. A thriving theater scene plus several art and history museums further add to the ambience. Most impressive, though, is the diverse population, with a strong sense of community pride and a fondness for the neighborhood's pretty tree-lined streets, proximity to the lake, and slightly off-the-beaten-path vibe.

◉ Sights

★ DuSable Museum of African American History

HISTORY MUSEUM | FAMILY | Sitting alongside the lagoons of Washington Park, the DuSable Museum, a Smithsonian Institution affiliate, offers an evocative exploration of the African American experience. The most moving display is about slavery—rusted shackles used on slave ships are among the poignant and disturbing artifacts. The museum also has a significant art collection. Rotating exhibits showcase African American milestones, achievements, and contributions. ✉ *740 E. 56th Pl., Hyde Park* ☎ *773/947–0600* ⊕ *www.dusablemuseum.org* ✉ *$10* ⊙ *Closed Mon. and Tues.* ♿ *Advance tickets required.*

★ Frederick C. Robie House

HISTORIC HOME | Named one of the 10 most significant buildings of the 20th century by the American Institute of Architects, the 9,063-square-foot Robie House (1910) is long and low. Massive overhangs shoot out from the low-pitched roof, and windows run along the facade in a glittering stretch. Inside, Wright's "open plan" echoes the great

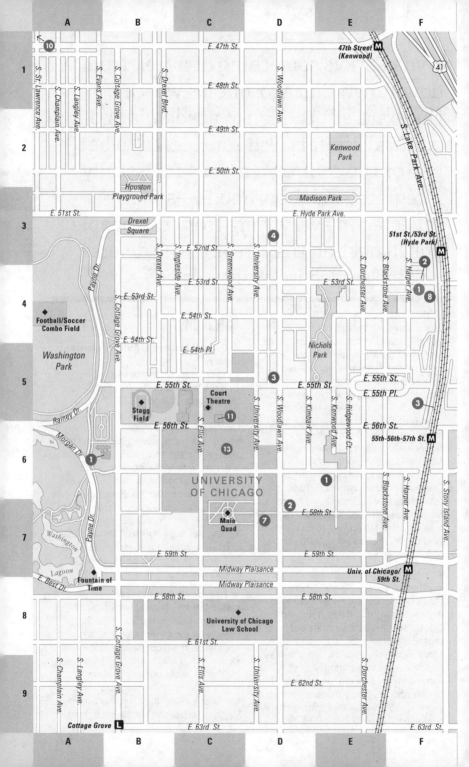

Hyde Park

KEY

1 Exploring Sights

1 Restaurants

1 Quick Bites

L CTA Lines

M Metra Lines

Shipwreck of
the Silver Spray

S. Lake Shore Dr.

Lake Shore Drive
Pedestrian Bridge

Model Yacht
Basin

Harold
Washington
Park

S. Cornell Dr.

S. Hyde Park
Blvd.

S. Everett Ave.

E. 55th St.

*Lake
Michigan*

Wallach
Fountain

9

E. 57th St.

41

Castaways Beach
and Park

6

57th Street
Beach

S. Cornell Dr.

Columbia
Basin

59th St. Harbor

0 ——— 1/4 mi

0 ——— 1/4 km

S. Lake Shore Dr.

S. Cornell Ave.

West Lagoon

East Lagoon

Wooded
Island

5

Jackson
Park

41

63rd Street
Beach

12
↓

World's Columbian Exposition

In 1893, the city of Chicago hosted the **World's Columbian Exposition.** The fair's mix of green spaces and Beaux-Arts buildings offered the vision of a more pleasantly habitable metropolis than the crammed industrial center that rose from the ashes of the Great Fire. However, a ruffled Louis Sullivan prophesied that "the damage wrought to this country by the Chicago World's Fair will last half a century." He wasn't entirely wrong in his prediction—the neoclassical style vied sharply over the next decades with the native creations of the Chicago and Prairie schools, all the while incorporating their technical advances. One of Hyde Park's most popular destinations—the Museum of Science and Industry—was erected as the fair's Palace of Fine Arts. It's the only exposition building remaining; other smaller buildings have been relocated.

outdoors, as one space flows into another, while sunlight streaming through decorative leaded windows bathes the rooms in patterns. The original dining room had a table with lanterns at each corner, giving the illusion that the table itself was a separate room. Other Wright innovations include a three-car garage (now the gift shop), an intercom, and a central vacuum-cleaner system. Check the website for tour options. It's a good idea to make reservations in advance. ⊠ *5757 S. Woodlawn Ave., Hyde Park* ☎ *312/994–4000* ⊕ *www.flwright.org* ▨ *Tours from $20* ◐ *Closed Tues.-Wed.*

Hyde Park Historical Society

VISITOR CENTER | To get a good overview of the neighborhood, contact the Hyde Park Historical Society, which sponsors lectures and tours. The society is housed in a building that once served as a waiting room for cable cars. The organization documents, preserves, and educates the public about the history of Hyde Park Township, which stretches from the north at E. 39th to E. 138th Streets on the south, and between Lake Michigan on the east and S. State Street on the west. ⊠ *5529 S. Lake Park Ave., Hyde Park* ☎ *773/493–1893* ⊕ *www.hydeparkhistory.org* ▨ *Free* ◐ *Closed weekdays.*

Isadore H. Heller House

HISTORIC HOME | When he designed this house in 1896, Frank Lloyd Wright was still moving toward the mature Prairie style achieved in the Robie House 13 years later. As was common with Wright's designs, Heller House is entered from the side. But rather than being long and low, this one has three floors, the uppermost one of which comes complete with pillars and sculptured nymphs. The building is not open to the public. ⊠ *5132 S. Woodlawn Ave., Hyde Park.*

Jackson Park

CITY PARK | This Hyde Park gem was designed by Frederick Law Olmsted (co-designer of New York City's Central Park) for the World's Columbian Exposition of 1893. It has lagoons, a Japanese garden (named Osaka Garden, for Chicago's sister city) with authentic Japanese statuary, and the Wooded Island, a nature retreat with wildlife and 300 species of birds. Its 63rd Street Beach is a popular summer destination, and the state-of-the-art fitness center means there's entertainment rain or shine. ⊠ *Between E. 56th and 67th Sts., S. Stony Island Ave. and the lakefront, Hyde Park* ☎ *773/256–0903* ⊕ *www.chicagoparkdistrict.com/parks/jackson-park.*

Robie House is emblematic of Frank Lloyd Wright's Prairie style.

★ Museum of Science and Industry

SCIENCE MUSEUM | FAMILY | The MSI is one of the most-visited sites in Chicago, and for good reason. The sprawling space has 14 acres of exhibit space on three floors, with new exhibits added constantly. The museum's high-tech interior is hidden by a Classical Revival exterior, designed in 1892 by D.H. Burnham & Company to house the Palace of Fine Arts for the World's Columbian Exposition. Beautifully landscaped Jackson Park and its peaceful, Japanese-style Osaka Garden are behind the museum. ⊠ *5700 S. Lake Shore Dr., Hyde Park* ☏ *773/684–1414* ⊕ *www.msichicago.org* ☏ *$22.*

Oriental Institute Museum

ART MUSEUM | This gem began with artifacts collected by University of Chicago archaeologists in the early 20th century (one is rumored to have been the model for Indiana Jones) and has expanded into an interesting, informative museum with a jaw-dropping array of artifacts from the ancient Middle East. With the largest collection of such antiquities in the United States, you'll see amulets, mummies, limestone reliefs, gold jewelry, ivories, pottery, and bronzes from the 8th millennium BC through the 13th century AD. A 17-foot-tall statue of King Tut was excavated from the ruins of a temple in western Thebes in 1930. ⊠ *1155 E. 58th St., Hyde Park* ⊕ *oi100.uchicago.edu* ☏ *Suggested admission $10* ⊗ *Closed Mon.* ⚷ *Advance reservations required.*

The Promontory

NOTABLE BUILDING | The tan brick building, designed by Mies van der Rohe and completed in 1949, was named for nearby Promontory Point, which juts out into the lake. Mies's first residential high-rise exemplifies the postwar trend toward a clean, simple style. Even from street level, the Lake Michigan views here are breathtaking. Note the skylines and belching smokestacks of Gary and Hammond, Indiana, to the southeast. ⊠ *5530–5532 S. Shore Dr., Hyde Park* ☏ *773/493–5599.*

Mr. Obama's Neighborhood

Hyde Park's most famous family spends its time between multiple locations these days, and street barriers prevent visitors from getting close to their Chicago home. Still, you can experience many of the former First Family's favorite neighborhood haunts. Start at the University of Chicago, where Barack Obama taught law from 1992 to 2004. Make sure to look up: you'll see the university's iconic gargoyles on some buildings. From there, poke around at 57th Street Books (*E. 57th St. and Kimbark Ave.*, 773/684–1300), recommended by Michelle Obama for its extensive collection of fiction and nonfiction and its youth-oriented programs. The store's tagline is "The South Side's community bookstore." With mind fed, it's time for some fresh air. Head east to Lake Shore Drive and walk to Promontory Point (*5491 S.*

Lake Shore Dr.) for a stunning view of Lake Michigan. If you walk to the lake along East Hayes Drive, you'll pass by the basketball courts where former President Obama has enjoyed shooting hoops with his brother-in-law, Craig Robinson, who has coached college basketball and worked for NBA teams.

Over in Jackson Park, nearby, the long-awaited groundbreaking of the Obama Presidential Center took place in the South Side park in August 2021. Construction on the 19.3 acre site is expected to last four years and when completed it will not only celebrate Barack Obama and Michelle Obama, the United States' first African American President and First Lady, it will provide new gardens, outdoor spaces for visitors of all ages, and a new branch of the Chicago Public Library.

Promontory Point
CITY PARK | It's tough to top the view of Chicago's skyline from the Point—a scenic, man-made peninsula, which projects into Lake Michigan. Opened in 1937 as part of Burnham Park, this 40-acre peninsula, which was originally called 55th Street Promontory, is entered via a tunnel underneath Lake Shore Drive at 55th Street or the Lakefront Trail. The fawn-shape David Wallach Memorial Fountain is located near the tunnel. The park's field house is a popular wedding venue, so you may catch a glimpse of a beaming bride during your visit. ✉ *5491 S. Shore Dr., Hyde Park* ☎ *312/742–5369* ⊕ *www.chicagoparkdistrict.com/parks/burnham-park* 🎫 *Free.*

Saint Gabriel Catholic Church
CHURCH | A tower, arched doorways, and a large round window form bold masses on the exterior of this church, designed

in 1887 by Daniel Burnham and John Root. The Romanesque interior, with vaulted arches, gives a feeling of breadth and spaciousness. The parish was organized to serve Irish workers at the nearby Union Stock Yards. Take Interstate 94 south from the Loop (43rd Street exit), or take Bus 8 to Halsted and 45th streets and walk east on 45th Street for a few blocks. ✉ *4500 S. Wallace St., Canaryville* ☎ *773/268–9595* ⊕ *www.saintgabes.com.*

★ Smart Museum of Art
ART MUSEUM | If you want to see masterpieces but don't want to spend a long day wandering around one of the major art museums, the Smart may be just your speed. Its diverse exhibition program features art from around the globe. ✉ *5550 S. Greenwood Ave., Hyde Park* ☎ *773/702–0200* ⊕ *www.smartmuseum.uchicago.edu* 🎫 *Free* ⊙ *Closed Mon.*

South Shore Cultural Center

NOTABLE BUILDING | Listed on the National Register of Historic Places, this opulent clubhouse on Lake Michigan is one of the last remaining Mediterranean resort–style buildings in the Midwest. The posh country club looks like something out of an F. Scott Fitzgerald novel. It boasts meeting rooms, horse stables, a 9-hole golf course, beach, and an art gallery. With magnificent crystal chandeliers, balconies, pillars, and a vaulted ceiling, its ballrooms and grand lobby wow visitors, including President Barack Obama and First Lady Michelle Obama, who chose the center for their wedding reception. Referred to by many as the "Gem of the Southside," it is also the home of the South Shore Cultural School of the Arts. ✉ *7059 S. Shore Dr., Hyde Park* ☎ *773/256–0149* 🌐 *www.chicagoparkdistrict.com/parks-facilities/south-shore-cultural-center-park* 🎟 *Free.*

★ **University of Chicago**

COLLEGE | Intellectuals come to the University of Chicago to breathe in the rarified air: after all, the faculty, former faculty, and alumni of this esteemed institution have won more Nobel prizes than any school in the country—94 in total, awarded in every field, including President Obama's 2009 Peace Prize. History buffs and art lovers are drawn by the Oriental Institute, Reva and David Logan Center for the Arts, and Smart Museum of Art, while the University's professional theater company Court Theatre stages new and classic works. Architecture aficionados won't be disappointed either.

The dominant building here, Rockefeller Memorial Chapel, is a neo-Gothic beauty complete with glorious stained-glass windows, a vaulted ceiling, 72-bell carillon (the single largest musical instrument ever built), and 207-foot-high stone tower. In sharp contrast, the Booth School of Business is very modern looking; its horizontal accents imitate the Frank Lloyd Wright Robie House (1910), located directly across the street. Mid-century buildings designed by Ludwig Mies van der Rohe and Eero Saarinen, as well as contemporary award-winners by MacArthur Fellow Jeanne Gang, postmodernist Helmut Jahn, and husband-and-wife duo Tod Williams and Billie Tsien, are also worth seeking out. Self-guided tours of campus highlights points of interest and public art on campus can be found at visit.uchicago.edu/campus-guides. ✉ *1101 E. 58th St., Hyde Park* ☎ *773/702–1234* 🌐 *visit.uchicago.edu.*

🍴 Restaurants

Restaurants in intellectual Hyde Park have a welcoming "come as you are" air about them that's a pleasant surprise for a neighborhood that houses a top-tier university and an Obama residence. Perhaps the area's proximity to downtown has made flashy eateries and big-name chefs unnecessary. It might be for the best, since visitors tend to feel comfortable in any restaurant, regardless of how much foodie cred they bring to the table. In the compact heart of the area, expect to find a little of everything, from Thai eats to pizza spots, bakeries, and coffee shops.

Chant

$$ | **ASIAN** | **FAMILY** | Asian fusion is the name of the game at this lively Hyde Park restaurant, where Chinese, Korean, Thai, Japanese, and other influences mingle on a menu that ranges from classic to creative and even includes some American staples for tamer diners. With an energetic atmosphere, plenty of dishes for sharing, and a menu that takes dietary restrictions into account, Chant is an easy spot for groups to gather. **Known for:** signature martinis and cocktails; relaxed atmosphere; live music. [$] *Average main: $20* ✉ *1509 E. 53rd St., Hyde Park* ☎ *773/324–1999* 🌐 *www.chantchicago.com.*

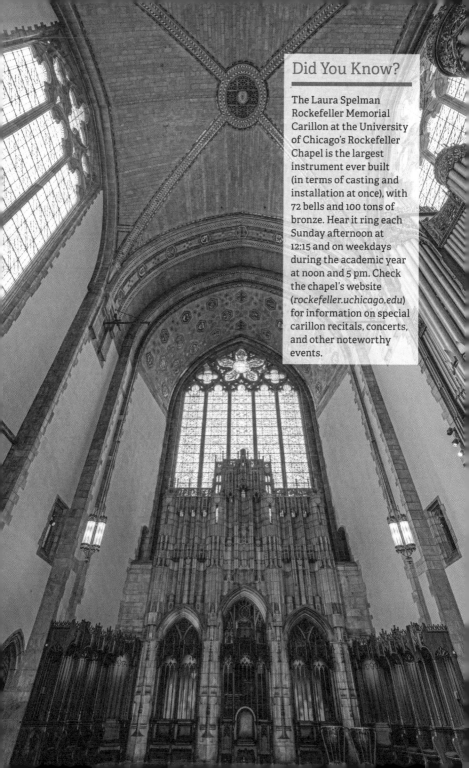

Did You Know?

The Laura Spelman Rockefeller Memorial Carillon at the University of Chicago's Rockefeller Chapel is the largest instrument ever built (in terms of casting and installation at once), with 72 bells and 100 tons of bronze. Hear it ring each Sunday afternoon at 12:15 and on weekdays during the academic year at noon and 5 pm. Check the chapel's website (*rockefeller.uchicago.edu*) for information on special carillon recitals, concerts, and other noteworthy events.

Coffee and Quick Bites

Woodlawn Tap

$ | **AMERICAN** | At this favored, no-frills tavern, locals and university students gather for beer, burgers, and Reuben sandwiches. On Sunday nights, jam sessions complement the pub grub. **Known for:** university crowd; burgers; 70-plus year history. [$] *Average main: $6* ✉ *1172 E. 55th St., Hyde Park* ☎ *773/643–5516* 🌐 *www.josephsittler.org/jimmys* 💳 *No credit cards* ⏱ *Closed holidays.*

Medici on 57th

$$ | **AMERICAN** | Opened almost 60 years ago, Medici has served generations of University of Chicago students and faculty, many of whom carved their name on the tables and walls. **Known for:** relaxed and welcoming atmosphere; pizza and burgers; popularity with locals. [$] *Average main: $10* ✉ *1327 E. 57th St., Hyde Park* ☎ *773/667–7394* 🌐 *www.medici57.com.*

Valois

$ | **AMERICAN** | This cash-only Hyde Park institution serves big portions of no-frills diner classics cafeteria-style. President Obama ate here often during his University of Chicago days, and the restaurant still posts a "President Obama's Favorites" menu. **Known for:** friendly staff; breakfast; loved by all walks of life. [$] *Average main: $6* ✉ *1518 E. 53rd St., Hyde Park* ☎ *773/667–0647* 🌐 *www.valoisrestaurant.com* ⏱ *No dinner* 💳 *No credit cards.*

Performing Arts

CLASSICAL MUSIC

Mandel Hall at the University of Chicago

MUSIC | Mandel Hall is one of the largest performing arts and events venues on the University of Chicago campus—the Victorian performance space can accommodate nearly 1,000 audience members. Mandel Hall is also home to the University's symphony orchestra and annual international folk festival. ✉ *1131 E. 57th St., Hyde Park* ☎ *773/702–2787.*

THEATER

Court Theatre

THEATER | This professional theater on the campus of the University of Chicago has a mission of producing "classic theater," but it's expanded the definition of that term well beyond Shakespeare and the Greeks. You'll find those here—and done exceptionally well—but Court also produces stunning reinventions of musicals, works by August Wilson and Pearl Cleage that have helped it tap into Hyde Park's largely black population, and the occasional new play dealing in classical themes. ✉ *5535 S. Ellis Ave., Hyde Park* ☎ *773/753–4472* 🌐 *www.courttheatre.org.*

Chapter 9

DAY TRIPS FROM CHICAGO

Updated by
Jessica Mlinaric

⊙ Sights	🍴 Restaurants	🛏 Hotels	🛍 Shopping	🍸 Nightlife
★★★★★	★★★☆☆	★☆☆☆☆	★☆☆☆☆	★☆☆☆☆

WELCOME TO DAY TRIPS FROM CHICAGO

TOP REASONS TO GO

★ **Stop and smell the flowers:** Admire over 2 million plants at the Chicago Botanic Garden; strolling woods, prairie, river corridor, and lakes and shores habitats all in one day.

★ **See the animals:** Get a fish-eye view of polar bears swimming underwater from the belowground viewing area at the Brookfield Zoo's Great Bear Wilderness Habitat.

★ **Get to know Frank Lloyd Wright:** Take a trip back to 1909, the last year the famed architect lived and worked in his Oak Park home and studio.

★ **Enjoy a picnic:** Pack up a candelabra and some foie gras—or just a blanket and some bug spray—and head to the Ravinia Festival for a night of music under the summer stars.

★ **Visit the Bahá'í Temple:** Stroll the beautifully landscaped gardens, or watch the sunset from the peaceful grounds of this majestic temple in Wilmette.

1 **Aurora.** Known for architect Ludwig Mies Van der Rohe's Farnsworth House, among other attractions.

2 **Brookfield.** Head here for the vast Brookfield Zoo.

3 **Evanston.** A pretty town, home to Northwestern University, museums, and good dining.

4 **Glencoe.** The Chicago Botanic Garden is the big attraction here.

5 **Glenview.** Kids love the Kohl Children's Museum.

6 **Highland Park.** Home of the famed summertime Ravinia Festival.

7 **Lisle.** The Morton Arboretum has miles of walking and biking trails.

8 **Oak Park.** The place to get familiar with Frank Lloyd Wright's architecture.

9 **Skokie.** The Illinois Holocaust Museum and Education Center is a moving place to learn about this part of world history.

10 **Vernon Hills.** The Cuneo Mansion and Gardens is an early-20th-century house museum.

11 **Wheaton.** Home to museums and Cantigny Park's many attractions.

12 **Wilmette.** The Bahá'í Temple House of Worship is visually stunning and has fascinating exhibits at the welcome center.

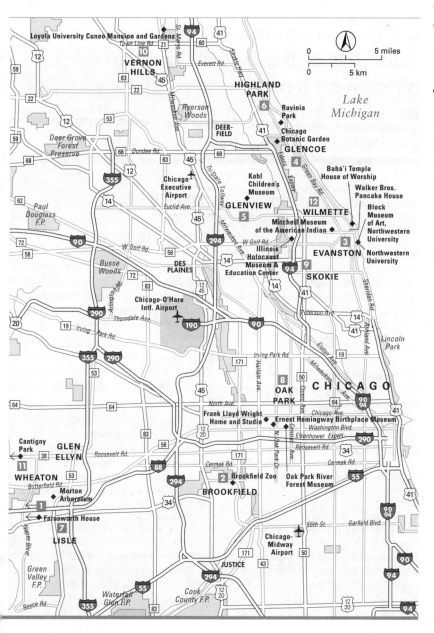

Loyola University Cuneo Mansion and Gardens
Town Line Rd. 21
10
12
59
VERNON HILLS
83
22 45
22

94
41
60
Everett Rd.
St. Marys Rd.
Saxony Hwy.

HIGHLAND PARK
6
Ravinia Park
Chicago Botanic Garden
Lake Michigan

59
12
53
Ryerson Woods
DEER-FIELD
41

GLENCOE
4
Green Bay Rd.
Edens Expwy.

68
Deer Grove Forest Preserve
Dundee Rd.
83 45
68

Bahá'í Temple House of Worship
Walker Bros. Pancake House

62
Paul Douglass F.P.
14
Chicago Executive Airport
Euclid Ave.
45

Kohl Children's Museum
GLENVIEW
5
12
WILMETTE
Block Museum of Art, Northwestern University

72
58
90
W. Golf Rd.
58
294
Milwaukee Ave.
W Golf Rd.
Mitchell Museum of the American Indian
Illinois Holocaust Museum & Education Center
14
EVANSTON
3
Northwestern University

20
Busse Woods
72
355 290
Arlington Rd.
DES PLAINES
83
14
94
9
SKOKIE
41
Sheridan Rd.

19
Irving Park Rd.
Chicago-O'Hare Intl. Airport
Thorndale Ave.
190
90
Peterson Ave.
14
41
Elston Ave.
19
Lincoln Park
Ashland Ave.

355 290
53
171
Irving Park Rd.
Milwaukee Ave.

64
64
45
North Ave.
171
8
OAK PARK
50
64
CHICAGO
90 94
41

Cantigny Park
38
GLEN ELLYN
Roosevelt Rd.
56
Frank Lloyd Wright Home and Studio
Ernest Hemingway Birthplace Museum
Chicago Ave.
Washington Blvd.
Eisenhower Expwy.
Roosevelt Rd.
290

11
WHEATON
53
Butterfield Rd.
Morton Arboretum
Farnsworth House
7
LISLE
12 20
88
Cermak Rd.
294
2 Brookfield Zoo
BROOKFIELD
171
Cermak Rd.
Oak Park River Forest Museum
55
41

1
34
Green Valley F.P.
55
355
Waterfall Glen F.P.
Royce Rd.
83
Cook County F.P.
JUSTICE
171
294
12 20
43
50
Chicago-Midway Airport
55th St.
Garfield Blvd.
90
94
12 20
94

0   5 miles
0   5 km

Chicago's suburbs aren't just for commuters. The towns that lie to the north, west, and south of the city are rich in history, culture, and outdoor activities. Add a day or two to your trip and get out of town for a concert, architecture tour, or zoo visit; the journey to the 'burbs is well worth the additional vacation time.

The suburbs closest to the city limits have excellent theaters and museums that rival their urban cousins. The farther away you go, the more likely you are to find the wooded parks and wider streets that characterize towns outside just about any major city. But Chicago's bedroom communities aren't mirror images of others that dot the map. Far from the ho-hum, they are destinations in their own right. Brookfield and Lisle, to the west, have top-notch zoos and exquisite gardens; along the North Shore, Highland Park and Evanston attract talented musicians and house internationally acclaimed art collections; and Oak Park is so rich in architectural history and diversity that you can't help but wish you had more time to simply stay put.

Forget strip-mall fast food, too—it's not uncommon to find decidedly urban types doing a reverse commute to visit a trendy new restaurant or ethnic eatery outside the city limits. With Chicago's bus and train system reaching some of the nearer ones, the trips are painless. In short, don't overlook the 'burbs when planning your Chicago trip. If you do, you'll miss out on some of the very best things the metropolitan area has to offer.

Planning

Getting Around

To get around using the El, take the Purple Line to Evanston and Wilmette, the Green Line to Oak Park, and the Yellow Line to Skokie. Many suburbs can also be reached by the Metra commuter rail system.

Making the Most of Your Time

There's a lot worth seeing and doing in the suburbs. Spend at least half a day in historic Oak Park to learn about famous residents Ernest Hemingway and Frank Lloyd Wright. A second day devoted to points farther west can take you to the Brookfield Zoo or the Morton Arboretum. Chicago's picturesque North Shore won't disappoint either: enjoy a collegial day wandering Northwestern University's campus and downtown Evanston or take in a concert at Ravinia Park in Highland Park and the Chicago Botanic Garden in Glencoe.

Aurora and Vicinity

41 miles west of downtown Chicago.

The Aurora vicinity has overcome lean times as a tourist destination and now offers something for everyone. Rent a kayak and float on the Fox River. Explore the sunken gardens, hiking paths, and zoo at Phillips Park. Or check out the plethora of art galleries in downtown Aurora.

Sights

★ Farnsworth House

HISTORIC HOME | This 1951 minimalist dwelling by Ludwig Mies Van der Rohe sits just down the Fox River from Aurora. Constructed of steel, wood, and travertine marble, it appears to nearly float against a backdrop of serene river views and woodland landscapes. Now operated as a museum by the National Trust for Historic Preservation, Farnsworth House may only be seen by guided tour (advance reservations are required). Note that the house is a half-mile walk from the visitor center. ⊠ *14520 River Rd., Plano* ☎ *630/552–0052* ⊕ *www. farnsworthhouse.org* ⊠ *$25, purchase at least 24 hrs in advance* ⊘ *Closed Mon. and Tues. Apr.-Nov. Closed weekdays in winter.*

Brookfield

10 miles west of downtown Chicago.

Brookfield makes a great day trip for families, thanks to the Brookfield Zoo.

Sights

★ Brookfield Zoo

ZOO | FAMILY | There are more than 2,000 animals at this gigantic zoo and highlights include the 7½-acre Great Bear

Wilderness exhibit, a sprawling replica of North American woodlands for the zoo's population of grizzlies, polar bears, bison, Mexican gray wolves, and bald eagles. Watch the polar bears from the popular underwater viewing area. Elsewhere, monkeys, otters, birds, and other rain-forest fauna cavort in a carefully constructed setting of trees, shrubs, pools, and waterfalls at Tropic World, while at the Living Coast you can venture through passageways to see sharks, rays, and Humboldt penguins.

One of the best educational exhibits is Habitat Africa, where you can explore the dense forest section, with animals like the okapi (an animal that looks like a cross between a zebra, giraffe, and horse). In the savannah section, which has a water hole, termite mounds, and characteristic rock formations, you can spy such tiny animals as the 22-inch-tall klipspringer antelope.

The Swamp is about as realistic as you would want an exhibit on swamps to be. It has a springy floor and open habitats with low-flying birds that vividly demonstrate the complex ecosystems. For hands-on family activities, visit the Hamill Family Play Zoo, where kids can play zookeeper, gardener, or veterinarian. Special events—most notably Holiday Magic, which lights up the zoo on select December evenings—are also worth checking out. If you don't want to trek around the 216-acre property, don't worry. You can hop aboard a motorized safari tram ($6) on weekends in warm weather months. ⊠ *1st Ave. at 31st St., Brookfield* ☎ *708/688–8000* ⊕ *www.czs. org* ⊠ *$25; parking $15.*

Continued on page 246

FRANK LLOYD WRIGHT

1867-1959

The most famous American architect of the 20th century led a life that was as zany and scandalous as his architectural legacy was great. Behind the photo-op appearance and lordly pronouncements was a rebel visionary who left an unforgettable imprint on the world's notion of architecture. Nowhere else in the country can you experience Frank Lloyd Wright's genius as you can in Chicago and its surroundings.

Born two years after the Civil War ended, Wright did not live to see the completion of his late masterpiece, the Guggenheim Museum. His father preached and played (the Gospel and music) and dragged the family from the Midwest to New England and back before he up and left for good. Wright's Welsh-born mother, Anna Lloyd Jones, grew up in Wisconsin, and her son's roots would run deep there, too. Although his career began in Chicago and his work took him as far away as Japan, the home Wright built in Spring Green, Wisconsin—Taliesin—was his true center.

Despite all his dramas and financial instability (Wright was notoriously bad with money), the architect certainly produced. He was always ready to try something new—as long as it fit his notion of architecture as an expression of the human spirit and of human relationship with nature. By the time he died in 1959, Wright had designed over 1,000 projects, more than half of which were constructed.

Robie House, Chicago

242

WELCOME TO OAK PARK!

★ Fodor's Choice

Oak Park is a leafy, quiet community just 10 miles west of downtown Chicago. Get maps and visitor information at www.visitoakpark.com.

Wander to the **Frank Lloyd Wright Home and Studio**. From the outside, the shingle-clad structure may not appear all that innovative, but it's here that Wright developed the architectural language that still has the world talking.

Financed with a $5,000 loan from his mentor, Louis Sullivan, Wright designed the home when he was only 22. The residence manifests some of the spatial and stylistic characteristics that became hallmarks of Wright's work: there's a central fireplace from which

other spaces seem to radiate and an enticing flow to the rooms. In 1974, the local Frank Lloyd Wright Home and Studio Foundation, together with the National Trust for Historic Preservation, embarked on a 13-year restoration that returned the building to its 1909 appearance.

STROLLING OAK PARK

A leisurely stroll around the neighborhood will introduce you to plenty of **Frank Lloyd Wright houses.** All are privately owned, so you'll have to be content with what you can see from the outside. Check out 1019, 1027, and 1031 Chicago Avenue. These are typical Victorians that Wright designed on the sly while working for Sullivan.

GETTING HERE

To get to the heart of Oak Park by car, take the Eisenhower Expressway (I-290) west to Harlem Avenue. Head north on Harlem and take a right on Lake Street to get to the Oak Park Visitors Center at Forest Avenue and Lake Street, where there's ample free parking. You can also take the Green Line of the El to the Harlem Avenue stop, or Metra's Union Pacific West Line from the Ogilvie Transportation Center in Citicorp Center downtown (500 W. Madison) to the Oak Park stop at Marion Street.

WOMEN, FIRE, SCANDAL . . . AND OVER 1,000 DESIGNS

Dana Thomas House interior, 1904

1885   Wright briefly studies engineering at the University of Wisconsin.

1887   Wright strikes out for Chicago. He starts his career learning the basics with J. L. Silsbee, a residential architect.

1889   Wright marries Catherine Tobin; he builds her a home in suburban Oak Park, and they have six children together. In 1898 he adds a studio.

"WHILE NEW YORK HAS REPRODUCED MUCH AND PRODUCED NOTHING, CHICAGO'S ACHIEVEMENTS IN ARCHITECTURE HAVE GAINED WORLD-WIDE RECOGNITION AS A DISTINCTIVELY AMERICAN ARCHITECTURE."

For a look at the "real" Wright, don't miss the **Moore–Dugal Home** (1895) at 333 N. Forest Avenue, which reflects Wright's evolving architectural philosophy with its huge chimney and overhanging second story. Peek also at numbers 318, 313, 238, and 210, where you can follow his emerging modernism. Around the corner at 6 Elizabeth Court is the **Laura Gale House,** a 1909 project whose cantilevered profile foreshadows the thrusting planes Wright would create at Fallingwater decades later.

A landmark profile: the eastern facade of the architect's home and studio, Oak Park.

Between 1889 and 1913, Wright erected over two dozen buildings in Oak Park, so unless you're making an extended visit, don't expect to see everything. But don't leave town without a visit to his 1908 **Unity Temple**, a National Historic Landmark. Take a moment to appreciate Wright's fresh take on a place of worship; his bold strokes in creating a flowing interior; his unfailing attention to what was outside (note the skylights); and his dramatic use of concrete, which helps to protect the space from traffic noise.

Exterior, Unity Temple, Oak Park

1893	Wright launches his own practice in downtown Chicago.
1905	Wright begins designing the reinforced concrete Unity Temple.
1908	Construction begins on the Robie House in Chicago's Hyde Park neighborhood.
1909	Wright leaves for Europe with Mamah Cheney, the wife of a former client; Mrs. Wright does not consent to a divorce.
1911	Wright and Cheney settle at Taliesin, in Spring Green, Wisconsin.

GUIDED TOURS

A great way to get to know Oak Park is to take advantage of the guided tours. Well-informed local guides take small groups on tours throughout the day, discussing various architectural details, pointing out artifacts from the family's life, and often telling amusing stories of the rambunctious Wright clan. Reservations are required for groups of 10 or more for the home and studio tours. Note that you need to arrive as early as possible to be assured a spot. Tours begin at the **Home and Studio Museum Shop.** The shop carries architecture-related books and gifts. You can pick up a map ($3.95) to find other examples of Wright's work that are within easy walking or driving distance, or you can join a guided tour of the neighborhood led by volunteers.

THE HEMINGWAY CONNECTION

Frank Lloyd Wright wasn't the only creative giant to call Oak Park home. Ten years after Wright arrived, Ernest Hemingway was born here in 1899 in a proper Queen Anne, complete with turret. Wright was gone by the time Hemingway began to sow his literary oats. Good thing, too. It's doubtful the quiet village could have handled two such egos. ⇨ *See* **listings in this chapter for more information.**

Frank Lloyd Wright's distinctive take on a modern dining room.

TIPS

■ Tickets go on sale every October for the eagerly awaited annual **Wright Architectural Housewalk** in May, your chance to see the interiors of some of Oak Park's most architecturally notable homes. Check out ⊕ *www.gowright.org* for more details.

■ The Blue Line also stops in Oak Park, but we recommend sticking to the Green Line, as the Blue Line stop leaves you in a sketchy neighborhood.

Taliesin, Spring Green, Wisconsin

1914   Mrs. Cheney, her two children, and several other people are killed by a deranged employee, who also sets fire to Taliesin.

1915   With new mistress Miriam Noel in tow, the architect heads for Japan to oversee the building of the Imperial Hotel.

1922   Wright and his wife Catherine divorce.

1924   Wright marries Miriam Noel, but the marriage implodes three years later.

1928   Wright marries Olga (Olgivanna) Lazovich Milanoff. They have one daughter together.

245

Focus | FRANK LLOYD WRIGHT

PRAIRIE STYLE PRIMER

Primarily a residential mode, Wright's Prairie style is characterized by ground-hugging masses; low-pitched roofs with deep eaves; and ribbon windows. Generally, Prairie houses are two-story affairs, with single story wings and terraces that project into the landscape. Brick and stone, earth tones, and unpainted wood underscore the perception of a house as an extension of the natural world. Wright designed free-flowing living spaces defined by alternating ceiling heights, natural light, and architectural screens. Although a number of other Chicago architects pursued this

"ALL FINE ARCHITECTURAL VALUES ARE HUMAN VALUES, ELSE NOT VALUABLE."

emerging aesthetic, Wright became its acknowledged master. Though Wright designed dozens of Prairie style homes, the most well-known is Robie House, in Chicago's Hyde Park neighborhood. A dynamic composition of overlapping planes, it seems both beautifully anchored to the ground and ready to sail off with the arrival of a sharp breeze.

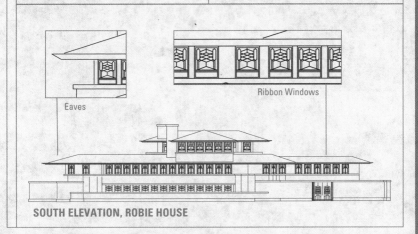

Ribbon Windows

Eaves

SOUTH ELEVATION, ROBIE HOUSE

Nathan G Moore-Dugal house, 1923

1930 The Taliesin Fellowship is launched; eager apprentices arrive to learn from the master.

1935 Fallingwater, the country home of Pittsburgh retailer Edgar J. Kaufmann, is completed at Bear Run, Pennsylvania.

1937 Wright begins construction of his winter getaway, Talesin West, in Scottsdale, Arizona.

1956 Wright designs the Guggenheim Museum in New York. It is completed in 1959.

1957 Wright joins preservationists in saving

Did You Know?

Brookfield Zoo gained international recognition for using moats rather than cages to separate animals from each other and from visitors. Today it continues to push the envelope with its immersive environments; instead of separating animals by type, in some exhibits those that share an ecosystem in the wild share a space at the zoo, too.

Evanston

10 miles north of downtown Chicago.

The home of Northwestern University is a pretty-as-can-be town in its own right, perched along the lake and studded with some magnificent homes and charming shops. As the birthplace of the temperance movement, Evanston was a dry town for decades. These days, it's brimming with innovative dining and drinking offerings. With a buzzing central business district, theaters, museums, and other cultural offerings, you almost forget that you're in the suburbs.

Sights

Block Museum of Art, Northwestern University

ART MUSEUM | Comprised of three galleries, this multipurpose space is among the most notable sights on the Northwestern University campus. The impressive rotating collection includes prints, photographs, and other works on paper spanning the 15th to 21st centuries. An outdoor sculpture garden features pieces by Joan Miró and Barbara Hepworth. Workshops, lectures, and symposia are also hosted here, and the museum's Block Cinema screens classic and contemporary films. ✉ *Northwestern University, 40 Arts Circle Dr., Evanston* ☎ *847/491–4000* 🌐 *www.blockmuseum.northwestern.edu* 🎫 *Free* 🕒 *Closed Mon. and Tues.*

Mitchell Museum of the American Indian

INDIGENOUS SIGHT | **FAMILY** | Founded in 1977, the Mitchell Museum houses more than 10,000 Native American artifacts from the Paleo-Indian period through modern times. Permanent exhibits focus on tribes in the Plains, Southwest, Northwest Coast, Woodlands, and Arctic areas. Guided tours, lectures, and kids' craft mornings (weekends only) are a regular part of the programming here. ✉ *3001 Central St., Evanston* ☎ *847/475–1030* 🌐 *www.mitchellmuseum.org* 🎫 *$7* 🕒 *Closed Mon.-Tues., Thurs.-Fri., and Sun.*

Northwestern University

COLLEGE | This private university, founded in 1851 by town namesake John Evans, puts Evanston on the map. Its sprawling Evanston campus hugs Lake Michigan. Strolling around its ivy-covered walls while listening to the crashing waves hitting the shore is a delightful experience. The campus is home to highly regarded undergraduate and graduate schools (the Medill School of Journalism and Kellogg School of Management among them) as well as the Block Museum of Art, which has more than 4,000 works in its permanent collection. Northwestern's Big Ten athletics program draws a mix of students and locals to games, especially when the Wildcats football team play at Ryan Field. ✉ *633 Clark St., Evanston* ☎ *847/491–3741* 🌐 *www.northwestern.edu.*

Coffee and Quick Bites

Edzo's Burger Shop

$ | **AMERICAN** | **FAMILY** | Northwestern students and suits line up at this casual counter service joint for burgers ground daily in-house. Beyond the griddled burger patties that you can order stacked two or three high, Edzo's slings Chicago classics like the Maxwell Street Polish and Chicago-style hot dog. **Known for:** huge 8-ounce char burger; truffle salt and Parmesan french fries; Nutella milk shake. [$] *Average main: $7* ✉ *1571 Sherman Ave., Evanston* ☎ *847/864–3396* 🌐 *www.edzos.com* 🕒 *Closed Sun.-Mon.*

Glencoe

19 miles north of downtown Chicago.

Glencoe is home to the Chicago Botanic Garden, the perfect place to take a break from the big city and experience nature.

 ## Sights

★ **Chicago Botanic Garden**
GARDEN | FAMILY | Among the 27 different gardens here are the three-island Malott Japanese Garden, the 5-acre Evening Island, and the Grunsfeld Children's Growing Garden. Three big greenhouses showcase desert, tropical, and semitropical climates where beautiful and fragrant flowers bloom year-round. Weather permitting, 40-minute trams tours ($8) are offered daily from 10 to 4, April through October. Special summer exhibitions include the 7,500-square-foot Model Railroad Garden with 17 garden-scale trains traveling around nearly 50 models of American landmarks, all made from natural materials. Butterflies & Blooms, a 2,800-square-foot white mesh enclosure, is filled with hundreds of colorful butterflies interacting with plant life; an $8 admission fee applies for each. ⊠ *1000 Lake Cook Rd., Glencoe* ☎ *847/835–5440* ⊕ *www.chicagobotanic.org* ⛵ *$25 parking including admission, purchase timed tickets online.* ♿ *Advance pre-registration required for non-members.*

Glenview

17 miles north of downtown Chicago.

In Glenview, the Kohl Children's Museum will keep kids busy with its interactive exhibits.

 ## Sights

Kohl Children's Museum
CHILDREN'S MUSEUM | FAMILY | Adults are hard-pressed to get youngsters to leave the 17 hands-on exhibits at this Glenview museum. Here toddlers to eight-year-olds can learn about solar power or how sounds make music. They can slip on a white jacket and be pretend doctors in a baby nursery or vets in an animal hospital. Kids can also get into home construction in "Hands on House" learn to change a tire, or paint their faces and don costumes. There's also a spot to put on raincoats and play in the water. When weather permits, the 2-acre "Habitat Park," just outside, is a great place for bug hunting, wall painting, and wandering through a grass maze. ⊠ *2100 Patriot Blvd., Glenview* ☎ *847/832–6600* ⊕ *www.kohlchildrensmuseum.org* ⛵ *$15* ⊗ *Closed Mon.*

Highland Park

26 miles north of downtown Chicago.

The town of Highland Park hosts the Ravinia Festival every summer, showcasing several musical acts, including the Chicago Symphony Orchestra.

 ## Sights

Ravinia Park
CITY PARK | FAMILY | If you enjoy music under the stars, the outdoor concerts at Ravinia are a stellar treat. Ravinia Festival, a summer-long series of performances, is the hot-months' home of the Chicago Symphony Orchestra, but the festival also features popular jazz, chamber music, rock, pop, and dance acts. Pack a picnic, bring a blanket or chairs, and sit on the lawn for little more than the cost of a movie (free to $50). Large screens are placed on the lawn at some concerts so you won't miss anything. Seats are also available in the pavilion for a significantly higher price ($25 to $215). There are restaurants and snack bars on the park grounds, so if you forget your goodies you still won't go hungry. Concerts usually start at 7:30

Did You Know?

In addition to all the plants to see at the Chicago Botanic Gardens, events on the grounds include light shows, flower shows, farm dinners, craft workshops, farm dinners, and more.

or 8 pm; the park usually opens three to four hours ahead to let everyone score spots and get settled. Weekend-morning concerts are aimed at kids. They feature a "KidsLawn" before or after the concert with an interactive music experience, an "instrument petting zoo," and occasional live performances. ⊠ *200 Ravinia Rd., Highland Park* ☎ *847/266–5100, 847/266–5000* ⊕ *www.ravinia.org.*

Lisle

25 miles southwest of downtown Chicago.

Visit Lisle to enjoy the natural beauty of woodlands, wetlands, and prairie at Morton Arboretum.

◉ Sights

Morton Arboretum
GARDEN | At this 1,700-acre outdoor oasis, you can hike some of the 16 miles of manicured trails, or drive or bike along 9 miles of paved roads bordered by trees, shrubs, and vines. Every season is magnificent: spring's flowering trees, summer's canopy-covered trails, fall's dazzling foliage, and winter's serene beauty. Bike, snowshoe, and cross-country ski rentals are available. If you have kids, check out the award-winning 4-acre Children's Garden, which is stroller- (as well as wheelchair-) friendly. A 1-acre maze garden will delight as you wind your way to the lookout platform. ⊠ *4100 Illinois Rte. 53, Lisle* ☎ *630/968–0074* ⊕ *www.mortonarb.org* ⌗ *$16; $11 on Wed.; 1-hr tram tours $9, purchase timed tickets online.* ♿ *Advance reservations required for non-members.*

Oak Park

9 miles west of downtown Chicago.

Oak Park is an architecture lover's dream with more Frank Lloyd Wright buildings than anywhere in the world. Tour Wright's Home and Studio before visiting the birthplace of another native son, Ernest Hemingway. The artsy town boasts its own symphony and outdoor theater with galleries, restaurants, and boutiques centered on the nine-block Oak Park Arts District. Oak Park's leafy suburb status was formally recognized as the first "municipal arboretum" in Illinois.

◉ Sights

Ernest Hemingway Birthplace Museum
HISTORIC HOME | Part of the literary legacy of Oak Park, this three-story, turreted Queen Anne Victorian, which stands in frilly contrast to the many streamlined Prairie-style homes elsewhere in the neighborhood, contains period-furnished rooms and many photos and artifacts pertaining to Hemingway's early life. Museum curators have restored rooms to faithfully depict the house as it looked at the turn of the 20th century. You can poke your head inside the one in which the author was born on July 21, 1899. ⊠ *339 N. Oak Park Ave., Oak Park* ☎ *708/445–3071* ⊕ *www.hemingwaybirthplace.com* ⌗ *$18* ⊗ *Closed Mon.–Thurs.*

★ Frank Lloyd Wright Home and Studio
HISTORIC HOME | Wright designed and built his first home in 1889, on the strength of a $5,000 loan from his then employer and mentor, seminal Chicago architect Louis Sullivan. Only 22 at the time, he would continually remodel the modest dwelling over the next two decades, so a visit here provides a unique look into the architect's developing ideas. This is where Wright's nascent architectural

Did You Know?

Before he was an influential novelist and famed adventurer, Ernest Hemingway was a teenager growing up in this Oak Park home. Glimpses of his future can be seen in his early years—he boxed, participated in track and field, played football, and wrote for the school newspaper. He also earned high marks in English.

339

BIRTHPLACE HOME OF
ERNEST HEMINGWAY
JULY 21, 1899

OPEN TO THE PUBLIC:
Sunday to Friday 1pm - 5pm
Saturday 10am - 5pm

His Oak Park home was the first building fully designed by Frank Lloyd Wright.

philosophy first bloomed; the house was intended not only to hold his rapidly growing family, but also to showcase his then revolutionary notions. It combines elements of the 19th-century Shingle style with subtle innovations that stamp its originality.

Wright established his own practice in 1893 and added a studio to the house in 1898. In 1909, he spread his innovative designs across the United States and abroad (at this time he also abandoned his wife and six children for the wife of a client). He sold his home and studio in 1925, which was later turned into apartments that eventually fell into disrepair. In 1974, a group of local citizens calling itself the Frank Lloyd Wright Home and Studio Foundation, together with the National Trust for Historic Preservation, embarked on a 13-year restoration that returned the building to its 1909 appearance. Today, Wright's Oak Park Home and Studio are owned by the Frank Lloyd Wright Trust.

Wright's home, made of brick and dark shingles, is filled with earth-tone spaces. The architect's determination to create an integrated environment prompted him to design the natural wood furniture as well—though his apparent lack of regard for comfort is often the subject of commentary. The lead windows have colored-glass designs, and several rooms have skylights or other indirect lighting. A spacious barrel-vault playroom on the second floor includes a hidden piano for the children's theatrical productions. The adjacent studio is made up of four spaces—an office, a large reception room, an octagonal library, and an octagonal drafting room that uses a chain harness system rather than traditional beams to support its balcony, roof, and walls.

To see the interior, you must take one of the small-group tours, led by well-informed guides who discuss the architecture, point out artifacts from the family's life, and tell amusing stories about the rambunctious Wright clan. Reservations are advised: without one, you'll need to arrive as early as possible to snag a spot—not later than early afternoon to make the last tour on any given day. Tours begin at the Frank Lloyd Wright Home and Studio Museum Shop, which carries architecture-related books and gifts. You can pick up a map noting other examples of Wright's work that are within easy walking or driving distance; guided tours and self-guided audio ones of the neighborhood are also available.

The annual Wright Plus Architectural Housewalk on the third Saturday in May offers interior tours of private homes designed by Wright and his contemporaries in Oak Park and other nearby villages. ✉ *951 Chicago Ave., Oak Park* ☎ *312/994–4000* 🌐 *www.flwright.org* 🎟 *$20; area walking tour $15.*

Oak Park River Forest Museum
HISTORY MUSEUM | FAMILY | Housed in an 1898 firehouse, this small but interesting museum chronicles the Oak Park and River Forest area's most notable people, events, and places. Famous residents including Frank Lloyd Wright and his son, John Lloyd Wright (creator of Lincoln Logs), Edgar Rice Burroughs (creator of Tarzan), James Alexander Dewar (creator of Twinkies), Ray Kroc (founder of McDonald's), and Dr. Percy Julian (a scientist and civil rights activist) are highlighted. Some Ernest Hemingway memorabilia, once part of the former Hemingway Museum, have also found a new home here. A World War I exhibit features the author's ambulance driving days and uniforms worn by former resident veterans. A hands-on kids section has old toys and a tiny reproduction of a little old school. ✉ *129 Lake St., Oak Park* ☎ *708/848–6755* 🌐 *www.oprfmuseum.org* 🎟 *$7* 🕒 *Closed Sun.–Tues.*

☕ Coffee and Quick Bites

Petersen's Ice Cream
$ | ICE CREAM | FAMILY | Step back in time at this old-fashioned ice-cream parlor, which celebrated its 100th anniversary in 2019. Choose from homemade ice cream in flavors like cappuccino and butter pecan complete with a cone dipped in chocolate. **Known for:** sundaes; vintage charm; homemade waffle cones. [$] *Average main: $5* ✉ *1100 Chicago Ave., Oak Park* 🌐 *www.facebook.com/PetersensOldFashionIceCream* 🕒 *Closed Jan. and Feb.*

Skokie

12 miles north of downtown Chicago.

Just north of Evanston is Skokie, which is home to the powerful Illinois Holocaust Museum & Education Center.

👁 Sights

Illinois Holocaust Museum & Education Center
COLLEGE | In the 1970s, a group of neo-Nazis planned a march in the predominantly Jewish suburb of Skokie, and local Holocaust survivors reacted by creating the Holocaust Memorial Foundation of Illinois, a group determined to educate the public about the atrocities of World War II. It took years of planning, but in 2009 the foundation finally unveiled a gem of a museum. The 65,000-square-foot building houses more than 11,000 Holocaust-related objects. An early-20th-century German railcar—of the type used by the Nazis during the Holocaust—serves as the central artifact. Permanent exhibits include the Legacy of Absence Gallery, which evokes other contemporary genocides and atrocities through art, and the Harvey L. Miller Family Youth Exhibition, which aims to teach kids about respecting differences.

Did You Know?

There are only nine Bahá'í temples in the world and the Wilmette's Bahá'í House of Worship is the oldest of the lot and the only one in North America. Bahá'ís consider the number nine (the highest single number) a symbol of oneness, comprehensiveness, and unity.

The newest addition is an interactive 3-D hologram exhibit, in which Holocaust survivors are projected onstage to tell their stories. ⊠ *9603 Woods Dr., Skokie* ☎ *847/967–4800* ⊕ *www.ilholocaust-museum.org* ⊠ *$15* ⊘ *Closed Mon. and Tues.* ⚐ *Advance tickets required.*

Vernon Hills

40 miles northwest of downtown Chicago.

Head to Vernon Hills to explore the beautiful Cuneo Mansion and Gardens.

Sights

Loyola University Cuneo Mansion and Gardens
HISTORIC HOME | Samuel Insull, partner of Thomas Edison and founder of Commonwealth Edison, built this mansion as a country home in 1916. After Insull lost his fortune, John Cuneo Sr., the printing-press magnate, bought the estate and fashioned it to suit his own taste. The skylighted great hall in the main house resembles the open central courtyard of an Italian palazzo, the private family chapel has stained-glass windows, and a gilded grand piano graces the ballroom. Tours highlight the antique furnishings, 17th-century Flemish tapestries, and Italian paintings that fill the interior. ⊠ *1350 N. Milwaukee Ave., Vernon Hills* ☎ *847/362–3042* ⊕ *www.luc.edu/cuneo* ⊠ *$10* ⊘ *Closed Sun.–Thurs.*

Wheaton

30 miles west of downtown Chicago.

Wheaton is home to Cantigny Park, which offers several different attractions, including a military history museum, walking trails, and the Robert R. McCormick Museum.

Sights

Cantigny Park
HISTORIC HOME | **FAMILY** | The 500-acre estate of former *Chicago Tribune* editor and publisher Robert McCormick (1880–1955) has multiple attractions. For starters, there's the First Division Museum, an impressive military history museum that has interactive, immersive exhibits. The sweeping landscape also incorporates formal gardens, picnic grounds, walking trails, and its own 27-hole public golf course with a separate 9-hole course for kids. The centerpiece, however, is the Beaux-Arts–style McCormick House. This 35-room mansion contains the Joseph Medill Library, the stately wood-paneled Freedom Hall, and an art deco movie theater. The hidden Prohibition-era bar alone is worth a visit—we won't ruin the surprise by revealing where it is. ⊠ *1S151 Winfield Rd., Wheaton* ☎ *630/668–5161* ⊕ *www.cantigny.org* ⊠ *$5 per car* ⊘ *Closed Jan. and Mon.–Thurs. in Feb.*

Wilmette

14 miles north of downtown Chicago.

The gorgeous Bahá'í Temple House of Worship is located in Wilmette.

Sights

★ Bahá'í Temple House of Worship
GARDEN | Your mouth is sure to drop to the floor the first time you lay eyes on this stunning structure, a nine-sided building that incorporates architectural styles and symbols from many of the world's religions. With its delicate lacelike details and massive dome, the Louis Bourgeois design emphasizes the 19th-century Persian origins of the Bahá'í religion. The formal gardens are as symmetrical and harmonious as the building they surround. The Bahá'í faith advocates spiritual unity, world peace, racial unity,

and equality of the sexes. Stop by the welcome center to examine exhibits that explain it; you can also ask for a guide to show you around. ✉ *100 Linden Ave., Wilmette* ☎ *847/853–2300* 🌐 *www.bahaitemple.org* 🎫 *Free* 🕓 *Welcome Center closed Mon. and Tues.* ☞ *Enter at lower level.*

Coffee and Quick Bites

★ **Walker Bros. Original Pancake House**
$ | **AMERICAN** | **FAMILY** | Be prepared to stand in line for the mouthwatering apple cinnamon pancakes, a massive disk loaded with apples, or the German pancake, a puffy oven-baked circle topped with powdered sugar. There are several branches, but the original Wilmette restaurant is where scenes from the 1980 movie *Ordinary People* were shot. **Known for:** pancakes as big as your plate; oven-baked omelets; stained glass and wood ambience. [$] *Average main: $15* ✉ *153 Green Bay Rd., Wilmette* ☎ *847/251–6000* 🌐 *www.walkerbros.net* 🕓 *No dinner.*

Index

Photo Credits

Front Cover: Adam Jones/Getty Images [Description: Kayakers on Chicago River and Chicago skyline, Chicago, IL].
Back cover, from left to right: UWMadison/iStockphoto, JaySi/Shutterstock, Ja'Crispy/iStockphoto. **Spine:** FeyginFoto/Shutterstock. **Interior, from left to right:** Richard Cavalleri/Shutterstock (1). Ellesi/Dreamstime.com (2-3). Chris Pritchard/iStockphoto (5). **Chapter 1: Experience Chicago:** cendhika/Shutterstock (6-7). Julien-grondin/Dreamstime (8-9). Atosan/Shutterstock (9). Kirkikisphoto/Dreamstime (9). Page Light Studios/Shutterstock (10). Michael Rosebrock/Dreamstime (10). alisafarov/Shutterstock (10). PkingDesign [CC BY-NC-ND 2.0]/Flickr (10). R. Gino Santa Maria/Dreamstime (11). Shinyshot/Shutterstock (12). Thomas Barrat/Shutterstock (12). Cmlndm/Dreamstime (12). Stefania Rossitto/Dreamstime (12). Chicago Cubs/Stephen Green Photography (13). Tea/Dreamstime (13). James Kirkikis/Dreamstime (14). Qoqazian/Dreamstime (14). Songquan Deng/Shutterstock (14). Jkirsh/Shutterstock (15). Bjphotographs/Dreamstime.com (20). Choose Chicago (20). Portillo's (20). Adam Madey/Shutterstock (21). Adam Alexander Photography/Choose Chicago (21). Nejdet Duzen/Shutterstock (22). City of Chicago Photo Courtesy of Choose Chicago (22). BorisVetshev/Shutterstock (22). Courtesy of Illinois Office of Tourism (23). Vlad Ghiea/Dreamstime (23). marchello74/Shutterstock (24). Thomas Barrat/Shutterstock (24). Fernando Espinosa/Shutterstock (24). Courtesy of Graham Chapman (24). Photo Courtesy of Abel Arciniega (25). Ranvestal Photographic Photo Courtesy of Choose Chicago (25). Maciej Bledowski/Shutterstock (25). Jes Farnum/Shutterstock (25). NMMA Michael Tropea (26). Patrick L. Pyszka/City of Chicago (26). Courtesy of The Lincoln Lodge (26). Michelle Duster (26). Dan Rest/Courtesy of Wabash Arts Corridor (27). **Chapter 3: The Loop:** Ffooter/Shutterstock (55). Camille Tsang/Dreamstime (61). Rudy Balasko/Shutterstock (63). f11photo/Shutterstock (65). f11photo/Shutterstock (66-67). TC, Fodors.com member (69). Rcavalleri/Dreamstime (71). Felix Lipov/Shutterstock (72). Photo Spirit/Shutterstock (74). The Art Institute of Chicago (74). The Art Institute of Chicago, Robert A. Waller Fund (75). The Art Institute, Gift of Arthur M. Wood in memory of Pauline Palmer Wood (75). The Art Institute of Chicago: Friends of American Art Collection (75). The Art Institute of Chicago, Friends of the American Art Collection (75). CharlesG.Young/Interactive Design Architects (76). DaveJordanoPhotography/Inc. (76). Charles G. Young, Interactive Design Architects. (76). DaveJordanoPhotography/Inc. (76). Sean Pavone/Shutterstock (82). Jim Lambert/Shutterstock (87). Ben Collins-Sussman [CC BY-ND 2.0]/Flickr (95). **Chapter 4: Near North and River North:** Richard Cavalleri/Shutterstock (103). Alexander Cimbal/Dreamstime (109). Rudy Balasko/Shutterstock (110-111). f11photo/Shutterstock (113). Alisonh29/Dreamstime (114). dibrova/Shutterstock (117). StephenFinn/Shutterstock (118). Therese McKeon/iStockphoto (118). dibrova/Shutterstock (118). Keith J Finks/Shutterstock (119). Tosca66/Shutterstock (119). Chris Pritchard/iStockphoto (119). Vladislav Mikhailov/Dreamstime (121).ErikLattwein/Dreamstime (124). NJCoop, Fodors.com member (132). Jim Roberts/Dreamstime (140). **Chapter 5: Pilsen, Little Italy, and Chinatown:** Juliscalzi/Dreamstime (145). Marina Endermar/Dreamstime (150). Stefania Rossitto/Dreamstime (152). Page Light Studios/Shutterstock (155). Thomas Barrat/Shutterstock (157). Jim Roberts/Dreamstime (158). **Chapter 6: Lincoln Park and Wicker Park:** Jim Roberts/Dreamstime (161). ThomasBarrat/Shutterstock (165). Sean Pavone/Dreamstime (170-171). City of Chicago/GRC (175). City of Chicago/GRC (175). Rosa's Lounge (175). Marcin Wichary [CC BY 2.0]/Flickr (175). James Fraher (176). Chansley Entertainment Archives (176). Alexapicso/Shutterstock (176-177). Joseph A. Rosen (177). Ray Flerlage/Chansley Entertainment Archives (177). Joe Sohm/Dreamstime (178). James Andrews1/Shutterstock (182). Antwon McMullen/Shutterstock (193). **Chapter 7: Lakeview and the Far North Side:** James Andrews/Dreamstime (201). Carlos Yudica/Shutterstock (206). Steve Broer/Shutterstock (210). James Andrews/Dreamstime (214). **Chapter 8: Hyde Park:** STLJB/Shutterstock (223). Adam Alexander Photography/Courtesy of Illinois Office of Tourism (229). Cafebeanz Company/Dreamstime (231). EQRoy/Shutterstock (233). **Chapter 9: Day Trips from Chicago:** Lmphot/Dreamstime (235). Alexandre Fagundes De Fagundes/Dreamstime (240). Marek Lipka-Kadaj/Shutterstock (241). Library of Congress Prints and Photographs Division (241). Carol M. Highsmith/Library of Congress Prints and Photographs Division (242). Benkrut/Dreamstime (243). Library of Congress Prints & Photographs Division (243). Aaron of L.A. Photography/Shutterstock (244). Tim Long. Courtesy of Frank Lloyd Wright Preservation Trust (244). Khairil Junos/Dreamstime (245). OGI75/Shutterstock (246). Ganesh005/Dreamstime.com (249). Manuel Hurtado Ferrández/Dreamstime (251). Man Hurt/Shutterstock (252). Nejdet Duzen/Shutterstock (254). **About Our Writers:** All photos are courtesy of the writers.

Every effort has been made to trace the copyright holders, and we apologize in advance for any accidental errors. We would be happy to apply the corrections in the following edition of this publication.

Notes

Notes

Notes

Notes

Notes

Notes

Notes

Notes

Fodor's CHICAGO

Publisher: Stephen Horowitz, *General Manager*

Editorial: Douglas Stallings, *Editorial Director;* Jill Fergus, Amanda Sadlowski, Caroline Trefler, *Senior Editors;* Kayla Becker, Alexis Kelly, *Editors;* Angelique Kennedy-Chavannes, *Assistant Editor*

Design: Tina Malaney, *Director of Design and Production;* Jessica Gonzalez, *Graphic Designer;* Sophia Almendral, *Design and Production Intern*

Production: Jennifer DePrima, *Editorial Production Manager;* Elyse Rozelle, *Senior Production Editor;* Monica White, *Production Editor*

Maps: Rebecca Baer, *Senior Map Editor;* David Lindroth, Mark Stroud (Moon Street Cartography), *Cartographers*

Photography: Viviane Teles, *Senior Photo Editor;* Namrata Aggarwal, Payal Gupta, Ashok Kumar, *Photo Editors;* Rebecca Rimmer, *Photo Production Associate;* Eddie Aldrete, *Photo Production Intern*

Business and Operations: Chuck Hoover, *Chief Marketing Officer;* Robert Ames, *Group General Manager;* Devin Duckworth, *Director of Print Publishing*

Public Relations and Marketing: Joe Ewaskiw, *Senior Director of Communications and Public Relations*

Fodors.com: Jeremy Tarr, *Editorial Director;* Rachael Levitt, *Managing Editor*

Technology: Jon Atkinson, *Director of Technology;* Rudresh Teotia, *Lead Developer;* Jacob Ashpis, *Content Operations Manager*

Writers: Matt Beardmore, Cate Huguelet, Jessica Mlinaric, Kris Vire

Editors: Caroline Trefler (lead editor), Angelique Kennedy-Chavannes

Production Editor: Elyse Rozelle

32nd edition

ISBN 978-1-64097-487-6

ISSN 0743-9326

All details in this book are based on information supplied to us at press time. Always confirm information when it matters, especially if you're making a detour to visit a specific place. Fodor's expressly disclaims any liability, loss, or risk, personal or otherwise, that is incurred as a consequence of the use of any of the contents of this book.

SPECIAL SALES

This book is available at special discounts for bulk purchases for sales promotions or premiums. For more information, e-mail SpecialMarkets@fodors.com.

PRINTED IN CANADA

10 9 8 7 6 5 4 3 2

MIX
Paper from responsible sources
FSC® C016245

About Our Writers

 Matt Beardmore grew up in the Chicago suburbs, but he's called the Second City his home for more than a decade. He lives on the North Side with his wife, Ewelina, and their young son, Adam, and he enjoys exploring the city's many amazing museums, biking and running on the Lakefront Trail, and trying as many new restaurants as possible. His work has appeared in *The New York Times*, *Chicago Tribune*, *Chicago Sun-Times*, *ESPN The Magazine*, and numerous other publications. For this edition, Matt updated the Near North and River North, and Hyde Park chapters.

 Chicago native **Cate Huguelet** spent several years in Ireland and Tennessee, but her heart belongs in her hometown, Chicago, where she lives in the Bridgeport neighborhood with her husband and two daughters. When she's not writing about food and travel for publications like *Chicago magazine*, *Saveur*, and *The New York Times*, she's working on a culinary school degree in baking and pastry. Follow her on Instagram @thepastrymethod.

 Jessica Mlinaric is the author of *Chicago Scavenger and Secret Chicago: A Guide to the Weird, Wonderful, and Obscure*. Her writing and photography covering culture and travel has appeared in *Condé Nast Traveller*, *GQ*, *The Architect's Newspaper*, *Chicago Magazine*, and more. She lives in Wicker Park with her husband, Brett, and their cats Coltrane and Zelda. Follow her latest writing at urbnexplorer.com.

 Kris Vire spent a decade as a staff writer and editor for *Time Out Chicago* covering the performing arts. More recently, Kris has served as a theater critic for the *Chicago Sun-Times* and writes regularly for *Chicago magazine* and *American Theatre*. He lives in North Center with his partner.